GENESIS AND
THE LAMB LIES DOWN ON BROADWAY

Genesis and *The Lamb Lies Down on Broadway*

KEVIN HOLM-HUDSON
University of Kentucky, USA

ASHGATE

Published by
Ashgate Publishing Limited
Gower House
Croft Road
Aldershot
Hampshire GU11 3HR
England

Ashgate Publishing Company
Suite 420
101 Cherry Street
Burlington, VT 05401-4405
USA

www.ashgate.com

British Library Cataloguing in Publication Data
Holm-Hudson, Kevin
    Genesis and *The lamb lies down on Broadway*. – (Ashgate popular and folk music series)
    1. Genesis (Musical group). Lamb lies down on Broadway
    I. Title
    782.4'2166'0922

Library of Congress Cataloging-in-Publication Data
Holm-Hudson, Kevin.
    Genesis and *The lamb lies down on Broadway* / By Kevin Holm-Hudson.
        p. cm. – (Ashgate popular and folk music series)
    Includes bibliographical references (p.   ) and index.
    ISBN 978-0-7546-6139-9 (alk. paper)
    1. Genesis (Musical group). Lamb lies down on Broadway. I. Title.

ML421.G46H65 2008
782.42166092'2–dc22

                                            2007050738

ISBN 978-0-7546-6139-9 (Hbk)
ISBN 978-0-7546-6147-4 (Pbk)

Bach musicological font developed by © Yo Tomita.

Contents

List of musical figures

General Editor's Preface

The upheaval that occurred in musicology during the last two decades of the twentieth century has created a new urgency for the study of popular music alongside the development of new critical and theoretical models. A relativistic outlook has replaced the universal perspective of modernism (the international ambitions of the 12-note style); the grand narrative of the evolution and dissolution of tonality has been challenged, and emphasis has shifted to cultural context, reception and subject position. Together, these have conspired to eat away at the status of canonical composers and categories of high and low in music. A need has arisen, also, to recognize and address the emergence of crossovers, mixed and new genres, to engage in debates concerning the vexed problem of what constitutes authenticity in music and to offer a critique of musical practice as the product of free, individual expression.

Popular musicology is now a vital and exciting area of scholarship, and the Ashgate Popular and Folk Music Series presents some of the best research in the field. Authors are concerned with locating musical practices, values and meanings in cultural context, and draw upon methodologies and theories developed in cultural studies, semiotics, poststructuralism, psychology and sociology. The series focuses on popular musics of the twentieth and twenty-first centuries. It is designed to embrace the world's popular musics from Acid Jazz to Zydeco, whether high tech or low tech, commercial or non-commercial, contemporary or traditional.

Professor Derek B. Scott
Professor of Critical Musicology
University of Leeds

Acknowledgments

The Lamb Lies Down on Broadway is an album with a good story behind it. I don't mean the story of Rael, although that too is very good, if maddeningly obscure at times. *The Lamb*'s other story is one of great creativity and personal turmoil within the band, of rapid change in the music industry at the time, and of the great economic and political stresses in the US and the UK during the time *The Lamb* was composed, recorded and performed on tour. In these respects *The Lamb,* like the Beatles' *Sgt. Pepper*, Pink Floyd's *The Wall*, Nirvana's *Nevermind*, Radiohead's *OK Computer*, and Green Day's *American Idiot*, marks a pivotal point in a band's trajectory and it both illustrates and resonates with its time.

For this story to be told, however, it required many contributors along the way. I would like to thank Heidi May, commissioning editor at Ashgate, and Derek B. Scott, editor for Ashgate's Folk and Popular Music series, for graciously answering questions, providing feedback, and in general making the entire editorial process very smooth. I am grateful for their professionalism. The University of Kentucky College of Fine Arts graciously awarded me with a sabbatical that provided needed time for writing. I am grateful to my colleagues for their congeniality and encouragement. My graduate students in my Progressive Rock seminars at the University of Kentucky have been an enthusiastic sounding board for my ideas over the years, and a rich source of new perspectives and suggestions for new directions of inquiry.

For academics "searching printed word" (as Gabriel would memorably describe my line of work in "The Chamber of 32 Doors"), or searching web sites, serendipitous avenues of research can pop up. I would like to thank two anonymous file-sharing bloggers who provided me with valuable material, at just the right time, without even knowing it. The first posted the entire Shrine Auditorium show in its "rough" pre-*Archive* form to a music blog. When a concert-streaming web site threatened litigation, the blogger hastily withdrew the files, but then subsequently posted the seven-CD bootleg *In the Beginning*, which contains a number of key *Lamb* demos; at almost exactly the same time, a second collector, who had managed to download the Shrine show in the brief time it was up, re-posted it on a mirror site. My thanks go out to both. Even if they never read this, their generosity significantly furthered my research; my comparative discussion of the Shrine Auditorium recordings, for example, would not have been possible.

It was my high-school friend and college roommate Mike Bowman who introduced me to Gabriel-era Genesis in general, and *The Lamb* in particular. Thanks, Mike; you were often in my thoughts as I wrote this book. Another longtime friend, Gary Zenker, has been a constant source of unconditional encouragement.

Finally, my wonderful family—my wife Karen, and our kids, Miranda and Toby—were a constant source of love, patience and support at all times, quiet and solitude when needed, and smoothies and caramels without my asking. Miranda and Toby, I pray that your careers, whatever they turn out to be, will be as motivating and rewarding for you as they are for your Mom and Dad. Thanks, Mom, for making me stick with those music lessons, and thanks as well to anyone whom I have neglected to mention here.

All musical examples in this book are the result of my own transcription efforts and analysis directly from the recordings; any errors are my own. All songs were written by Tony Banks, Michael Rutherford, Peter Gabriel, Steve Hackett, and Phil Collins, published by © Genesis Music Ltd. / Hit & Run Music (Publishing) Ltd.

It's quite a barrage of words and there should be an award for people who go through it!
—Peter Gabriel (Welch, 1975)

—Kevin Holm-Hudson

Introduction
"This is the story of Rael"

I do like to have the detail there so if anyone did want to spend their life rooting around the lyrics, it would be like a little paper chase for them – very unnecessary, but great fun!

—Peter Gabriel, March 1973[1]

The crowd files into Los Angeles's Shrine Auditorium on a cold January evening in 1975. It's the familiar audience for a mid-1970s "progressive" rock concert, mostly white college-age males. The group they have come to see, Genesis, has not as yet received widespread airplay in the US. The band had played LA only once before, a storied three-night stint at the Roxy back in December 1973. Based on those shows and a handful of other performances in large East Coast cities (New York, Philadelphia, Miami) as well as a handful of important collegiate markets (Boston's Tufts University, Ypsilanti, Michigan), the audience had heard stories of a British band with an epic, theatrical sound and strange songs about watchers from the skies and ancient Roman hermaphrodites. They knew something of this group's singer who would tell tales of a senile lawnmower or a malevolent sex-obsessed ghost named Henry, or portray the spirit of Britannia herself. He wore his long, dark hair with a prominent bald spot shaven in front and was also known for donning flower masks and fox heads. There was still something of a novelty to their show. It was a bit like a cross between Yes and David Bowie, people said—a cult attraction.

All the same, audience members expecting to see an elaborate set of the sort that Yes used were in for a surprise. The stage was starkly minimal by 1970s concert standards, with even the amplifiers hidden from view. Writing in *Circus* magazine, Ron Ross described it this way:

Where groups from the Who to ELP [Emerson, Lake and Palmer] impress their fans visually with walls of amplified thunder-machinery, Genesis' [sic] set is virtually bare of electric equipment. Steve Hackett and Mike Rutherford's amps are so well hidden that their music often appears to emanate from the air itself. No mountains of synthesiser technology surround Tony Banks. Aside from the panoramic three-part slide screen and an odd little rock formation at the center of the stage, the most striking "prop" is Phil Collins' beautifully complete and well-ordered drum kit. It is almost a sculpture in itself, but, of course, its function is strictly musical. (Ross, 1975, p. 70)

---

[1]   Quoted in Bowler and Dray, 1993, p. 68.

When Genesis took to the stage, their charismatic front man, Peter Gabriel, was wearing none of the fanciful accoutrements that had distinguished their earlier Roxy appearance. Instead, he looked much like any no-nonsense pub-rocker of the mid-seventies, wearing a black leather jacket and jeans, his famously long hair cut short. Instead of the glam-like fluorescent eye-shadow and lipstick he had worn for shows on the previous tour, his only make-up this time was some skin base to darken his complexion and a dab of football-player-style blackener below the eyes. As the crowd hushed in anticipation, Gabriel addressed the crowd before a note was played.

> Good evening. We've written a big lump of story and music and we'd like to play the whole thing for you tonight. It tells of how a large black cloud descends into Time Square and straddles out across 42nd Street, turns into a wall and sucks in Manhattan Island. Our hero, named Rael, crawls out of the subways of New York and is sucked into the wall, to regain consciousness underground. This is the story of Rael.

And with that, with Tony Banks's now-familiar electric-piano trills introducing the title song, the group launched into their new release, a double-album dramatic work entitled *The Lamb Lies Down on Broadway*. The show was unlike anything Genesis had done before, surprising even fans who were familiar with the group's previous music. The purpose of the minimal staging was then made clear—to focus the audience's attention on Gabriel as he acted out the role of Rael.

Even more unusual, the group had decided to begin the show with this new, largely unfamiliar 90-minute opus in its entirety. Even by the excessive standards of 1970s rock shows, this was a risky undertaking. Only Yes, on their *Tales from Topographic Oceans* tour, had previously attempted introducing so much new material to their audience without the relief provided by "the hits," or at least older, more familiar material. And Yes had failed—after only a few shows the group was forced to begin their concerts with familiar material, moving the complete *Tales* to the end of the show, and eventually they were forced to edit down *Tales* itself for live performance. And Yes, of course, were one of the top progressive-rock concert draws of the 1970s, with two top-10 albums prior to the release of *Tales*. Although *The Lamb* had been released about five weeks prior to this performance, it is a fair assumption that this music would be completely new to most of the audience who had come to this show out of curiosity regarding the group's reputation. Compared to the prog-rock giants such as Emerson, Lake and Palmer or Yes, Genesis was still regarded as an "underground" group with no hits to speak of stateside. How would their story of an American street punk named Rael and his strange journey into a metaphysical realm of the subconscious be received?

As it turns out, very well. While *Tales from Topographic Oceans* never quite recovered from the critical vilification heaped upon both the album and the tour that followed (even today, it symbolizes the excesses of progressive rock's "golden years" from 1969 to 1977), the reputation of *The Lamb Lies Down on Broadway* has steadily increased over the years. Although the album received only lukewarm critical response on its release, the tour that followed greatly enhanced Genesis's standing in the US, then the largest market for popular music. So successful was the tour, and Gabriel's personification of Rael, that Gabriel came to be seen as the major creative figure in Genesis; and when Gabriel announced his departure from the group in 1975, critics were prepared to write off the group's future. Unbeknownst to the public at large, however, the experience of recording *The Lamb* fortified the group for working without Gabriel; the follow-up album *A Trick of the Tail* heralded the beginning of Genesis's hugely successful period with Phil Collins as singer and charismatic front man.

Writing in 1986—the peak of Genesis's post-Gabriel popularity—*Village Voice* critic Barry Walters wrote a surprisingly appreciative assessment of *The Lamb* that indicates something of its staying power nearly 12 years after it was released:

> With more braggadocio than L. L. Cool J and a harder gangster attitude than Schooly-D, Rael Imperial Aerosol Kid was also the way Gabriel saw himself, especially in relation to the future AOR horrors he then sang and conceptualized for, Genesis. During the oblique narrative course of *The Lamb Lies Down on Broadway*'s four sides, Rael joins the Grand Parade of Lifeless Packaging, gets shot up by the Supernatural Anaesthetist, suffers castration, and finally dissolves to be reborn. It seemed incomprehensible in 1974, but *The Lamb* basically is a confined artist's struggle for liberation. (Walters, 1986)

One of the reasons that *The Lamb Lies Down on Broadway* has aged so well over the years is that its lyric content may be seen as allegorical on several levels. First, it may be enjoyed at face value as a consummately bizarre surrealist epic—the logical extension of the fanciful and bizarre stories that Gabriel began improvising on stage to cover the awkward moments of tuning guitars between songs. It is also a religious allegory, which Gabriel has compared to John Bunyan's epic *Pilgrim's Progress*. As such it is a notable example in the long line of songs with religious themes in Gabriel's output, beginning with the songs on Genesis's debut *From Genesis to Revelation* and continuing through "Visions of Angels" and "Supper's Ready" all the way to later solo songs such as "Blood of Eden" and the *Passion* soundtrack for Martin Scorsese's film *The Last Temptation of Christ*. The album also has intriguing psychological themes, which again characterize both Gabriel's work with Genesis ("The Musical Box") and his solo work ("No Self Control," "We Do What We're Told [Milgram's 37]").

Moreover, *The Lamb Lies Down on Broadway* holds up well as a historical document. It is a product of its time, reflective of the general economic and social turmoil of the early 1970s. It was a time of unprecedented economic expansion for the music industry, but the same economic conditions conveyed in the album's title track ultimately prefigured the industry's recession-era implosion and retrenchment. *The Lamb Lies Down on Broadway* is one of the last classic concept albums of the 1970s, released at a time that concept albums were—thanks to albums such as *Tales from Topographic Oceans*—decidedly out of fashion. Beyond all that, it is—as Walters (1986) put it—"the funkiest, most tuneful progressive rock album."

This book examines *The Lamb Lies Down on Broadway* from all of these perspectives. In Chapter 1, I examine the social and economic contexts in which *The Lamb* was released. The emergence of progressive rock as a genre— and, indeed, as a marketing category—is situated within the globalization and consolidation of the music industry and the emergence of related industries such as concert promotion and merchandising. At the same time, I also examine social and political conditions in the US (then the world's largest market for recorded music, and the market in which Genesis was poised for a significant breakthrough in 1975) and the UK. Sociocultural tensions engendered by the Watergate crisis and the OPEC oil embargo of 1973–74, for example, were manifested in the popular music of the era, and Genesis was no exception. The energy crisis, in fact, directly contributed to structural changes in the music industry in the mid-1970s—among these changes, it can be argued, was the demise of progressive rock, an inherently cost-ineffective "art for art's sake" genre that was difficult to promote to radio and expensive to mount on tour. Chapter 1 also includes a brief survey of Genesis's career up until the recording of *The Lamb*; although this information is found in each of the many books that have been written about Genesis (Bowler and Dray, 1993; Fielder, 1984; Gallo, 1980; Hewitt, 2000), its inclusion helps to situate *The Lamb* within the emergent career of this prominent and uniquely theatrical British band. Chapter 1 accordingly closes with some observations on the role that theatre played in Genesis's performances, and the relation of Gabriel's adaptation of various stage personae to the glam rock movement that was at its peak in the UK during the same period.

Chapter 2 details the process of composing and recording *The Lamb*. Again, although this information has been covered in the various biographical accounts of the band, this section brings together the various strands of information into one narrative. Gabriel's different versions of the story line, both from the album packaging and in press interviews, are also brought together for comparison and commentary.

Chapter 3 is a detailed musical and textual analysis of *The Lamb,* song by song. While some fan documents (see, for example, Hoppe, 1998; McMahan, 1998) provide some textual analysis, the actual musical content is generally passed over. In the spirit of music theorists such as Walter Everett (1999, 2001) and John Covach and Graeme Boone (1997), I believe that an informed musical analysis can enhance appreciation of the listening experience, and consequently I attempt to place musical analysis on equal footing with the textual component. Although the ability to read music will be helpful to derive maximum benefit from some parts of this chapter, I have attempted to steer clear of overbearing technical jargon. Musical examples are only provided inasmuch as they help to clarify points in the text, and CD timings are provided for easy aural reference. Nevertheless, readers may pass over the passages of musical analysis if they see fit, with no disruption of the reading flow.

Chapter 4 examines the public reception to *The Lamb,* considering reviews of both the recording and the world tour that followed. Chapter 5 is a survey of different interpretations of *The Lamb* as allegory, addressing the album's psychological themes, its musical references (mostly to 1960s and 1970s pop and rock songs), and its religious imagery. In so doing I draw upon some of the existing fan interpretations of this album (found on the Internet and elsewhere) while adding some of my own. Finally, Chapter 6 considers the lasting influence of *The Lamb* on both Gabriel's solo career and the career of the band he left behind after six studio albums, as well as *The Lamb*'s continued longevity through neo-progressive bands and Genesis tribute bands such as The Musical Box.

Although *The Lamb Lies Down on Broadway* may not have the iconic stature of Pink Floyd's *Dark Side of the Moon* or Yes's *Tales from Topographic Oceans*, it nonetheless manages to encapsulate both the zenith of progressive rock and the decline of the 1970s. Like *Dark Side of the Moon*, *The Lamb* possesses a timeless quality that transcends the historical period in which it was made, retaining its emotional and dramatic power even today. At the same time, it represents the culmination of a period when record companies and producers took on the role of impresarios, providing seemingly unlimited financial resources for the creation of music guided by the principle of "art for art's sake." After *The Lamb*—and perhaps spurred by the debacle surrounding *Tales from Topographic Oceans*—economic constraints began to curtail the wilder creative flights of fancy (some would say excesses) of progressive rock musicians. The economic and social conditions that led to the "retreat to simplicity" epitomized by punk and new wave are in fact prefigured by *The Lamb*, which manages to comment upon the period in which it was created even as one may listen to it without being reminded of that period.

This, then, is the story of Rael … .

Chapter 1

"It's the last great adventure left to mankind": Situating *The Lamb*

With the marvelous complicity of its entire population, New York acts out its own catastrophe as a stage play.

—Jean Baudrillard[1]

New York has inspired creative visionaries for decades. In transferring its rhythm and energy into words, Walt Whitman's poetry burst through the boundaries of classical meter. George Gershwin captured the vitality of New York's jazz age in works such as "Rhapsody in Blue." Leonard Bernstein, Steven Sondheim and Jerome Robbins supercharged a Shakespeare story with inspirations from two of New York's prominent subcultures and contemporary accounts of juvenile delinquency to create *West Side Story*. Whether one considers the diversity of literary styles between, for example, F. Scott Fitzgerald and Allen Ginsberg, or between filmmakers Martin Scorsese and Woody Allen, or between musicians John Cage and Bob Dylan, New York has provided inspiration for all of them.

New York in the 1970s was altogether less romantic. The city was in the grip of a persistent fiscal crisis that bankrupted the city by the end of the decade. Between 1970 and 1980, 824,000 residents deserted the city (Markowitz, 2003); corporations likewise pulled out, and the widespread perception of New York was of a city sinking into a seedy decline, from which it would not effectively emerge until the mid-1990s. Yet as New York lost much of its romantic allure in the 1970s, it still provided a rich source of inspiration, at least for rock musicians. Lou Reed and Paul Simon each provided their own literate, witty spins on tales of New York's denizens, its high- and low-lifes. Punk rock was to emerge here from bands such as the Ramones, Television, and others who played at Hilly Kristal's club CBGB. By the end of the 1970s, a thriving avant-garde renaissance would be in full flower in the "downtown" SoHo district, spearheaded by such soon-to-be-prominent musicians and artists as Philip Glass, Keith Haring, and Laurie Anderson.

This gritty urban scene would seem to be an odd backdrop for a British progressive-rock band's concept-album fantasy, but just as New York had inspired Walt Whitman and Andy Warhol, so it also came to enthrall a young upper-middle-class English rock musician named Peter Gabriel. Like Baudrillard—and Charles Dickens, who visited the city in 1842 and was appalled by the poverty and squalor

---

[1]   From Jean Baudrillard, *America*, translated by Chris Turner (1989), p. 22.

he saw, describing it as worse than London's—Gabriel was fascinated by New York's "catastrophe" acted out "as a stage play." He responded by creating his own "stage play" for which the "catastrophe" of "early morning Manhattan" could serve as a fitting location. New York, it would seem, never leaves those who have lived there. The experiences of young Rael—the half-Puerto-Rican "street punk" Gabriel created as his protagonist for *The Lamb Lies Down on Broadway*—would be altogether different if Rael were, for example, an East-End Londoner.

In the 1970s, if you were young and artistically ambitious, it seemed as if writing the "Great American Novel" was no longer a worthy pursuit; instead, chances are you were a rock musician trying to record the ultimate concept album. The concept album—a collection of songs (or sometimes a even single album-length song) arranged around a single subject ("concept") or narrative structure, became the rock version of the nineteenth-century song cycle. It became the vehicle of choice for exploring "deep" philosophical ideas in a sustained manner, an invitation for the listener to join in the artist's contemplation and enter their artistic universe for a while. Music critic Jon Landau once asserted, "The criterion of art in rock is the capacity of the musician to create a personal, almost private, universe and to express it fully" (Garofalo, 1997, p. 249). If Landau is correct, the concept album was one of the most prominent and distinctive manifestations of rock's "art" impulse in the late 1960s and early 1970s.

Art and commerce: Progressive music and "progressive" marketing

"Nobody went around actually *calling* themselves progressive," recalls Tom Newman, a musician who wound up working as engineer on Mike Oldfield's gargantuan *Tubular Bells* album—the album that launched a record mega-label (Virgin) and embodied progressive aesthetic with its epic pseudo-classical structure and its look-mum-I-can-play-it-all-myself conceit. "The press did, the industry did" (Stump, 1997, p. 76). Before 1972, at least, progressive rock was "hardly a unified style," according to musicologist Allan Moore, in his book *Rock: The Primary Text* (one of the first to objectively examine progressive rock's aesthetics). Moore notes that at one point the term "extended from 'art' rock on the one hand through 'hard' rock to styles of 'folk' rock" (2001, p. 69). The commonality among all these styles involved extending rock's formal and musical syntaxes "through infusion with a variety of foreign influences" (ibid.), especially "musical features seeming to have little in common with those of Afro-American musical traditions" (p. 102). Even as late as 1973—by which time, thanks to the success of albums such as Pink Floyd's *Dark Side of the Moon* and Yes's *Close to the Edge*, the music industry was moving toward excising non-"symphonic" elements from accepted definitions of "progressive" style—Lester Bangs cast a very wide stylistic net for his discussion of what he called "the Progressives." Bangs's article covered groups as diverse as Traffic, Soft Machine, Jethro Tull, Emerson, Lake and Palmer (ELP),

Pink Floyd, Procol Harum, The Band, the Grateful Dead, the Allman Brothers, and Johnny Winter:

> Why do we call 'em the Progressives? Because that's what they are ... . They have the common aim in mind of advancing the whole of rock as an art form through the systematic and craftsmanlike absorption of the likeliest elements from every other style of music known to this planet. You might not like to hear rock 'n' roll called "art," and some of the musicians in this chapter would agree with you. Some of them would even say that the term "rock 'n' roll" is too inhibiting. Why put labels on anything anyway? Just let the music be what it is. Others among this motley crew would insist that rock *must* fulfill itself as art to transcend its crude beginnings. And, further, that they are the ones who are enabling it to do that so that it may survive. (Bangs, 1973, p. 87)

Originally, then, "progressive" artists sought to expand the commonly accepted boundaries of what was considered to be "rock." At the same time, these musicians sought to validate their work as art; and, even though few of them had extensive training in "classical" music, such music provided a ready model for their cultural aspirations. Journalist Paul Stump, in his book *The Music's All That Matters*, writes that this music was "'progressive' in the sense that the sounds these musicians made seemed to shake up, superficially, existing popular-music expression and urge it vaguely towards modernist/Romantic art music" (1997, p. 90). It was "a beseeching of—or a defiant gesture towards—a parental generation that had explicitly belittled the idea that their children's music could ever attain artistic credibility" (p. 50).

The seven-inch 45 RPM single, the medium associated with rock and roll since its beginnings, came to be seen as something to be transcended. Few pop singles were longer than three and a half minutes long; the seven-inch single represented, by virtue of its own limitations, the temporal limits imposed by commercial radio. Albums, at least until 1966 or so, were usually marketing afterthoughts intended to compile successful singles; the single was what drove the market. In the mid-1960s, artists began to work toward circumventing the three-minute limit. Back in 1964, for example, producer Phil Spector misrepresented the length of the Righteous Brothers single "You've Lost That Loving Feeling" on the record's label as 3:05 (rather than its true length of 3:50) so that it would get airplay, and Bob Dylan's "Like A Rolling Stone" (1965) was so long it was split across both sides of the 45, resulting in many stations playing the album track instead.

The real difference between progressive rock and "pop" of the day, according to Moore, "lay in the connotation the style had for its audience; for few students and hippies did the music function primarily as entertainment" (p. 69). Indeed, for rock's student and hippie cognoscenti music was a ritualistic backdrop—for getting high, for discussing philosophy and politics, and ultimately for defining one's social and subcultural identity. Paul Willis, in his important study of the hippie subculture *Profane Culture*, notes that music occupied a central role in the hippie lifestyle, and it held pride of place in the hippies' construction of identity because of its ambiguous "meaning" for outsiders: "It was impossible to decode. It could safely hold contradictory, otherwise unexpressed or profound meanings" (1978, p. 106). Music was part of what Stump describes as "an entire leisure *commodity*" that "immediately began generating its own signs and signifiers: dislocation, sensory autonomy, pluralism. The discourse, the Romantic individualism consecrated by the Beats in the 1950s, was beginning to assume its own concrete identity" (1997, p. 29). This ethic of "Romantic individualism" can be traced back in part to the success of the Beatles as original songwriters, which "nullified mediation between performer and production process, a luxury unavailable to most popular entertainers outside the jazz world" (Stump, 1997, p. 40). Referring to music as part of a "leisure commodity," on the other hand, suggests that this lifestyle could be packaged and marketed. This is exactly what the music industry set out to do, and exactly what Frank Zappa recognized as early as 1967's prescient *We're Only In It For the Money* album.

When the Beatles released *Sgt. Pepper's Lonely Hearts Club Band* in June 1967, they were already at the top of the global music industry. Its commercial success was thus virtually pre-ordained; its artistic success, however, while not unexpected given the experiments already glimpsed on *Rubber Soul* (1965) and *Revolver* (1966), was unprecedented. The success of *Sgt. Pepper* was pivotal in establishing the progressive aesthetic. Moore credits *Sgt. Pepper* with the "realignment of rock from its working-class roots to its subsequent place on the college circuit" (2001, p. 65).

Granted, other albums—such as Frank Zappa and the Mothers of Invention's *Freak Out!* (1966)—had already begun to breach the boundary between "disposable" pop and "serious" rock. *Sgt. Pepper* merely gave an established "commercial" rock voice to an alternative youth culture that had been brewing in London as early as 1961, around a "loose coalescence of jazz, Beat poetry and avant-garde art" (Stump, 1997, p. 24). By 1964, with Britain in the grip of Beatlemania and the first wave of British Invasion bands succeeding in the American pop charts, Britain's "art-school preoccupation with art's sacred stature, the primacy of individual expression, had been filtered through jazz to young British musicians who now saw the Beatles pointing a guitar-led route to riches" (Stump, 1997, p. 25).

Musicologist Edward Macan, in his study of English progressive rock and its roots in the counterculture *Rocking the Classics*, defines progressive rock as an extension and consolidation of earlier psychedelic music. He summarizes psychedelic and progressive rock's original subculture, as it coalesced between 1966 and about 1971, as "regionally distinct" and "essentially homogeneous in terms of its members' ages and class origins":

> Like the musicians, the audience was young (under thirty); it was centered above all in southeastern England; its socioeconomic background was solidly middle class and it shared the musicians' general educational backgrounds, and thus their familiarity with the art, literature, and music of high culture. The only major difference between audience and performers at this time involved gender: while the audience seems to have

had a roughly equal female–male ratio, the performers were overwhelmingly male. (Macan, 1997, pp. 151–152)

Stump also connects the subculture with Britain's universities, asserting that "redbrick colleges practically kept Progressive alive" in its early years, helping to create "an audience for Progressive as a lifestyle, as a separate culture, a signifier for a newly-defined 'other'" (1997, p. 73).

Macan argues that there is a homologous relationship between the musical elements that characterize progressive rock and the values of the hippie counterculture. For example, he finds that "the consistent use of lengthy forms such as the programmatic song cycle of the concept album and the multimovement suite underscores the hippies' new, drug-induced conception of time" (1997, p. 13). Elsewhere he provides other homologies:

> Progressive rock's attachment to dense arrangements, complex mazes of shifting meters, and spasmodic solos created the sense of unpredictability, tension, and nonconformity which the hippies found so spectacularly lacking in the Establishment-approved pop styles. Furthermore, its complexity served as a symbol of resistance against the Establishment, as a gate that separated the uncomprehending "straights" from the mysteries of the hippie subculture. (Macan, 1997, p. 51)

This last point is important, for it brings to mind the modernist and somewhat exclusivist stance on art espoused famously by Arnold Schoenberg: "If it is art, it is not for all, and if it is for all, it is not art" (1975, p. 124). The "resistance" inherent in musical complexity is an implicit point in Schoenbergian apologist Theodor Adorno's neo-Marxist critique of popular music, which in its formal standardization was found to embody the ethic of capitalist mass-production and unquestioning acceptance of the "culture industry."[2] Nonetheless, with a few notable exceptions (Henry Cow and the "Rock in Opposition" subgenre of progressive, for example), progressive rock was notably apolitical, especially when compared with some of the American psychedelic (Jefferson Airplane) and hard rock (Steppenwolf) groups of the period. As Allan Moore puts it:

> Some musicians were associated with the ("progressive") aims and ambitions of late-1960s' counter-culture, always more apparent in the USA than in the UK, but "association" was normally as far as any relationship went … . Few of the musicians were as politically involved either as their audiences believed, or indeed as many of those audiences themselves were. (Moore, 2001, p. 64)

Some of the comments made by progressive rock musicians themselves confirm Moore's statement. For example, Genesis's keyboardist Tony Banks, referring to

---

[2] For a summation of this critique, to which progressive rock offers a surprisingly nuanced response, see especially Adorno, 1989.

the group's first overseas gig in Belgium in 1971, noted that the group's song "The Knife" was a particular favorite among audiences. "They seemed to go for the pseudo-revolutionary thing which was very tongue-in-cheek from our point of view, but they seemed to take it seriously and they loved it" (Russell, 2004, p. 203).

If the musicians saw no inherent politicization in their musical complexity, then, some fans certainly did. The music industry—which was already cashing in on radical chic with advertising slogans such as Columbia Records' "The Man can't bust our music"—was quick to oblige in furthering this perception. Thus, popular music scholar Reebee Garofalo's critique that the label of "progressive" rock was "a term which resonated nicely with the radical rhetoric of the era" (1997, p. 244), while perhaps somewhat cynical, is not inaccurate. It was all too convenient a label for describing and positioning this nascent musical style.

Popular music sociologist Simon Frith has outlined the procedures for the emergence of what he has calls new "genre worlds" in the music industry. Once a musical style seems to spontaneously emerge from the "streets" or from the "ground up," as it were, the music industry isolates particular features of that style and thus constructs the new genre as a *marketing* category. Frith writes that a new "genre world" is "first constructed then articulated through a complex interplay of musicians, listeners, and mediating ideologues, and this process is much more confused than the marketing process that follows, as the wider industry begins to make sense of the new sounds and markets to exploit both genre worlds and genre discourses in the orderly routine of mass marketing" (1996, p. 88). The music industry sets such "genre boundaries" through its marketing and distribution practices: financially successful bands tend to receive higher production and promotional budgets, which in turn tend to further the successes of those groups; more marginal groups receive less support and accordingly often remain marginal, "cult" bands. At the same time, new groups are often formed in emulation of successful examples. Moore's observation that "once the norms of any style have been set, many less well-known musicians work quite happily within them" (2001, p. 68) is thus true in a marketing as well as a musical sense.

Progressive rock emerged, rather uniquely, through the "trial and error" of testing such genre boundaries, much in the same way that record companies did in the mid-1950s as rock and roll was emerging into mainstream popular culture:

> Initially, the record companies could not tailor the music to the masses, as they did with so many other styles of popular music; they could only react to demands for the new music by signing a wide range of acts and carefully monitoring what sold and what didn't ... . Record company "turbulence" during the late 1960s and early 1970s gave artists recording at this time a creative control over their music that was virtually unprecedented in the history of popular music. There is also no doubt that without this leeway for experimentation, the economic conditions would have never existed for · progressive rock's appearance. (Macan, 1997, p. 18)

Moore also concurs that "the economic situation of the record companies, effective employers of bands" was the paramount factor in encouraging such experimentation:

> Not only did they see the world market rapidly expanding, but the consumer boom in the UK yielded them large returns, enabling them to invest in their artists without requiring an immediate financial return ... and also to relinquish a degree of control over the resultant product and its marketing. (Moore, 2001, p. 65)

In summary, Macan attributes the sea-change in pop music that began in mid-1960s Britain to the:

> specific alignment of cultural and economic forces—the appearance of the counterculture, the formation of the psychedelic style, the rise of a network of clubs, radio stations, and publications around the music, and an entirely new relationship between the musicians and the record companies. (Macan, 1997, p. 18)

Money was "the engine room of the underground," fueling these experiments (Stump, 1997, p. 27).

"By 1968," Simon Frith observes, "the commercial viability of 'progressive' rock was obvious" (1983, p. 97). Marketing of the new "progressive" product was facilitated by its being distinguishable from its more light-weight "pop" counterpart, being released on separate "progressive" labels aimed at the college-circuit market (Moore, 2001, p. 65). In the words of Dave Betteridge, a manager at the time for then-independent Island Records: "there was a college circuit being built and a new audience was emerging. And we were running in tandem, *supplying their needs*" (Stump, 1997, p. 76, emphasis added).

EMI was the first label to start its own "progressive" imprint, setting up Harvest in 1968; other labels were quick to follow. For example, Philips had Vertigo, RCA had Neon, and Decca had Deram Nova; major labels also quickly snapped up distribution deals for independent labels such as Island and Charisma (Stump, 1997, p. 73). These labels had a mystique such that consumers would buy previously unheard groups on those labels simply on the grounds of the labels' reputation for "artistic integrity" (Stump, 1997, p. 78). Noted broadcaster John Peel, whose *Top Gear* show on BBC Radio 1 provided invaluable exposure for the new emerging style, later recalled that "in those days the labels seemed to know they had a responsibility beyond straight-forward commerce. They'd set these things up ... knowing they might make a loss, but knowing they might find something profitable" (Stump, 1997, p. 76). In 1969, rock album sales surpassed pop single sales for the first time; the album, rather than the single, accordingly became the dominant focus of the music industry (Stump, 1997, p. 73). *Sounds*, the first British publication specifically devoted to progressive music, began publication in October 1970 (Stump, 1997, p. 91), and the BBC television show

The Old Grey Whistle Test, a kind of *Top of the Pops* (another BBC television show) for the progressive set, went on the air in the same year (p. 92).

If fusions with "classical" music styles came to be marketed as "progressive rock," the musicians themselves certainly helped it to happen. Macan notes that progressive rock's continual references to classical music are:

> emblematic of the musicians' middle- and upper-class backgrounds. Progressive rock as an idiom can be understood as a forum in which the musicians attempt to forge a dialectical relationship between the high culture of their parents and the popular culture that they grew up in, dominated by African-American musical forms. (Macan, 1997, p. 13)

More accurately:

> Progressive rock is thoroughly grounded in African-American musical concepts such as group composition, improvisation (or at least the performer's right to realize certain aspects of a piece differently in each performance), and a general lack of reliance on notation. At the same time, however, progressive rock musicians thoroughly absorbed the essence of European programmatic forms such as the song cycle and the multimovement suite, and this point cannot be overstated. (Macan, 1997, pp. 165–166)

The use of classical music is also seen by some as more than a mere consequence of musicians' socioeconomic background. Some musicians—such as Yes's Jon Anderson—came from working-class backgrounds. Allan Moore notes that:

> "classical" music is popularly perceived as having its own aesthetic, based on its lack of "survival value" (in that, unlike heat and water, it is not a commodity necessary to survival), giving it an apparent autonomy, to which rock has always been equivocal. These pretensions clearly suggest that rock musicians were asking for their product to be judged as art. (Moore, 2001, p. 92)

The "art for art's sake" aesthetic inherent in progressive rock once again dovetails with the hippie culture's propensity for the obscure and arcane.

Another essential element in the construction of progressive rock, perhaps fostered by its musicians being almost exclusively white males, is the influence of fantasy and speculative fiction. Allan Moore cites musicians' "concentration on obscure and occult (in the sense of 'hidden') matters, their lack of obvious personal reference and their clear attempt to provide an alternative way of looking at things, even if this was not clear to the uninitiated" (p. 110). He writes:

> The importance of the fantastic in rock seems predicated upon gnosis … . Classically, gnostic faiths are based on beliefs that salvation is gained by knowledge, rather than by faith or by works or some other means … . Obscurity is hence to be striven for in their construction, since it intensifies the achievement of the goal … . This sealing-off is typical of a gnostic attitude: whereas in the summer of 1967 salvation had seemed open

to all (even if it wasn't), very soon the language's obscurity encouraged separation. (Moore, 2001, pp. 111–112)

Indeed, an American English literature student was reportedly able to devote an entire master's thesis to interpreting the lyrics to Procol Harum's "A Salty Dog" (Stump, 1997, p. 57).

The gnostic qualities of progressive rock helped to "set [progressive] bands apart from the 'commercial' end of the market" (Moore, 2001, p. 110), so these features were certainly foregrounded by record companies, graphic designers, and so forth as a "positioning" device. (Interestingly, today a progressive-rock fan web site, consisting mainly of album reviews, calls itself "Gnosis" [http://gnosis2000. net].) The visual sense of the entire genre was shaped largely through the album covers of the graphic design firm Hipgnosis (the name punning on both the chic of "hip" and the obscurity of "gnosis") (Stump, 1997, p. 95). Storm Thorgerson and Aubrey "Po" Powell, the founders of Hipgnosis, were friends of Pink Floyd who ultimately designed virtually every Pink Floyd cover from *A Saucerful of Secrets* (1968) through *Animals* (1977), as well as a host of other memorable covers such as Led Zeppelin's *Houses of the Holy* (1973). When Genesis wanted the cover of *The Lamb Lies Down on Broadway* to break away from the bizarre fantasy elements that had become associated with them largely through the covers of Paul Whitehead (*Trespass*, *Nursery Cryme*, *Foxtrot*), they approached Hipgnosis.

Progressive rock writ large: The concept album

Macan observes that psychedelic music shared with nineteenth-century music a Romantic worldview, "sharing the same cosmic outlook, the same preoccupation with the infinite and otherworldly, the same fondness for monumental statement (often conveyed through very long pieces), and the same concern with expressing epic conflicts" (1997, p. 41). These same concerns are present, to a hyperbolic degree, in progressive rock. In fact, the most distinctive formal archetype in progressive rock—the "concept album"—is an inherently Romantic form. Progressive rock musicians "used the term 'concept' in exactly the same sense that nineteenth-century composers used the term 'program'" (Macan, 1997, p. 58).

As I have already pointed out, most progressive rock musicians actually lacked formal training in the very style of art music they were imitating. Thus, artists who created vast concept albums appeared to be unaware that "very few classical pieces attempt to achieve a sense of unity across spans in excess of half an hour" (Moore, 2001, p. 97). Nevertheless, these musicians evidently intended for concept albums to do exactly that, sometimes—in the case of a double album—for up to an hour and a half.

The changing fortunes of the concept album may be observed in comparing two representative examples recorded by Jethro Tull, 1972's *Thick as a Brick* and 1973's *A Passion Play*. Both albums consisted of album-length multi-movement suites, even though individual sections were not given titles or labeled as "movements" as such. Both albums were commercial successes, reaching positions 5 and 13 respectively in the British album charts (Moore, 2001, p. 92). In the US, both albums reached #1 (Whitburn, 1995, p. 159). However, "live performances of *Passion Play* were poorly received, and both albums (but particularly this one) received such critical panning in the UK that leader Ian Anderson vowed not to tour again (a promise he kept for a year)" (Moore, 2001, p. 92). The negative critical response and lukewarm audience reception to performances of *Passion Play* and Yes's *Tales from Topographic Oceans* (also released in 1973) led to the concept album largely being considered "passé" in some quarters by 1974, when Genesis began work on *The Lamb*.

Progressive rock was thus disseminated to its audiences primarily through the acquisition of albums and through concert performances. Longer tracks, especially album- or side-length suites such as comprised the two aforementioned Jethro Tull concept efforts, were simply too long for most commercial radio stations, even in the pre-format early 1970s (Macan, 1997, p. 57). Thus, the album and the concert performance became inextricably linked in the 1970s, and the quasi-liturgical experience offered by a progressive rock show[3] was increasingly supplanted by the more materialist and utilitarian role of promoting the most recent recording, as guitarist Robert Fripp of King Crimson explains:

> The musicians in King Crimson [in 1973–74] didn't get paid for live work: wages were not budgeted into the tour accounts. The rationale was that album and publishing royalties generated from the sale of the records we had "promoted" was our payment. Management deducted their percentage from the fees from live work, which we didn't see, as well as from records and publishing, the companies of which they owned. (Fripp, 1992, p. 4)

Moore asserts that the *notion* of the "concept album," in fact, has since "grown to the extent that all rock tours have acquired particular identities, existing largely to promote a particular album or set of material as a package" (2001, p. 92). *The Lamb* tour thus may be seen as a very early example of this direction toward all-encompassing promotional spectacles such as Pink Floyd's *The Wall* performances and U2's *Zoo TV* tour.

Progressive rock in changing social contexts

Macan sees in progressive rock's adoption of intricate forms, such as the multi-movement suite and the concept album, a "tacit acknowledgment that some

---

[3]   Macan argues that progressive rock concerts had an almost "liturgical" function for fans, because "the counterculture had fully accepted the Romantic notion of the Artist as Prophet or Seer" (1997, p. 68).

sort of order, however loose, would be necessary after all in order to avoid total incoherence," concluding that such formal constraints poignantly reflect "the hippies' ultimate accommodation to the conventions of industrial society" (1997, p. 56). The change from the theoretically "wide-open" jamming style of psychedelia (the Grateful Dead's "Dark Star," for example—or even Iron Butterfly's "In-A-Gadda-da-Vida" with its potentially endless drum solo) to the narrowly proscribed musical mannerisms of Yes or Genesis also perhaps symbolizes the change in societal beliefs, from the unbridled idealism of the Kennedy years to the recognition in the 1970s that seemingly everything had limits and limitations (a point I explore at the end of this chapter).

At the point in progressive rock's history at which Genesis released *The Lamb Lies Down on Broadway*, progressive's traditionally "reconciliatory" stance toward stylistic appropriation became balanced with "regressive" tendencies that work to "recapture past glories, from within rock itself" (Moore, 2001, p. 67). Bands such as Yes and ELP were seen by the critics (though perhaps not by fans) to be treading water stylistically by the mid-1970s. Perhaps sensing this stagnation themselves, both ELP and Yes spent some time on self-searching hiatus in 1975–76. The members of Yes, from vocalist to drummer, all engaged in making solo albums. ELP, having reached the zenith of their style with 1973's *Brain Salad Surgery* and the gargantuan world tour that followed (amply documented on a triple live release) spent a lengthy period out of the spotlight. They would not re-emerge until 1977's *Works Volume 1*; the structure of that album—three solo sides followed by a group side—shows the same pattern of individualistic retrenchment as Yes's solo releases while hearkening back to the structure of Pink Floyd's *Ummagumma* (1969). *The Lamb* addresses pop's "former glories" in a different way, however. It is unique among Genesis's 1970s releases in its musical and textual references to rock and pop's past, specifically the early 1960s (a point that I will take up in more detail in Chapters 3 and 5).

"Art for art's sake, Money for God's sake": Progressive rock's decline

If progressive rock was so closely aligned with the values of the counterculture that spawned it, why did it so quickly fall from favor? Several factors contributed to its decline. Robert Fripp ascribes at least part of the blame to the changes in the music industry that occurred in the decade following 1968:

> In the Sixties, rock music could change the world. In the Seventies and Eighties, politics and economics did change the world, and the music business ... .

> The record industry in the period 1968–78 was a seemingly unstoppable growth industry. The early amateurism surrounding the rock business had professionalized by about 1974, although this increased throughout the Seventies and Eighties. Records became "product" and "units" which moved, audiences became "consumers" whose

"behavioral patterns" were charted by "demographics". Something went terribly, terribly wrong in our sense of values. Pragmatics replaced Principle. Quantity replaced Quality. (Fripp, 1992, p. 4)

Martin (1998) has situated progressive rock within what he calls the "popular avant-garde" (p. 96) of the late 1960s and early 1970s, noting that label executives and producers accordingly "played the important role of patrons and impresarios" (p. 95). In the case of Genesis, the unstinting support provided by Charisma Records and its founder Tony Stratton-Smith certainly allowed the group to develop its own distinctive voice and following. The idealistic scenario soon unraveled, however, in the face of "business as usual."

> The pre-Progressive bourgeois youth adoption of jazz and art-school aesthetics, the consciously slumming aspirations to lower-class values and styles, had now become a new middle-class aspiration governed by material privilege. The play ethic of the late 1960s had been replaced by a studio-bound work ethic. While this would produce unique and excellent music, it also produced a sessionman-virtuoso culture. (Stump, 1997, pp. 206–207)

A song from the fall of 1975 by British "progressive pop" group 10cc summed up the change: "Art for art's sake, Money for God's sake."

The gleefully eclectic stylistic pluralism that Lester Bangs celebrated in his essay "The Progressives" and that the UK scene had witnessed in the period from 1968 to 1972 had, by 1975, come to be whittled down. "Progressive" rock was by now almost exclusively associated with the "symphonic" style of classical-rock fusion promulgated by the genre's most commercially successful bands—Yes, ELP, and Genesis. Bands that formerly had been key to progressive rock's development—such as Jethro Tull, Pink Floyd, and Procol Harum—were accordingly shunted to other marketing categories such as "psychedelia" or "hard rock."

All three of progressive rock's main chroniclers—Macan, Stump, and Moore—agree that in the early 1970s, progressive rock came to be defined by the music industry in terms of a narrow set of stylistic parameters, and that such stylistic barriers helped lead to the genre's stagnation. For example, Macan observes that by 1972, "the formation of progressive rock as a distinct style was essentially complete" (1997, p. 25); after 1972 new groups that emerged were essentially continuations or slight modifications of the templates established by established bands (p. 26). While Macan chooses to optimistically refer to the period from 1971 to 1976 as English progressive rock's "golden age" (1997, p. 27), Stump notes that as early as 1973 progressive rock had "found its voice and the acts to put it across," diminishing the music industry's "desire to unearth new talent" (1997, pp. 109–110). The industry's aforementioned practice of establishing and defining genre norms through marketing had a stagnating effect on progressive rock by the mid-1970s; although it was commercially successful, the music was no longer "progressing" (Moore, 2001, p. 66).

Macan correctly connects the fragmentation of the counterculture's rock into various "formats"—glam rock, progressive rock, heavy metal, et al.—to the "fragmentation of the essentially unified youth culture that existed between 1966 and 1970 into a number of distinct subcultures along national, regional, and class lines" (1997, p. 19). At the same time, however, it should be pointed out that record companies were getting savvier about their consumers as well. Radio was soon to catch on; in America, for example, the emergence in the mid-1970s of AOR (Album Oriented Radio) and other radio formats, specifically targeted to particular demographics, further discouraged extended musical experiments, which increasingly came to be regarded as self-indulgent. The same "alignment of cultural and economic forces" between record companies, radio, and the press that fostered the emergence of progressive rock thus shifted allegiances, leading to an economic stranglehold on progressive rock.

In Britain, the audience itself changed, as hippie idealism soured under persistent economic hardship and the explosion in numbers of unemployed youth on the dole. Allan Moore writes that the "gnostic ideology inherent in the use of fantastic and obscure imagery, itself supported by the apparent 'strangeness' of the stylistic fusions" ultimately became too obscure for many British listeners, especially working-class consumers, who "did not feel part of this music at all" (2001, p. 114). Along with the potential alienating effects of a gnostic aesthetic, the audience's engagement with progressive rock changed with the change of the music's performance venues in the early 1970s, as it went from small clubs (chiefly in Britain) to large-scale tours of arenas (chiefly in the US). Such gigantic tours "became necessary to generate the huge volume of sales that record company executives increasingly expected" (Macan, 1997, p. 28). This change particularly affected progressive rock's fan base in Britain, where fans might go for years between opportunities to see their favorite band in live performance. It didn't help perceptions among what was left of the British counterculture in the mid-1970s that major artists also began to record and live outside Britain, in order to avoid punitive British tax codes. This further contributed to progressive rock's estrangement from the counterculture that had nurtured the genre.

Progressive rock's high ambition also admittedly carried with it a high price tag. The genre depended on "the visual qualities associated with large-scale staging, and on good studio recordings, both of which required heavy investment and therefore high commercial returns" (Moore, 2001, p. 69). Major labels such as CBS increased the financial advances offered to bands in the early 1970s. While such arrangements facilitated the production of exacting and expensive studio recordings, they also resulted in "increasing the numbers of sales necessary for break-even and, inevitably, the amount one had to spend on promotion" (Stump, 1997, p. 205). This led to a kind of indentured servitude, the artists themselves being "deeply in hock to record-company capital, an arrangement that alienated audiences and made bands' own survival even more dependent on industry whim" (Stump, 1997, p. 204). Progressive rock's economic foundation was ultimately cut out from under it by the considerable expenses involved in its production and promotion, as diminishing amounts of money were "spread thinner over fewer bands" (Stump, 1997, p. 110). When compared with progressive rock, punk was seen as simply more "realistic," closer to many listeners' working-class experiences; it was easier for musicians to "break into the business" playing, and easier for record companies to produce and promote.

Even in the face of the uprising of punk, however, progressive rock still maintained its commercial viability in 1976–77, at least among listeners in Britain. While the much-touted Sex Pistols placed fifth among the top five British bands in *Melody Maker*'s end-of-year readers' poll in 1977, three of the remaining four groups (Genesis, Yes, Led Zeppelin, and ELP) were progressive rock bands (Platts, 2001, p. 107).

Genesis and the progressive paradigm

Stump identifies three cardinal points of progressive ideology: First, "the cosmology of English eccentricity, mysticism and pastoralism"; second, "a spiritual autonomy of the musician-creator always close to Romantic ideology"; and third, "the notion of Bohemian community" (p. 111). All three points resonate with Genesis's history as a band and its emergence as a leading group in the progressive rock genre. Therefore, although the group's history has been well covered in various biographies, a summary is necessary here, in order to explore how these ideological strands were deeply woven throughout Genesis's early career and to situate *The Lamb Lies Down on Broadway* as the culmination of the band's progressive trajectory.

The story of Genesis begins at the Charterhouse School, one of those English "public schools" thoroughly steeped in British tradition and rigorous (some would say cruel) discipline. Charterhouse was founded in London in 1611; the school was relocated to Godalming, Surrey in 1872 (Bright, 1988, p. 19).

> "I hated Charterhouse, it was terrible."
> —Peter Gabriel (Bowler and Dray, 1993, p. 6)

> "I went through periods of being extremely unhappy. I was shy and liked to be on my own a lot and the Charterhouse system is not good for people like that."
> — Tony Banks (ibid.)

> "It wasn't a good place for any of us. We weren't right for it—they're easier if you're into sport and activities which we weren't."
> —Michael Rutherford (ibid., p. 10)

> "Without playing and writing I'd have gone crazy."
> —Anthony Phillips (ibid.)

Peter Gabriel was, along with Tony Banks, the first future member of Genesis to arrive at Charterhouse; the two arrived in September 1963, when they were 13. Banks was already something of a boarding-school veteran, having already entered Boarzell prep school in Hurst Green when he was only seven years old (Bowler and Dray, 1993, p. 6). Michael Rutherford came to Charterhouse next, in September 1964, just before his 14th birthday; Anthony Phillips arrived in the following spring, in April 1965 (Bowler and Dray, 1993, p. 10). For four shy, awkward teenagers, Charterhouse could be a repressive and intimidating place. Music, particularly pop and rock music in the "swinging London" era of 1965–66, became a source of refuge and escape:

> Inevitably, a group of adolescent boys housed in the repressive atmosphere of an English public school, one of the last great repositories of Victorian values and the spirit of Empire, would find concepts such as revolution, freedom and the overthrow of the old guard in favour of a more creative way of life very attractive. However, as boarders, reality meant that uniforms still had to be worn, hair kept short, lessons attended and standards upheld—failure to do so would mean punishment … .

> Weekends were a little more relaxed and, inspired by the hits of the day, groups of boys would gather to attempt to recreate these songs and write their own. The very fact that the members of the fledgling Genesis were virtually forced to stay within the confines of the school grounds enabled them to apply the fullest concentration to their music. In the "outside world", people of their own age had any number of leisure activities with which they could fill their spare time, but Banks, Gabriel, et al., had little choice—sport or music being the only real options available to them. (Bowler and Dray, 1993, pp. 5–6)

The billiards room was the only place in Charterhouse where students were allowed to play records. Gabriel told his biographer Spencer Bright, "It had this really beaten-up, old Dansette record player in a wooden cabinet. You could only play it for about an hour and a half every day. I used to take my Otis Redding records in there and turn them up full volume and dance until I was in a frenzied sweat. This ritual gave me an immense feeling of relief" (p. 25).

The "lack of black influence" perceived in progressive rock was a frequent critical point of contention (Moore, 2001, p. 74). While the "whiteness" of progressive rock was arguably true—largely because of the socioeconomic background of most progressive rock artists and the extreme "other" status of blacks living in Britain in the late 1960s,[4] Peter Gabriel was perhaps the exception to the critical generalization. Gabriel viewed the music of black American soul

---

[4]   An obvious and vivid illustration of this racial "otherness," much commented upon, is the attention that was paid to Jimi Hendrix upon his arrival in London in 1966 and his perceived "novelty" as a black rock musician. For another example, the subculture of Jamaican expatriates that were already living in London in the 1960s did not come to widespread attention until Chris Blackwell of Island Records began marketing reggae

artists as something of a cathartic antidote to the "repressive atmosphere" he experienced at Charterhouse: "to hear things like Otis Redding and the Stax and Motown artists, they seemed very free and open and liberating ... . I think these were pivotal experiences that made us want to get involved with music" (Bowler and Dray, 1993, p. 9). Gabriel and Tony Banks used to sneak to the local "Record Corner" store in Godalming to listen to records by singers such as Otis Redding and James Brown. "We'd sneak there very bravely," Gabriel remembers, "because loafing around in cafés and record shops of the town was out and if were caught we would have been punished" (Bright, 1988, p. 25).

One of Gabriel's most powerful musical experiences was seeing Otis Redding perform live, in a club in Brixton on September 18, 1966 (Bright, 1988, p. 24):

> It is still my favourite gig of all time ... . He was my hero as a singer, definitely, and a lot of that music was part of what drove me to consider music for myself. I was a teenager, very impressionable and very ready to be impressed. (Bright, 1988, p. 25)

The soul influence is perhaps more obvious in Gabriel's post-Genesis soul music; "Sledgehammer" is a deft distillation of Marvin Gaye's "Grapevine" mannerisms, while "Steam" is more of a tribute to the Stax sound of Otis Redding. Nonetheless, one need not look farther than the opening to "Looking for Someone" (the opening track on Genesis's second album, *Trespass* [1970]) for the earliest evidence of soul music in Gabriel's singing. Likewise, although Moore is correct in asserting that "there tends to be an absence of such things as the extended use of vocal melismas" in progressive rock (2001, p. 74), that is exactly what happens in the vocal cadenza at the end of "Counting Out Time" on *The Lamb Lies Down on Broadway*. In some live performances of that song the melismatic coda would be extended for over a minute in length (Couture, n.d.).

Gabriel's first band was the Milords, which he joined as a drummer when he was fifteen (Bright, 1988, p. 26). In the summer of 1966, he became the drummer for a rhythm and blues group called the Spoken Word (Bright, 1988, p. 27). Gabriel was looking for an outlet for the songs he was writing, however. "Then I tried writing with Tony Banks, and he could play piano better than I could" (Bright, 1988, p. 28). Soon Gabriel and Banks began writing their own songs together, and eventually they formed a group that called itself the Garden Wall, with Gabriel singing and Chris Stewart on drums (Platts, 2001, p. 9).

Meanwhile, soon after Anthony Phillips's arrival at Charterhouse in April 1965, he put together his own band called Anon, with Rivers Job (bass), Rob Tyrell (drums), and Richard MacPhail (vocals); MacPhail would later become Genesis's sound mixer and equipment roadie in the group's early days. The group soon added Michael Rutherford as a second guitarist (Platts, 2001, p. 8). Phillips

---

music in 1972, by which time progressive rock was already a prominent and fully-formed musical genre.

and Rutherford began writing their own songs together in 1966, basing their style on the unique texture created by their interlocking 12-string guitar arpeggios.

The two bands that ultimately merged to become Genesis came together at a fateful concert in July 1966. Anon and the Garden Wall performed together at an end-of-school concert in Charterhouse; Anthony Phillips recalls the school's headmaster "with his hands firmly stuck in both of his ears because he couldn't take the noise" (Platts, 2001, p. 9):

> The school wasn't keen on us; pop bands were regarded as anarchists. There was a music teacher called Jeffrey Ford—a bit precious, but he let us do this unofficial concert—a beat concert, in the main hall! Not the official end-of-winter-term school concert. "Only one condition," he told us, "no announcements. Like a classical thing!" In the second half … Anon went onstage and one of the leads blew. Embarrassing silence … so Richard McPhail [*sic*], who was singing, said, "Sorry, ladies and gents, it's all part of the act—and now, we'd like to do one of our own songs." And there was a Vesuvian Jeffrey Wood in the wings, going, "Right, last number—off!" And he stopped the concert. He stopped the concert, and there was nearly a riot. (Stump, 1997, p. 49)

Anon broke up soon afterward, but Phillips and Rutherford continued to work together. When they had an opportunity in early 1967 to record a demo of their songs, they invited Tony Banks to play organ on the session. Banks in turn brought along Gabriel to record one of their own songs, "She is Beautiful" (which turned up on their first album, *From Genesis to Revelation*, as "The Serpent") (Platts, 2001, p. 9). At this time, the group thought of themselves more as a "songwriters club" than as a professional working band. "We thought these masterpieces were ready to be recorded by thousands of Number One recording stars," Gabriel later recounted (Platts, 2001, p. 10).

Gabriel now says that the Charterhouse experience:

> made us more original … . I think it gave us a classical influence, it gave us a sort of the idea of using the intellect in rock music, if you like, which is good and bad. Really, we did it without realizing it at all. We just did what we wanted. There were people that I tried to copy then, like Otis Redding, Nina Simone and Roger Chapman, and I've got no qualms about admitting that at all. (Gallo, 1980, p. 154).

The still un-named group received their first "break" courtesy of Jonathan King, a recent Charterhouse graduate who had made his mark with a pop hit entitled "Everyone's Gone to the Moon." They passed their demo tape to King via a friend who left it in King's car. King financed a second demo of the group in the summer of 1967, and was pleased enough with the results to secure them a deal with Decca Records. By that August, Rutherford was doubling on bass as well as guitar (Platts, 2001, pp. 10–11).

King was not sympathetic toward the group's more "progressive" tendencies, however, particularly Banks's "organ rubbish": "I told Tony Banks to cut his rather self-indulgent keyboard solos by three quarters, which he resented" (Platts, 2001, p. 11). Since King preferred Genesis's acoustic guitar-and-piano sound in a three-minute pop format, Banks and Gabriel responded with a tune called "The Silent Sun," which was modeled after the soft pop material that the Bee Gees were known for at the time. "The Silent Sun" was recorded at Regent Sound A in London in late December 1967; as Banks and Gabriel predicted, King decided this song was good enough to be their first single (Platts, 2001, p. 12). The song was released on February 22, 1968, but "mercifully," according to Phillips, "it wasn't successful" (Platts, 2001, p. 13).

It was King who named the group Genesis and who also provided the concept for *From Genesis to Revelation*. That album was recorded in a single marathon session, from 9 AM until midnight on September 4, 1968, at London's Regent Studio B (Platts, 2001, p. 15). According to Anthony Phillips, King:

> let us do this album, which was kind of much more visionary. The songs weren't particularly commercial. They didn't really have build-ups to the choruses. They weren't aimed specifically at the singles market. He just basically let us do our own thing, up to a point. (Platts, 2001, p. 14)

Robin Platts speculates that with the success of other early "concept" albums, such as the Moody Blues's *Days of Future Passed*, King may have thought that Genesis could tap into the same nascent progressive vibe (2001, p. 14). Unfortunately, the album only sold about 650 copies and was largely overlooked, both by the record-buying public and by their record company.

The group and their would-be pop mentor "went our separate ways," Phillips continues:

> And then the group was forced, slightly reluctantly, into going on the road and thereby, through a lot of grief and hard work, sort of found its truly original voice … . Everyone wanted to be composers … and just write, or just be a studio band. But it didn't work. So it was either give up or try and turn ourselves into a playing band. It was a voyage into the dark, really. (Platts, 2001, p. 19).

At this point, Richard MacPhail—who had been a friend from Anon—re-entered the story and made a decisive impact on the group's development. He offered the fledgling group the use of a cottage in Dorking, which his parents planned to put on the market in the spring. From November 1969 to April 1970 they worked intensively, composing and rehearsing the material that eventually became their second album *Trespass* (Bowler and Dray, 1993, pp. 27–28). Michael Rutherford confirms the importance of the Dorking cottage days in establishing the band's new musical direction: "We were completely removed from the business and any other outside music really. That was when we first learnt the way that we were going to be Genesis" (Bowler and Dray, 1993, pp. 27–28). Tony Banks remembers the period as one in which "the whole idea moved from a band trying to have a hit single to one that was trying to do something adventurous musically" (Bowler and Dray, 1993, p. 28). This sense of taking chances artistically influenced their live performances as well. Banks recalls:

> One thing we seemed to have as a group was a really good idea of pacing, we were a long-winded group and some people will hate that and that's fine. We spent a lot of time on the set order and I think it makes a big difference. The way you juxtapose your songs can really sell them to an audience. You have to build people up then let them go, build them up again, and we had very dynamic music and the whole set structure was very important to us. (Russell, 2004, p. 203)

Charisma Records staff producer John Anthony, who would later produce the *Trespass* album, saw Genesis at one of their early shows:

> When I first heard Genesis I always thought of William Blake. I was quite taken with the band because I was interested in classical music, mythology, history and the general Englishness of things. I was genuinely enthralled. They were a very strong band with a commanding presence and an emotive energy. (Bright, 1988, p. 42)

Anthony was particularly impressed by Anthony Phillips' song "Visions of Angels," which was an early highlight of the band's style, although "The Knife" would attract wider attention.

The intense and rapid stylistic development that characterized the creation of *Trespass*, and the album's strong pastoral and fantasy imagery and distinctive 12-string guitar work, can be connected with hippie culture's preoccupation with pastoralism and "getting back to the land," the first of Stump's three central threads of progressive ideology. "Rock musicians," Stump writes, "adopted an emphatically Romantic attitude that affirmed that inspiration derived from subjective experience of non-urban places" (1997, p. 62). Thus, Led Zeppelin retreated to the Welsh countryside of Bron-yr-Aur to write several of the songs that appeared on their largely acoustic third album in 1970. Richard Branson's newly established Virgin Records set up a studio in an old manor house in Oxfordshire, which they fittingly called "the Manor." Virgin's star artist Mike Oldfield composed much of his follow-up album to *Tubular Bells*, the unsung *Hergest Ridge* (1974), at Kington in Herefordshire. Genesis not only retreated to the Dorking cottage to create *Trespass*, but also essentially repeated the experience by relocating to Headley Grange to write the music for *The Lamb Lies Down on Broadway* four years later.

While such pastoral experiments may be chalked up to fashionable rock-star behavior in the early 1970s, and admittedly the "back to the land" movement had its adherents in America as well as throughout Europe, Stump also connects it with British youth's rediscovery of past traditions. Such rediscovery is congruent with an "Anglicization of rock discourse that would characterize mature Progressive ... . There was now a prestige, abstracted consciously or subconsciously, in the folk roots of both modern and pre-modern Britain that gave indirect strength to musical expression" in songs such as Spectrum's "Portobello Road," Donovan's "Sunny Goodge Street," the Kinks' "Waterloo Sunset," and Pink Floyd's "Grantchester Meadows" (Stump, 1997, p. 60).

Signs of this new cultural pride—and connection with Britain's past—were widespread. For example, Fairport Convention's *Liege and Lief* album, released in 1969, introduced Britain's hippie youth culture to the traditional British ballads collected by Francis Child in an electrified format. Moreover, the album's liner notes were strongly didactic in nature, informing the listener about Morris dancing and other pre-industrial traditions. Even the album's originals, such as Sandy Denny's striking "Come All Ye," took the invocation-to-party-through-introducing-various-instruments-of-the-band approach found in Sly & The Family Stone's "Dance to the Music" and recast it as a seemingly ages-old broadside ballad.

Many of Genesis's later songs, such as "Can-Utility and the Coastliners" (with its oblique reference to King Canute), the "Willow Farm" section of "Supper's Ready," and much of *Selling England By The Pound*, celebrate this same Englishness. Peter Gabriel, described the lyrics to "Willow Farm," in fact, as exploring "this unreal world of [the] English subconscious" (Spicer, 2001, p. 75, n. 28). Anthony Phillips recalls of Gabriel's imagination in the *Trespass* days that it was:

> so bizarre, but he can be very articulate at times in trying to explain himself and because he wasn't completely on top of an instrument, he couldn't demonstrate things. He was interested in space and rhythm but we were powerful chord merchants, it was what we felt secure with. (Bowler and Dray, 1993, p. 29).

With these differing approaches, Genesis's music quickly attained a distinctive richness and stylistic depth. The time was also arduous for all concerned; composing and rehearsal sessions often lasted 10 or 11 hours a day (Bowler and Dray, 1993, p. 28). Rutherford remembers the cottage experience as "very claustrophobic. It wasn't a specially [*sic*] happy time in my memory though musically it was very formative. None of us had a social life. We were actually more interested in music than in sex in those days" (Bright, 1988, p. 40). Anthony Phillips agrees:

> We were just too young to know that if you live and work together for five solid months, fifteen hours a day, seven days a week, there's bound to be friction and people are going to suffer because of it. I felt the relationships in the group deteriorated because of the ridiculously extreme conditions under which we put ourselves. (Bright, 1988, pp. 40–41)

Gabriel's biographer Spencer Bright finds that "the tensions in the cottage" that resulted from "inhabitants who tended to bottle things up and then explode" in such intense living and working conditions was "channeled into the music which became more aggressive" (p. 40), with a particularly fine example from the period being their stand-out track "The Knife."

Soon after the release of *Trespass*, health issues and stage nerves forced the departure of Anthony Phillips from the band. He was eventually replaced by Steve Hackett, who was located via a *Melody Maker* ad offering his service to a band seeking to break through past "existing stagnant musical forms"—a perfect example of Stump's second central thread of progressive ideology, the Romantic ethos. The band also seized the opportunity to "clean house" in the drummer's seat, replacing John Mayhew with the altogether more assertive Phil Collins. The classic line-up now in place, they set about to record their third album, 1971's *Nursery Cryme*. It was during this time that Genesis received their first significant exposure, as part of a "package tour" of Charisma progressive bands. Audiences could pay six shillings to see Lindisfarne (then holding the number 1 album in the UK charts with their album *Fog on the Tyne*), Van der Graaf Generator, and Genesis.

Stump's third thread of progressive ideology—Bohemian communalism—is perhaps most evident in the group's unusual approach to songwriting. Like most progressive rock bands, Genesis worked out their arrangements communally, but unlike other bands, all of the song credits were shared by and attributed to the group as a whole:

> The first benefit from this was that royalties would be divided equally, so there was no financial necessity for anyone to push their songs ahead of those by other members. This in turn meant that, theoretically at least, the strongest material would get through irrespective of writer, an idea which appealed to the committee-style organization of the band … .

> It was also widely felt that no one member of the group was more important than any other and so by communal credit they hoped to deflect press attention away from individuals— an unwanted and often unwarranted spotlight which had torn apart many groups in the past—and towards Genesis as a working entity. (Bowler and Dray, 1993, p. 52)

The communal aesthetic underlying these decisions explains the tensions that Genesis experienced as Peter Gabriel came to attention in the press as the group's dominant personality. By the time *The Lamb Lies Down on Broadway* was released, it was widely known that Gabriel had written the story. Many assumed that Gabriel had written the music as well, reducing the rest of the band to the role of interpreters executing Gabriel's "grand vision" (the unintended negative "flip side" of progressive's Romantic aesthetic). Not surprisingly, the rest of the group resented that their role was seen as so passive, and it is significant that after Gabriel's departure, the group reverted to individual songwriting credits for all subsequent albums beginning with *A Trick of the Tail*.

This is not to say that the members of Genesis have been guarded about their individual contributions during the "communal" songwriting period. Tony Banks told Paul Russell, "The main [lyric] writing contributions came from Mike, Peter and I. Steve [Hackett] would write some stuff but he tended to stay more in his own corner" (Russell, 2004, p. 206). As far as instrumental contributions to the songwriting were concerned, Tony Banks says:

> Steve wrote, but got frustrated as an awful lot of what he wrote didn't get included, maybe he didn't shout as loud as the rest of us, I don't know. Phil didn't really write much then, but was very good at arranging and getting things together. (Russell, 2004, p. 206)

Mike Rutherford added, "Instrumentally it was the three of us; myself, Tony and Phil" (Russell, 2004, p. 206). Steve Hackett does confirm the traditional progressive approach to communal arranging:

> The arrangement was as important as the song itself. Just because someone comes up with the framework, it doesn't mean the spaces in between aren't important. We all had a crack at filling in the spaces, racking our brains to come up with original bits of detail, usually within each other's songs. We tried all the possible combinations, sometimes collective, sometimes individual, but at its best the group mind was in force. (Bowler and Dray, 1993, p. 52)

Once arrived at, the arrangements were essentially unchanged; unlike other progressive rock bands, there were usually no sections for extensive improvisation. "We, as a band, tended to be obsessed with the idea of the form of the song. Everything was written, everything was crafted," Hackett says. "Even the solos were worked out" (Platts, 2001, p. 35).

This is not to say that the group was free of in-rehearsal wrangling. Disputes over song selection, arrangement details, and so forth tended to fall into consistent "alliances" between Rutherford and Banks, and between Hackett and Gabriel, with Phil Collins sometimes acting as a go-between between the two factions (Platts, 2001, p. 104). (Evidence of these persistent rifts—especially between Banks and Gabriel—can still be seen in some of Banks's negative comments regarding *The Lamb Lies Down on Broadway*, which will be examined in more detail in Chapter 4.)

An interview exchange with Paul Russell reveals the challenges of working with Gabriel's unusual imagination and keen intellect even in the *Trespass* days:

> PHILLIPS: Some of the best stuff comes out under conflict .... I think [Peter] felt a bit lost without an instrument, he didn't have a power base. He would come up with moments of genius and then stuff that wasn't genius, and he got shot down quite a lot. It was like he was assuming a position, rather perverse at times.

> BANKS: With Peter, whenever he introduced an idea it meant everything stopped for a bit, because he would have to sit down at a piano or something to demonstrate the idea. Whatever flow we had going seemed to disappear at that point and it made the whole process somewhat difficult.

> PHILLIPS: For someone who was so articulate when he was acting, he couldn't articulate what he meant. A lot of the time he had these visions of arrangements and he couldn't get it across.

RUTHERFORD: Very soon after Pete left, his recording skills took off fantastically, but in our environment there was no room to breathe.

PHILLIPS: He had this thing about all the thick chords we were playing, we all loved chords and chord sequences and there were loads of them, everyone playing at once, and I think he was ahead of his time in the respect of the way he was always trying to break it down. (Russell, 2004, p. 199)

"Stepping one beyond your show": Genesis and the construction of rock theatre

Among progressive rock groups in the early 1970s—indeed, among most bands to have come out of the late-1960s counterculture—Genesis was a distinctively theatrical band. It was the group's theatrical approach—particularly the stories and costumes of Peter Gabriel—that attracted press attention to the band, more so perhaps than their actual music. *The Lamb Lies Down on Broadway* was the culmination of Genesis's contributions toward an emerging sense of rock theater, one which can also be seen in the ironic 50s-styled performances of Sha Na Na, the *Grand Guignol* spectacle of Alice Cooper, and the sci-fi transgenderism of David Bowie.[5]

In addressing Peter Gabriel's approach to constructing an on-stage persona for performance and how *The Lamb Lies Down on Broadway* was a groundbreaking example of rock theatre, I shall refer to the performative analysis of Philip Auslander in his book *Performing Glam Rock* (2006). Auslander justifies his analytical approach on the assertion that:

> no rock subgenre can ever be defined solely in musical terms, for each one entails an ideology that is manifest not only in music and lyrics, but also in the visual elements of performance (costume, staging, gesture, etc.) and the visual culture surrounding the music (album covers, posters, etc.). It is never enough for rock performers to play a certain kind of music in order to claim membership in a particular rock subgenre; they must also present the right kind of image onstage, on screen, and in print, even when part of the ideology is to deny the importance of the visual, as was the case in psychedelic rock. (Auslander, 2006, p. 39)

Thus, a study of Genesis's performance style is not only an essential part of the study of Genesis as the band's image was constructed in the early 1970s, but also— by extension—an analysis of how progressive rock's ideology was manifested in

---

[5]   Sha Na Na's frankly nostalgic and kitsch approach to 1950s sock-hop and greaser culture might appear to be an odd example alongside Bowie and Cooper. For a detailed analysis of Sha Na Na's and Alice Cooper's contribution to the 1970s conception of rock theatre, see Auslander, 2006, pp. 19–38.

its visual presentation (or lack thereof) and how Genesis often stood in marked contrast to the normal progressive ideology in the area of visual presentation.

Some may find my choice of Auslander's book for this discussion surprising; after all, glam rock (sometimes also called "glitter rock") would appear to be only tangentially related to a study of Genesis, for at no time were Genesis considered a "glam rock" group, and Auslander does not mention Genesis at all in his study. Nevertheless, there are some intriguing parallels that may be made between Genesis's theatrical style of progressive rock and glam rock's emphasis on persona and visual presentation. For example, some contemporary rock critics did not distinguish between Gabriel's onstage personae and the theatrical spectacle of Alice Cooper or David Bowie, as seen for example in this review of a 1973 concert written by Al Rudis for the *Chicago Sun-Times*:

> There is nothing like them [Genesis]. Period. And not only are they among the most creative and innovative musicians performing in pop music today, but they are masters of the magic that Alice Cooper and David Bowie are crudely (by comparison) grasping toward—theatre. (Gallo 1980, p. 61)

While comparing Genesis to Cooper and Bowie in the use of theatrical elements, Rudis at the same time emphasizes Genesis's uniqueness, perhaps distinguishing their more "classical" musical style from the hard-rock elements found in early-1970s glam ("There is nothing like them. Period"). Writing with about 25 years' hindsight, Edward Macan likewise connects Gabriel, indirectly, with glam rock. "Gabriel had much less impact on progressive rock—which seldom set out to be 'theatrical' ...—than on English glitter rock. The irony and sense of self-detachment fostered by this genre made it a more hospitable format for the development of this almost Brechtian conception of theatre, and Gabriel's approach was developed to its logical conclusion by glitter rock's most important exponent, David Bowie" (Macan, 1997, pp. 65–66). Interestingly, Genesis once opened for a Bowie performance at the Roundhouse in London in March 1970, when Bowie just beginning his own experiments with personae that ultimately led to the construction of Ziggy Stardust (Platts, 2001, p. 25).

I am not asserting here that Gabriel influenced Bowie or vice versa, but rather argue that Gabriel's and Bowie's approaches to theatrical performance of rock perhaps have common roots deep in English popular culture. Simon Frith writes that in the UK, "Rock 'n' roll never really made a decisive break from traditional English popular culture"; this would be particularly true of Genesis, given their tradition-bound Charterhouse formative years. Instead, Frith claims, British rock was rooted in the "show-biz tradition of *putting on the style*. It doesn't have much to do with rock, it emerged from music hall and pantomime, from drag acts and blue comics, from the notions of spectacle and all-round entertainment" (Frith, 1973, p. 44, emphasis added). Elsewhere, Frith has written that in the British tradition, popular music has always featured the character song … . The lyrical and narrative convention here is to use the song to portray a character while simultaneously drawing attention to the art of the portrayal. The singer is playing a part, and what is involved is neither self-expression … nor critical commentary … . The art of this sort of singing becomes a matter of acting, and there is always a question concerning the singer's relationship to his own words. (Frith, 1996, p. 171)

Persona, then, has always been an important element of British popular music performance, dating back at least as far as music hall and vaudeville. The Beatles' own music hall experiments ("When I'm 64"), as well as a large swath of Ray Davies's Kinks catalogue from the latter half of the 1960s into the 1970s, fit squarely into this tradition. Peter Gabriel also attributes the foregrounding of persona in British rock to good old-fashioned eccentricity:

There are two distinct traditions in rock, those of Europe and America. In Europe there is often no interest from record companies or agents unless the artist is different from everything else, whereas in America there is often no interest unless the artist is similar to everybody else. Particularly in England there is a tradition of eccentricity to the point of gimmickry. (Gallo, 1986, p. 68)

Nonetheless, progressive rock's "eccentricity" was usually manifested in its musical forms (the broad and seemingly incongruous stylistic appropriations, the gaudy excesses of multi-movement suites and concept albums) rather than its onstage presentation, at least in the early stages of its identity construction. Auslander notes that the counterculture was "ambivalent, at best, about theatricality, especially in musical performances" (2006, p. 10), and goes on to say that "psychedelic rock musicians usually appeared quite introspective on stage. They generally focused their attention on each other or their instruments, especially while playing a solo, and did not play to the audience extensively" (Auslander, 2006, pp. 16–17). (It should be noted that Auslander conflates the categories of "psychedelic" and "progressive" rock.)

The primary impression psychedelic rockers apparently wished to create was of seriousness and concentration—in keeping with the counterculture's valorization of virtuosity, they appeared to be focused on musicianship above all, which they implied to be more important than acknowledging their audiences or creating visually interesting effects. (Auslander, 2006, p. 18)

Macan attributes the generally static performance style of progressive rock to the complexity of the musical arrangements (1997, p. 64). However, we may extend what Auslander refers to as psychedelic/progressive rock's "antiocular bias" (2006, p. 15) to an *anti-corporeal* bias in general. Progressive rock was "head" music, rather than "body" music; it was intended for listening rather than dancing. Perhaps the most obvious manifestation of this aesthetic was progressive rock's propensity for unusual and frequently changing meters (Moore, 2001, p. 90). This was, again, a source for critical contention, as critics perceived a link between "conservatoire-type training" and cold, emotionless playing. Thus, "the concentration on technical craft was discredited, for it filtered 'natural expression'" (Moore, 2001, p. 90). A few examples will suffice. The music of King Crimson was described by the *Rolling Stone Record Guide* as "somewhat cold and aimless" and "icy abstractness" (Marsh and Swenson, 1979, p. 205); *New Musical Express*'s Nick Logan and Bob Woffinden wrote in 1977 that "latter-day activities" of Yes "have plunged headlong into … cold artistry" (p. 250); and Chris Welch of *Melody Maker* described *The Lamb* as "instrumentally lacking in character," played "with little fire or purpose" (1974, p. 41).

While there is no question that their performance style on stage was, with the exception of Gabriel, relatively inert, the members of Genesis might disagree with Welch's critique of their purported lack of emotional involvement in their music. It may be helpful at this point to make a distinction between two different types of theatrical presentation, which I call *totalist* and *particularist*. Totalist theatrics direct one's attention to the total performance space by providing a "larger-than-life" theatrical spectacle, not unlike Richard Wagner's vision of an all-encompassing *gesamtkunstwerk*, which invariably serves to distract one's attention from the performers themselves. (One is reminded of the Wizard of Oz's smoke-and-lights distractions and his plea to "pay no attention to the man behind the curtain.") Pink Floyd's stage show, for example, with its laser show, surround-sound mixing and props such as flying pigs and crashing airplanes, offered audience members a total theatrical experience while at the same time allowing the members of Pink Floyd virtual anonymity in public. Particularist theatrics, on the other hand, focus one's attention on a particular person on stage—usually the singer or a particularly virtuosic instrumentalist. Particularist theatrical devices would involve such accoutrements as costumes, make-up, and body language (including stage movement).

Here, then, is the chief distinction, in terms of theatrical presentation, between early-1970s progressive rock bands and glam or glitter rock artists: glam artists tended to be *particularist* in their theatrical style (consider, for example, the extravagant make-up and body language of Bowie's Ziggy Stardust character, or the futuristic costumes of Gary Glitter), whereas most of the major progressive rock bands tended to employ *totalist* theatrical devices. One reason that progressive rock theater tended to be totalist is that bands responded to the much larger performance venues in which progressive rock bands had to put their performances across (especially in the US) with accordingly exaggerated staging devices that could be seen and responded to in such enormous spaces. The emphasis on "total" spectacle may also be seen as a possible distraction from the relatively static performance style of progressive rock groups, itself a holdover from the counterculture's "antiocular" aesthetic of foregrounding musical content over stage charisma. Still another theme underlying the totalist theater of many progressive rock groups is a group-performance aesthetic of "collective virtuosity", in which the musical performance is moreover wedded to the lights, special effects, and stage design in performance (Macan, 1997, p. 67). Arguably, this emphasis on the group, rather than individuals, is another manifestation of the progressive ideology's theme of Bohemian collectivism (Stump, 1997, p. 111).

The danger of totalist theatre is that it runs the risk of being arbitrary, having little to do with the music that is ostensibly the focus of the performance. Macan cites this as a shortcoming of progressive rock theatrics in the 1970s:

> The problem with ELP's catapulting pianos and Pink Floyd's crashing airplanes is that the relationship between music and image became increasingly tenuous. As often as not, image was employed as a spectacle in and of itself, as an attempt to make up for the loss of a meaningful symbiotic relationship between musicians and audiences that occurred when progressive rock bands made the move from clubs and small venues to arenas and stadiums. (1997, pp. 63–64)

Genesis took pains to distance themselves from such arbitrary theatrical elements that were used for the sake of "flash" alone. "Visuals are only rubbish if they're not integrated with the continuity of the music," Gabriel told an interviewer during the *Lamb* tour (Ross, 1975, p. 70). "The most important thing to us is the songs, then the playing, and only then the presentation," Tony Banks would emphasize, reminding the press (and perhaps himself) of Genesis's earliest ambitions to be songwriters before they became a band. Banks distinguished Genesis from their contemporaries such as ELP: "We're not as concerned with flaunting musicianship; Yes and ELP are more dependent on solos. I'm not a soloist as such. I think of myself more as an accompanist who colors the sound" (Ross, 1975, p. 70). Even in 1974, the *Lamb* tour program book reminded audiences, "To this day, the band insist [*sic*] that they are primarily songwriters who play at being musicians and only later play at being presenters" (Platts, 2001, p. 78).

Gabriel's use of make-up, body language, masks, etc., was decidedly different from his progressive-rock peers (including those in his own band), placing him in a particularist theatrical aesthetic that worked as a foil (or a source of dialectical tension) with the totalist theatrical approach of the band as a whole. "I believe there is a ritualistic aspect to all performances just by the nature of the stage and an audience and the exaggeration that provides for gestures. Sometimes by moving very slowly and deliberately one can pinpoint a mood in a way that draws people into the music. When I go to a concert I want to be moved and excited by the passion or the ideas. That is my aim as a performer" (Gallo, 1986, p. 7).

The particularist nature of Gabriel's performances did tend to focus attention on him, almost to the exclusion of his bandmates. One of the sources for tension within Genesis prior to Peter Gabriel's departure, in fact, was the unusual degree of attention paid to Gabriel's status as "front man," which by *The Lamb* had grown so intense that many critics assumed Gabriel wrote the music to *The Lamb* as well as the lyrics (Bright, 1988, p. 61).

Gabriel began to extend his role beyond the mere singer for the band when he began to introduce songs with stories. Originally these stories had a strictly utilitarian function—they provided a diversion for the audience during the long awkward moments of silence that would occur while Phillips and Rutherford tuned their twelve-string guitars:

> The stories started very early. Mike and Ant came up with this beautiful twelve-string sound, and they needed time to tune their guitars in between numbers. I started filling in time with them, improvising the stories. And later on I enjoyed preparing them. (Gallo, 1980, pp. 154–155)

These stories, often surreal in nature, were often improvised and often had little or no relation to the songs they were purportedly introducing, only ending with the song's title functioning as a punch line. Thus, "Supper's Ready," Genesis's epic version of the Christian apocalypse, was frequently introduced with stories about worms emerging from the dirt after a heavy rain, which for the birds meant "supper's ready."[6] Gabriel's comment that he "later on … enjoyed preparing them" is reflected in the fact that the stories grew in length and detail. Certain songs also became "fixed" with particular stories. "The Musical Box," for example, was invariably introduced with the story of Henry and Cynthia, two children playing a game of croquet at which Cynthia murders Henry by decapitating him with her mallet. Years later, the dead Henry emerges as an old man from Cynthia's musical box and releases decades of pent-up sexual frustration by raping her.

Before long, costumes and masks were added to Gabriel's presentation. "The costumes were really an extension of the stories. They were there to concentrate people's attention, because we were all so busy playing and I felt that we needed a focus for the energy to come out" (Gallo, 1980, p. 154). Thus, for the closing section of "The Musical Box," Gabriel "became" Henry, slipping backstage during an extended instrumental passage and then emerging with "a disturbing, malevolent old-man mask, miming Henry's sexual climax and thus making further sense of the musical accompaniment in a tremendously strong piece of theatre" (Bowler and Dray, 1993, p. 75). Multiple costumes were used for "Supper's Ready," including a giant flower headpiece for the "Willow Farm" section, a box-shaped mask for the "Apocalypse" section that resembled a cubist depiction of an hourglass, and a black cloak that would be torn away in the concluding "As Sure as Eggs is Eggs" section "to reveal Peter in a shining white suit, the final triumph of good over evil" (Bowler and Dray, 1993, p. 75).

For "Watcher of the Skies," Gabriel wore a large set of bat wings affixed with a headband and ultraviolet-sensitive eye make-up that made his eyes appear to glow supernaturally under black light (Bowler and Dray, 1993, p. 74). Tony Banks later enthused about the dramatic power of "Watcher of the Skies," which was a

---

[6]   The *Genesis Archive 1967–1975* box set (Virgin, 1998) contains one such version of this story, recorded at the Rainbow Theatre in London on October 20, 1973.

favorite opening number in concert: "It was incredibly exciting and it just gave everything a power" (Bowler and Dray, 1993, p. 74).

> Coming to a Genesis concert that opened with "Watcher of the Skies" meant you weren't coming to see anybody else, it could only be one group really. The Mellotron and those rock chords plus the look of the stage and Pete with his batwings and glowing eyes, this could not be the Rolling Stones, this had to be Genesis. Just those opening two chords set you up for the next ten minutes of the show, we could have done anything after that, a very, very strong beginning. (Russell, 2004, p. 205)

The glowing eye make-up, at least, seems to have been a happy consequence of another staging decision: The band had been looking for a suitable way to hide their amplifiers and other equipment in order to give the stage an uncluttered, streamlined look:

> Their stage manager had come across a gauze curtain which was fine enough to be transparent to sound, but unfortunately it was also fine enough for people to see through. The problem seemed insoluble until they hit on the idea of shining ultra-violet light on to the curtain, which made it appear solid. (Bowler and Dray, 1993, p. 74).

Gabriel later explained his use of the masks:

> I strongly believe the mask is a device through which the performer can bring out parts of his personality better than a device to hide behind. Sometimes the mask would help create moods so strong that the audience became very uneasy, and other times I would feel like an overdressed turkey. (Gallo, 1986, p. 8)

During the *Lamb* tour he told a journalist:

> If the visual images are conceived at the time of writing and you don't use those visuals then you're not allowing the audience to listen to the song in the full strength of which it was created. That's what you're after, to give the audience as much in a song as you get from it. (Ross, 1975, p. 70).

Genesis biographers Dave Bowler and Bryan Dray comment that Gabriel "adopted and then shed costumes and personas as naturally as a snake sheds its skin" (1993, p. 75). This observation is suggestive of Bowie's flexible approach to persona, as described by Auslander: "Rather than developing a consistent persona, Bowie sang in many voices and from many subject positions without identifying clearly with any of them" (2006, p. 106). Auslander goes on to comment that Bowie's "basic assumptions concerning rock performance were analogous to those of a stage actor in that he saw himself moving from role to role rather than developing a single persona even as he positioned himself within the countercultural arena" (2006, p. 107). A comment by Gabriel indicates agreement with Bowie's approach to persona: "If you're going to get up on stage and occupy a role, you have to discard previous roles you've adopted and not simply adopt the standard rock role" (Bowler and Dray, 1993, p. 102).

Further comparison between Bowie and Gabriel may be made in their type of lyrics and vocalizations used to advance particular characterizations. As Simon Frith notes, the voice "may or may not be a key to someone's identity, but it is certainly a key to the way we change identities, pretend to be something we're not" (1996, p. 197). Addressing the case of Bowie, Auslander has commented on the singer's flexibility of persona, both as a songwriter and as a singer: "Some of his lyrics are in the first person, some in the third. His voice and accent change according to the character he portrays ..." (2006, p. 111). One may compare this fluidity of voicing with Gabriel's various personae adopted in such songs as "Get 'Em Out By Friday," "The Cinema Show," and "I Know What I Like." Despite the fact that Gabriel is virtually the only singer in all of these songs (Phil Collins contributed backing vocals on the chorus of "I Know What I Like"), each may be regarded as a miniature monodrama in which Gabriel "acts out" all of the parts, changing vocal timbre, accents, etc., with remarkable flexibility. Banks has said, for example, that "the idea of characterization" on "Get 'Em Out By Friday" was "almost a Gilbert and Sullivan operetta type thing" (Gallo, 1980, p. 55).

Popular music scholar Iain Chambers situates glam against the backdrop of changes in British social mores in the early 1970s, citing "mounting resistance" in the 1970s to changes of the 1960s: "the spaces for social experiments began closing down, earlier boundaries were pulled back and prospects retracted as the solid values of 'tradition' closed ranks." Glam brought "public attention to the details of sexuality ... when precisely at that time a new, authoritarian morality was spreading over Britain's cultural landscape" (Chambers, 1985, pp. 134–135). The same implicit social critique can be claimed for Gabriel's exploration of sexual undercurrents in society on songs such as "The Musical Box," "The Cinema Show," "The Fountain of Salmacis," and certain songs in *The Lamb* ("Slippermen," "The Lamia," "Counting Out Time"). Steve Hackett's comment that in his adaptation of the persona of Rael for *The Lamb*, Gabriel "wanted to get more outside himself with this new role ... Peter felt the need to be more butch" (Ross, 1975, p. 66) is telling, for it implies that on some level *The Lamb*—in fact, much of Gabriel's admittedly androgynous theatricality during his years with Genesis—was a response to the rise of glam culture in Britain.

Glam rock artists—with the exception of David Bowie—were not able to replicate their considerable British success in America. Likewise, Genesis's "conquest" of America was long in coming; not until the 1978 ... *And Then There Were Three* album—long after Gabriel's departure and with the group's change to a more radio-ready pop style well under way—did Genesis have their first US hit, "Follow You Follow Me."

Genesis made their American concert debut on December 16, 1972, at Brandeis University in Boston, Massachusetts; the following evening they played New York's Philharmonic Hall. This high-profile concert, arranged by Charisma and their American distributor, Buddah Records, was sponsored by WNEW-FM, who organized annual Christmas benefit shows for the Cerebral Palsy Fund. The group remembers the show as an artistic disaster because of inadequate sound-check time and electrical problems involving their gear's unsuitability for American voltages. Tony Banks later recalled:

> It was a bit of a nightmare at the time, we did a warm-up in Boston the night before and discovered that the Hammond organ was a cycle-controlled motor—50 cycles in England, 60 in the US ... . We had to get in touch with this legendary roadie called Baz, who used to work on Keith Emerson's organ, and they had to rebuild a complete power supply for me. I think we ended up going on stage about four hours late. It transpired that the power was too weak for the organ and, as usual, bicycle chains and vacuum cleaner motors were holding the Mellotron together. It was the usual nightmare.
>
> So we got to New York and I knew I could sort of get away with it, but Mike's bass guitar had this incredible buzz throughout, like you wouldn't believe. Peter was not as good as usual and we came off the stage so depressed because we thought it was our own big chance and we'd blown it. It was probably one of our worst shows of that era, but *the audience had never heard anything like it* and they seemed to like us. (Wilding, 2000, p. 24, emphasis added)

Afterwards, Banks recalls, "Strat [Tony Stratton-Smith of Charisma] came up and said, 'Look, 80% of Genesis is still pretty good,' so basically if were 20% off we were still able to get it across to the audience" (Russell, 2004, p. 203).

Although Rutherford remembers that when the group came back four months later "New York had forgotten us and the rest of the country never had a clue who we were" (Wilding, 2000, p. 20), the novelty of Genesis's music and theatrical approach attracted favorable critical attention, though they were still very much a cult band. Jim Knippenberg's review of a 1973 Cincinnati show, during their US tour in support of *Selling England By The Pound*, is illustrative in its efforts to describe exactly what was heard, chiefly by comparing their sound to well-established points of rock reference and ultimately concluding that they sounded like none of them:

> It is not boogie stuff. It's not for foot-stomping or hand-clapping. Lousy for singalongs. Not good to get drunk to. Not much better to get sober to.
>
> Nor is it hard-hitting, slammin' and smashin' English rock and roll like we get from so many other madmen across the waters.
>
> It's something entirely different and completely unique in a world of imitation and mimicry. Tasty; tight; literate; diversified; serious without being pseudo-profound.
>
> It's something you can listen to several hundred times without tiring out ... music that no other rock and roll group is currently offering; music that is good for both the mind and the body. (Gallo, 1980, p. 61)

A three-night, six-concert stand at the Roxy in Los Angeles in December 1973 attracted widespread industry attention. Reviewing the show, Richard Cronelin wrote that "the school of rock that [Genesis] represents emphasizes control and discipline over spontaneity and release," adding:

> Genesis's show is the most perfectly realized piece of rock theatre yet to come along ... a breathtaking mélange of science fiction and fairy tale overlaid with a mythic dimension ... it sweeps you from primitive gods and apocalyptic battles to futuristic watchers from the skies, from not-so-innocent childhood to malevolent senility. One needn't hear all the words nor spend time analyzing, because it's good theatre and these striking images hit responsive chords on an instinctual plane. (Gallo, 1980, p. 62)

Regardless of Cronelin's assessment of Genesis's performance as a "perfectly realized piece of rock theatre," the *Selling England By The Pound* tour of 1973 was when Banks started to think that

> the costumes got a bit out of control at times with all that Bodicea stuff or Britannia— whatever it was at the beginning of "Moonlit Knight". It just looked silly to me. I didn't like that. Some things were great, like the simplicity of "I Know What I Like." (Russell, 2004, p. 207)

The aesthetic differences between Banks and Gabriel would only grow more pronounced into 1974, with the composition, recording, and mixing sessions for *The Lamb Lies Down on Broadway*. Nonetheless, the success of the 1973 tour is evident in Genesis's selection as the "Top Stage Band" in 1974's *New Musical Express* Readers' Poll, beating out the Who and Pink Floyd (Bright, 1988, p. 58).

In spite of Genesis's apparent success and positioning for international rock stardom, their finances were in serious disarray. The group also realized that at last they needed a manager, so they hired Tony Smith (no relation to Charisma president Tony Stratton-Smith), whose father had organized some of the first Beatles concert tours. Smith later told Armando Gallo:

> When I first got involved with the band and looked at their finances it was bad. They were so in debt it just wasn't true. They were spending far more money on the show than they were earning, and their record deal was terrible. Charisma were [*sic*] a young, struggling label, and they didn't have much money to play with themselves. But the band needed to play, they needed to tour, because that was the only way to get the music to the people, in order to sell records. And as we were touring, I was finding out more and more about their finances, and how much they were in debt. And, oh boy! .... They had advances on records that had not been paid back, they owed money to me as their management company, the publishing company advances ... . It wasn't until the summer of 1976 that they actually got on an even keel. (Gallo, 1980, p. 64)

The actual amount varies from account to account, even among differing interviews with Smith. While he estimated their debt at 150,000 pounds in an interview with Bowler and Dray ("That's at 1972 values too. It'd be about a million now") (1993, p. 83), he told Gallo that the figure was about 200,000 pounds (1980, p. 64) Regardless of the specific amount, it was considerable, and it illustrates how Tony Stratton-Smith's support of the band was unwavering, with an understanding that this would be a band with a long-term growth curve. Tony Banks attributes at least part of the band's financial problems to inadequate record-keeping:

> We were protected from our debt by Charisma, but 1972/73 was a bad period, in the USA especially, as touring was very expensive without the receipts—on one tour, no receipts were kept for anything and the Inland Revenue decided we'd made a huge profit when we'd made a big loss. (Bowler and Dray, 1993, p. 83).

In today's music-business economic climate, where a band often has a chance at only one album to make an impact or else be dropped by their label, it is difficult to understand Charisma's largesse. Tony Smith recounted how Charisma's recognition of Genesis's potential was also fortuitously buffered by the considerable economic support they had just arranged by signing for distribution with Atlantic Records (who for their part were well on their way to merging with Warner Brothers and Elektra):

> What happened was that Atlantic Records had by now signed Charisma, and one of the bands that they happened to have was Genesis, and I don't think that they knew what the hell to do with Genesis. They didn't know how to handle it, or what it was. They had absolutely no idea, and obviously felt that they were a bit like Yes, and a bit like ELP, with an interesting stage show, and it might happen. (Gallo, 1980, p. 60)

By 1973, the music business had become a 2-billion-dollar industry, about as large as the sports and film industries combined (Garofalo, 1997, p. 240). The late 1960s and early 1970s saw an unprecedented period of mergers and corporate consolidation; by 1974:

> structural realignments had produced a level of concentration in the music industry that had not been witnessed since the postwar 1940s. The top four record corporations accounted for over 50 percent of all records and tapes sold. CBS and Warner Communications alone took in about 40 percent of the total. (Garofalo, 1997, p. 242)

Bill Martin ties this economic prosperity to the global situation:

> There was a relatively long period, perhaps from the late sixties to the late seventies, when record companies seemed to have more money than they knew what to do with … . This extravagance was financed by a decadent capitalist society that, despite international setbacks, was still riding fairly high in the global economic order. In

other words, extravagance in the West was connected, essentially, with poverty and exploitation in the Third World. (Martin, 1998, p. 96).

As it turned out, the global hegemony the US and Western Europe enjoyed was soon to be dealt a serious blow.

A decade of limitations: Progressive rock and social stagnation in the 1970s

Historian Peter Clecak writes that "by the end of the seventies, the belief that affluence would evolve into general abundance had ceased to be the controlling assumption of postwar American social criticism" (1983, p. 43). In other words, beginning in the mid-1960s and continuing to the end of the 1970s, "Americans were pushed into a rediscovery of limits and limitations of all sorts" (1983, p. 42). Persistent recessions and inflation eroded Americans' belief in an economy that could expand without limits; the slow, grinding denouement of the Vietnam war revealed that there were limitations to America's military power; and the Watergate scandal undermined Americans' faith in the honesty of government. The energy crises of 1973 and 1979, triggered by the Arab OPEC (Organization of the Petroleum Exporting Countries) nations, reminded Americans of the US's dependency on foreign oil; and the Three Mile Island nuclear accident in Harrisburg, Pennsylvania in 1979 demonstrated that nuclear power would not be an "easy way out" of America's energy dependency.

Clecak sees the 1970s as an anxious time of "transition from industrial to postindustrial society" (1983, p. 93). This transitional uncertainty is expressed, albeit allegorically rather than directly, in progressive rock. While it was true that progressive rock musicians were not themselves deeply involved in progressive politics, and that they did not tend to inject topical commentary into their songs (as, for example, Jefferson Airplane and John Lennon did), nevertheless progressive rock albums do reflect the anxieties of the period in which they were made. The transition from industrial to post-industrial society, for example, is the narrative thread that runs through much of ELP's *Brain Salad Surgery* album (1973). *Brain Salad Surgery* begins with an arrangement of the Anglican hymn setting of William Blake's "Jerusalem," a poem that was written in response to Britain's industrial revolution. In the same way that Blake's poem portrays the anxiety of an emergent and potentially dehumanizing technological age of "dark Satanic mills," the album's conclusion depicts the anxiety of an imminent post-industrial society dominated by computers, using a wildly accelerating synthesizer sequencer to depict a computer run amok in "Karn Evil 9, 3rd Impression."

According to Clecak, the anxiety of the 1970s was:

> heightened by a perception of the future as cramped. Doubts spread about the very idea of future space: the availability of raw materials, the capacity of the environment to bear unlimited industrial activity and population growth, and the possibility of maintaining

international security in an age of revolution and insane nuclear arms buildups. (Clecak, 1983, p. 42)

The frequency with which one encounters images of a society that has reached its limits in progressive rock indicates that Americans were not alone in having these beliefs. King Crimson's "Epitaph" portrays a bleak world in which "the fate of all mankind ... is in the hands of fools," concluding with the dire prediction: "if we make it, we can all sit back and laugh / but I fear tomorrow I'll be crying." In Genesis's "Get Em Out By Friday," an elderly couple is displaced from their home by some unspecified urban renewal, and a spokesman from "Genetic Control" announces new restrictions in "humanoid height" to fit more people into cramped quarters, a clear picture of overpopulation. Robert Fripp chose to disband King Crimson in 1974 in part because of his belief that a global social and economic collapse was imminent. Faced with such distress, large and unwieldy bureaucracies (the entire star-making machinery of the music industry, or "dinosaurs" as Fripp saw it), could not survive. The way to adapt would be to become what Fripp called a "small, mobile, intelligent unit" (Partridge, 1974). Gabriel echoed these sentiments in 1978 on his second solo album, which Fripp produced, in the song "D.I.Y.": "When things get so big, I can't trust them at all / You want some control, you've got to keep it small."

By the mid-1970s, "profound and deepening pessimism colored Americans' attitudes about the future. The rhetoric of impending disaster became popular. Population growth, economic collapse, limited resources, climatological disaster, and nuclear holocaust all seemed possible, and possibly inevitable" (Robertson, 1998, p. 3). Even as early as 1972, David Bowie's *Rise and Fall of Ziggy Stardust* began with the chilling "Five Years," a song depicting global hysteria in response to an announcement that Earth was "slowly dying" and had only five years left. Such apocalyptic or post-apocalyptic themes set in some unspecified future are also found in many movies of the period, such as *The Omega Man*, the *Planet of the Apes* films, and *Silent Running*.

In summary, the 1970s seemed "particularly bleak," Clecak concludes, "because in many ways they were" (1983, p. 36).

Historians tend to divide decades by social or cultural shifts rather than according to the calendar; thus the 1960s are commonly said to have begun not in 1960 but with the assassination of John F. Kennedy. Likewise, the 1970s are commonly regarded as "beginning" with the resignation of Richard Nixon in 1974. A more significant starting point for the 1970s, however—particularly in light of later events such as the Iranian Islamic revolution of 1979, the events of September 11, 2001, and the second wave of energy concerns that occurred beginning in 2005—would be October 16, 1973. On that day the flow of much of the Western industrialized world's oil supply abruptly ceased.

At dawn on October 6, 1973, the Jewish Yom Kippur holy day, Egyptian and Syrian armies invaded Israel. US policy officially remained pro-Israel, but President Richard Nixon and Secretary of State Henry Kissinger initially restricted military assistance to Israel in an effort to appease the oil-producing Arab nations. This decision "nearly strangled the Israeli effort" until a complete reversal of action—a massive airlift of weaponry and supplies—assisted Israel in driving back the invasion (Carroll, 1982, p. 117). In response, OPEC countries halted the flow of oil to the US.

The OPEC oil embargo lasted from October 16, 1973 to March 18, 1974. Between the fall of 1973 and January 1, 1974, the OPEC countries raised the cost of crude oil by 300 percent (Carroll, 1982, p. 131). The precipitous rise in oil prices constituted, according to economist David Brian Robertson:

> the most severe shock to the American economy since the early 1930s. The value of the American dollar dropped. The fixed price of gold ceased to anchor the international political economy … . Economic growth, which once seemed limitless, seemed increasingly difficult to sustain. (Robertson, 1998, p. 5)

The economic slow-down that began in 1973 was felt by nearly all industrialized countries; the rate of productivity growth declined sharply in 1974–75, "down to zero or below in many countries. It was this that was responsible for the slowness of productivity growth over the peak-to-peak period 1973–79 as a whole" (Matthews, 1982, p.1).

The embargo affected some members of the European Economic Community more than others. Although the UK had traditionally been an ally of Israel, and Prime Minister Harold Wilson's government had supported the Israelis during the 1967 Six Day War, Wilson's successor Edward Heath had reversed this policy in 1970 and called for Israel to withdraw to its pre-1967 borders. Consequently, the UK's supply was at first virtually unchanged from pre-embargo levels. However, increases in the cost of oil on the worldwide market, in the wake of the embargo, had a much greater impact in Britain than the embargo itself. The effect of the price increases was compounded by industrial actions by coal miners and railway workers demanding higher wages and an unusually harsh winter. These factors created a "second-wave" energy crisis in late 1973 and early 1974. Prime Minister Heath warned, "We shall have a harder Christmas than we have known since the war," calling for British citizens to heat only one room in their homes (Frum, 2000, p. 319). Stump ruefully refers to this period as a time of "strikes and teeth-brushing in the power-cut dark" (1997, p. 79).

In retrospect, the OPEC embargoes, and the resulting energy crises that gripped the US and Western Europe, represented "what may well be the most revolutionary shift of world power in the twentieth century" (Carroll, 1982, p. 117). They also permanently changed the economics of the music industry, as the cost of oil directly impacted the cost of vinyl used to make record albums. Some companies experimented with recycled vinyl, which was inevitably of poor quality; this in turn sparked a market among audiophiles for higher-quality import pressings of albums. Some companies experimented with thinner or lighter vinyl, such as RCA's "Dynaflex" pressings—these, however, were susceptible to warping and returns. Packaging, in general, became more expensive to produce, and so extravagances such as triple-gatefold sleeves, posters, and oddly shaped album covers (Bob Marley's lighter-shaped *Catch a Fire;* round covers such as the Small Faces' *Ogden's Gone Nut Flake* or Grand Funk Railroad's *E Pluribus Funk*) or die-cut cover packages (e.g. Led Zeppelin's *Physical Graffiti*) were curtailed. Back-catalogue albums with elaborate packaging were re-issued with simpler "no-frills" cover designs (for example, the extensive "newspaper" packaging included within the gatefold sleeve of Jethro Tull's *Thick as a Brick* album was omitted from later pressing runs).

In general, artistic experiments were supplanted with a concern for the bottom line. The economic uncertainties of the 1970s had the greatest effect on progressive rock, since the style depended on the economic largesse of a prosperous music industry for survival. As Paul Stump notes:

> Whether it was represented by *Topographic Oceans* or by Henry Cow, utopia was out. Whereas the likes of Fleetwood Mac and Rod Stewart could continue to market a commercially successful, artistically undemonstrative stance, Progressives, more connected, in their espousal in their morals and politics, with that other world, never stood a chance ... . Musically or politically, the 1960s were exposed and alone in a suddenly much colder climate. (Stump, 1997, pp. 231–232)

John Lennon sang "the dream is over" in 1970, but by 1979 it really appeared to be true.

Visiting America in 1979, the time of the second of the 1970s energy crises as well as the Iranian hostage crisis, Jean Baudrillard wrote:

> The fifties were the real high spot for the US ("when things were going on"), and you can still feel the nostalgia for those years, for the ecstasy of power, when power held power. In the seventies power was still there, but the spell was broken ... . The US, like everyone else, now has to face up to a soft world order, a soft situation. Power has become impotent. (Baudrillard, 1989, p. 107)

Americans sensed this impotence years before. A December 1973 Gallup poll found that 85 percent of those surveyed expected serious economic problems in 1974 (Carroll, 1982, p. 131). *The Lamb Lies Down on Broadway* bears the influences of this period of social, political and economic uncertainty, a time when "the gas station [couldn't] quench their thirst".

Thus it was that toward the end of the *Selling England By The Pound* tour, Genesis decided their next album would be a concept album. They believed that:

> using an underlying theme throughout the course of an album would give them the necessary space to develop some of their lyrics more fully, and the challenge of capturing specific moods and atmospheres in the music to help the story along also appealed. (Bowler and Dray, 1993, p. 88)

However, Gabriel, at least, was interested in developing a more "realistic" persona that reflected the harsher social and political climate of the 1970s. The extra amount of time that Genesis spent touring America in 1973 evidently also had an impact on him. "The idea [behind *The Lamb*] was to present someone earthy who people could relate to and who would be a point of reference in each situation," Gabriel said (Bowler and Dray, 1993, p. 102). Like Fripp, Gabriel sensed that major changes were imminent, but instead of thinking in terms of global cataclysm Gabriel was sensing seismic change in the music industry:

> This was 1974; it was pre-punk but I still thought we needed to base the story around a contemporary figure rather than a fantasy creation. We were beginning to get into the era of the big, fat supergroups of the seventies and I thought, "I don't want to go down with this Titanic". (Fielder, 1984, p. 90)

Chapter 2

"There's something solid forming in the air": Recording *The Lamb*

By early 1974, progressive rock was big business in the US. ELP's tour supporting *Brain Salad Surgery* set new box office records and new standards for arena-sized spectacle ("You've got to see the show … it's rock and roll," Lake appropriately sang on "Karn Evil 9, 1st Impression"). Pink Floyd's *Dark Side of the Moon*, released the previous year, was comfortably set atop the US album charts. Yes managed to recapture some of its momentum that had been lost with *Tales from Topographic Oceans* with the harder-edged *Relayer*, their star keyboardist Rick Wakeman replaced by the relatively unknown Patrick Moraz. Wakeman, meanwhile, was enjoying his own high-profile solo career.

Following the critical enthusiasm for their *Selling England By The Pound* tour, and with their first British hit in the song "I Know What I Like (In Your Wardrobe)," Genesis seemed at last poised to make a lasting imprint in the sizable US market. They had built an image as an eccentric and theatrical band, a group whose somewhat arcane song lyrics were set to suitably intricate musical arrangements. Gabriel ruefully noted that in Atlanta they were billed as "the hottest thing to come out of England's new Intellectual Rock movement" (Bell, 1975, p. 14). Writing in *Creem* magazine, journalist Barbara Charone described Genesis's image for American audiences as "so hazy, so off the wall, that it gets confusing. People come to shows expecting to see a half-assed circus act; they wait at the stage door to glimpse robed occultists" (1974, p. 37). Musically, she wrote, "they rip off their predecessors far more than Yes or Alice Cooper ever did. People murmur about theater rock, fantasy world, bloody faggots, and brilliant—all in the same breath" (pp. 36–37). Genesis was not (yet) a radio-friendly band, yet the considerable commercial momentum that progressive rock built in the US since 1972 seemed to virtually ascertain that Genesis could ride the coat-tails of the "big three" bands into the big time. The long-awaited payoff—both for the hardworking band and the investment made by their record label—appeared to be just around the corner.

The point at which Genesis found itself poised was thus a delicate one to negotiate. The group was seriously in debt to Charisma, who had invested heavily in the band's artistic promise and commercial potential. Given the recent economic setbacks caused by the energy crisis of the winter of 1973, there were no guarantees that such support would go on indefinitely. There was a great deal riding on the next album, the next tour. All Genesis had to do, it seemed, was nurture the cult following they had and give the fans what they had come to expect: quirky, literate, very "English" songs.

Instead of "staying the course," however, the next Genesis project would be an abrupt departure in several respects. First, it was a concept album; although the concept album was a beloved format for progressive rock groups, Genesis had not made a concept album before, though *Selling England By The Pound*—in its "Englishness" of subject matter throughout—may be regarded as a step in the concept album direction. By 1974, however, concept albums were losing much of their allure. Additionally, the philosophical preoccupations of *The Lamb*—its episodes in the after-life—was suspiciously similar to Jethro Tull's *A Passion Play*, which had been mercilessly maligned by critics and audiences alike. According to Gabriel, *The Lamb* was "an adventure through which one gets a better understanding of self—the transformation theme" (Bright, 1988, p. 61). In some ways, he says, it was "sort of a moral fable in a sense" (Gallo, 1980, p. 155); it was "a type of *Pilgrim's Progress* but with this street character in leather jacket and jeans" (Fielder, 1984, p. 90).

This use of a "street character" brings up the album's second departure from "typical" Genesis fare—its "American" protagonist and setting. Genesis's lyrics had always tended toward a "British" tone. The most extensive example of this, of course, is *Selling England By The Pound*, with its references to Labour Party slogans, Wimpy hamburger chains, "Father Thames," and London neighborhoods such as Epping Forest. Earlier examples include much of "Willow Farm" ("Winston Churchill dressed in drag / He used to be a British flag") and "For Absent Friends" (with its reference to a "pram" rather than a baby carriage). The subject matter of "The Return of the Giant Hogweed," an imported agricultural pest that was thoroughly familiar to British listeners, was misread by many American listeners as a science-fiction horror scenario, like *Day of the Triffids*. The pastoral theme—long familiar to readers of English romantic poets such as Keats and Wordsworth—was also a recurring element in Genesis's songs (Hoppe, 1988).

The Lamb Lies Down on Broadway, on the other hand, was thoroughly urban and "American," or at least its protagonist was Gabriel's conception of an American. Gabriel told *Melody Maker* journalist Chris Welch that the album's protagonist, Rael, is "half Puerto Rican and lives in New York, and he'd be the last person to like Genesis!" He then admitted, "I've yet to talk to the genuine article, but that's not important" (Welch, 1975). In creating the character of Rael, Gabriel looked towards *West Side Story* "as a starting point" (Fielder, 1984, p. 90). *New Musical Express* writer Max Bell finds in Rael "roots in the most obvious territory: a mixture of James Dean, Sal Mineo and Warren Beattie [*sic*] with a fair measure of Rod Steiger thrown in on top. A Lee Strasberg wet dream" (Bell, 1975, p. 14).

As often happened in the collective negotiations that ensued during rehearsal sessions, Gabriel had to strong-arm his idea across to the rest of the band. Michael Rutherford had suggested a concept-album adaptation of Antoine de Saint-Exupéry's *The Little Prince*, which Gabriel rejected as "too twee" (Fielder, 1984, p. 90). Instead, Gabriel wanted a story with a "street slant"; well before the emergence of punk, Gabriel now claims to have "felt an energy in that direction" (Bright, 1988, p. 61). Consequently, Gabriel said, "it seemed that prancing around in fairyland was rapidly becoming obsolete" (Bright, 1988, p. 61). Gabriel wanted to avoid "dressing it up in white-coated-hippy-flower-power ideals" and instead create a story for "the guy who has never seen this, the guy who is the most alienated city-oriented person you could find" (Gallo, 1980, p. 155). Rael is thus a kind of antihero, a "Puerto Rican that everybody abuses in New York," who "goes through a series of events from which he learns. I was basically trying to develop impressions of different emotional states" (Gallo, 1980, p. 155).

Although Pete Townshend of The Who had already created a "mini-opera" entitled "Rael" for the album *The Who Sell Out* (1967), Rael was Gabriel's made-up name. Spencer Bright explains that the name was "similar enough to the popular Spanish name Raoul to fit in with the character, but English enough to suggest both reality and fantasy" (p. 61); the name is also clearly a pun on the last part of Gabriel's own surname. At the same time, Michael Rutherford recalls that creating Rael as a central protagonist was a way of unifying and controlling Gabriel's wildly wayward imagination: "Rael wasn't the beginning at all. It was getting so obscure we needed a central character" (Bowler and Dray, 1993, p. 88).

The third significant departure for *The Lamb Lies Down on Broadway* was that it represented a change from Genesis's usual means of collective songwriting. Previously, all songs were credited to the group as a whole, a more communal version of, for example, Lennon and McCartney's practice of joint songwriting credit regardless of who wrote a particular song. Just as Lennon or McCartney would sometimes contribute a section or a lyric to complete the other's song idea, so the members of Genesis were accustomed to contributing collectively to the final product. For *The Lamb Lies Down on Broadway*, however, Gabriel broke with this practice by insisting on writing all of the lyrics himself.

"My argument was that there aren't many novels which are written by a committee," Gabriel said. "I said, 'I think this is something that only I'm going to be able to get into, in terms of understanding the characters and the situations'. I wrote indirectly about lots of my emotional experiences in 'The Lamb' and so I didn't want other people colouring it" (Fielder, 1984, p. 90). Although he later conceded that the story line "had a lot of faults," he still defended his decision to write it alone: "I think you need leadership in a lot of artistic work because committees spend a lot of time not being bold and going for compromise solutions. You need singular vision" (Bright, 1988, p. 60). Besides, Gabriel did not believe the others' lyrics were "real enough so far as shifting Genesis out of the sixties and into the seventies" (Gallo, 1980, p. 155).

Gabriel wrote a story to provide a backdrop for the rather allusive narrative contained in the songs; the story was contained inside the original gatefold album, whereas the songs' lyrics were printed onto the album sleeves. Gabriel felt proud enough of the story to have it copyrighted for himself (Bright, 1988, p. 123).[1]

For all of its obscure and mystic symbolism, *The Lamb* shares with contemporary 1970s styles such as glam rock and disco an avoidance of preachy didacticism, instead focusing on entertainment and escapism. Gabriel told Armando Gallo that "it was really supposed to be an adventure story, and I wanted to get away from all that writing about death, sex or God type of preaching approach, because that alienates people. I wanted it to be entertainment first, and to write what I think and feel through the entertainment, rather than be a politician and try and be entertaining" (Gallo, 1980, p. 155).

The story also had personal relevance for Gabriel, who projected some of his discomfort with stardom into the story. "I am sure that my own doubts and searches were built into the story I wrote for Rael," Gabriel told Armando Gallo, "although I didn't really understand the connection until I was performing 'The Lamb' live" (1986, p. 12). Genesis biographers Dave Bowler and Bryan Dray describe the *Lamb* album as a "form of therapy and an effective expression of [Gabriel's] erotic/neurotic fantasies" (Bowler and Dray, 1993, p. 96).

> Rael's story is that of a split-personality, a characteristic often attributed to Peter—the shy, retiring, inarticulate figure off-stage and the charismatic attention-seeker onstage. Similarly Peter professed to disliking the star machinery that was being created around him and yet there were many times when he courted that machine shamelessly, and his enthusiasm for the wonders of collaboration contrasted with his disdain for the committee. Rael is a character that, according to Peter, felt "as if he was a waste of material, part of the machinery. He doesn't even think about his position in society—all he can do is escape or give up." (Bowler and Dray, 1993, p. 96)

Nevertheless, both Rutherford and Banks felt they could have made important lyrical contributions to Gabriel's story. There was concern that Gabriel would not be able to come up with the required amount of material in the allotted time

---

[1]   Unfortunately, permission could not be obtained to reproduce the story in its entirety as part of this volume. The complete text may be found inside the gatefold sleeve of vinyl pressings of *The Lamb,* as well as in the CD booklet. On the Internet, McMahan (1998) and Finegan et al. (1994) intersperse the story text with lyrics and interpretations, each in a different font; this content is also mirrored on numerous other web sites. Other anonymous sources for the text include GenesisFan.net's (n.d.) "The Lamb Lies Down on Broadway Story" (http://genesisfan.net/content/view/14), "The Lamb Story" (n.d.) (http://members.aol.com/inthecage9/lambtext.html), "Historia en inglés de The Lamb Lies Down on Broadway—Genesis" (n.d.) (http://www.ferhiga.com/progre/notas/notas-genesis-tlldob-ingles.htm), "Genesis on Green Pages: The Lamb Lies Down on Broadway" (n.d. (http://www.venco.com.pl/~piotrus/greenpages/genesis/la~a.htm), and "The Lamb Lies Down on Broadway—Genesis—Traduções" (n.d.) (http://whiplash.net/materias/traducoes/052446-genesis.html); this last cited web page includes a parallel translation of the story and all of the lyrics into Portuguese.

(Bowler and Dray, pp. 88–89). In the end, Rutherford and Banks did write the lyrics for "The Light Dies Down on Broadway," the opening song's reprise found on Side Four of the double album. The lyrical style is notably different from the other songs, and there is also a confusion of timelines in its reference to Rael's New York home as being in "yesteryear" rather than in simultaneous "real time," as implied in the last paragraph of Gabriel's story: "All this takes place without a single sunset, without a single bell ringing and without a single blossom falling from the sky" (Gabriel, 1974).

Writing and rehearsals for the new album began in June 1974 (Platts, p. 74). The group spent June and July at Headley Grange, a manor house in Hampshire that had been previously used by Led Zeppelin. The house was in considerable disrepair; perhaps due to the house's "occult" reputation from its association with Led Zeppelin, Gabriel was disturbed by rumors that the house was haunted (Bright, 1988, p. 60). Steve Hackett concurs that the place had "a haunted house vibe. I used to hear weird scratching sounds at night," in all likelihood the rats that shared the house with their rock-star guests (Platts, 2001, p. 75).

Not long after the band settled in at Headley Grange, Gabriel received a phone call from film director William Friedkin, who was interested in securing Gabriel's involvement as a writer on his next film project. Friedkin was, at the time, a major director, responsible for commercial blockbusters such as *The French Connection* and *The Exorcist*; the offer must have been both enticing and flattering for Gabriel. The commonly accepted story is that Friedkin had seen Gabriel's story from the back of the *Genesis Live* album and that he thought it "indicated a weird, visual mind" (Fielder, 1984, p. 91). Spencer Bright offers as an alternative explanation that Friedkin had apparently seen Genesis at one of the group's December 1973 Roxy concerts in Los Angeles (Bright, 1988, p. 59). Perhaps both stories are true, but at any rate Friedkin was interested in working with "a writer who'd never been involved with Hollywood before" (Fielder, 1984, p. 91). Other artists to be involved with the project reportedly included Philippe Druillet (the co-founder of *Heavy Metal* magazine) and electronic musicians Tangerine Dream. Gabriel was to be the "ideas man" for the script (Bright, 1988, p. 59).

The story that appeared on the back cover of *Genesis Live*, released in 1973, was transcribed from one of Gabriel's in-concert introductions. A story of a woman who unzips herself from the inside out on a tube train, only to be interrupted by a passenger who shouts, 'Stop this, it's disgusting!', it is notable for its sense of the surreal and grotesque, as well as for its sexual overtones, all of which would also characterize parts of *The Lamb*. For his part, Gabriel was keenly interested in working with Friedkin, because Gabriel had long been interested in film; he had in fact received an offer to study at the London School of Film Technique after graduating from Charterhouse in the summer of 1969 (Bowler and Dray, 1993, p. 23). In support of his application, he wrote a screenplay based on his feelings of having run over and killed a bird while driving; ultimately he turned down going to film school to stay with Genesis (Bright, 1988, p. 125). Gabriel originally planned to work with Friedkin after finishing *The Lamb*, but the enormous success of *The Exorcist* meant that Friedkin's creative clout in Hollywood was then at its peak, and so Gabriel felt the need to act quickly (Bright, 1988, p. 59). Headley Grange did not have a phone, so Gabriel would have to "bicycle to the phone box down the hill and dial Friedkin in California with pockets stuffed full of 10p pieces" (Fielder, 1984, p. 91).

The rest of the group, understandably, did not share Gabriel's sudden enthusiasm for this outside project. According to Gabriel, his bandmates "thought I was going to use the group as a springboard to jump off for my own personal success and wasn't even bringing them along with me. But Friedkin didn't want Genesis. He only wanted me for weird ideas, not for music" (Fielder, 1984, p. 91). Forced between continuing to work with Genesis—a group in which Gabriel was beginning to feel creatively constrained—and the opportunity to realize a long-deferred dream of working in film, Gabriel left for about a week to work out screenplay ideas with Friedkin. During his temporary absence, Phil Collins suggested continuing as an instrumental group, "because we had a lot of music written"—Collins was already exploring instrumental music with his jazz-rock fusion outfit Brand X. Tony Banks, however, argued that "the song was the reason for Genesis' existence. Everything was based on the song, everything was complimentary to that." Collins soon acquiesced, agreeing that "Mike and Tony wrote songs that needed singing" (Bowler and Dray, 1993, p. 91).

When Charisma learned of Gabriel's departure, label president Tony Stratton-Smith intervened and convinced Gabriel to return; at the same time, Friedkin cooled to the project, not wanting to be responsible for breaking up the band (Fielder, 1984, p. 91). "So Peter made a definite commitment to finish the album before he did anything else," Banks continued. "But I think it made all of us feel that he was getting fed up and it was only a matter of time before he left" (Fielder, 1984, p. 91). Collins agrees: "Things were restored to normal but, from that moment on, I think we all felt that this could happen again at any time" (Fielder, 1984, p. 91).

The film Friedkin eventually made, *Sorcerer*, was released in 1977 and was a critical and commercial failure; the soundtrack was by Tangerine Dream.

Gabriel's temporary departure to work with Friedkin, coupled with his insistence on having total creative control on the story and lyrics, caused a rift between him and the rest of the band. It affected their working method: "Generally the group would write and rehearse in one room while Peter toiled in another working and revising the lyrics and vocal melodies" (Morse, 1999). Steve Hackett remembers that there were "long periods when the band didn't actually come together. I felt that the tension was really very, very strong" (Bright, 1988, p. 60). He told Tim Morse, "I think the band was starting to fall out of love with each other. It seemed to be disintegrating and then integrating again. I got the feeling that everything was being held together with cellophane tape. And in some instances it probably was" (Morse, 1999).

Perhaps because of the simmering tensions between Gabriel and the others, and the characteristic shyness and stiff-upper-lip reticence instilled in Gabriel, Banks and Rutherford during their years at Charterhouse, the lack of communication meant that a great deal of music was created as a means of avoidance. Hackett has said he was "not quite sure why" *The Lamb* became a double album:

> I think it was because we were all traumatized by Peter's departure [to work on the film project with Friedkin], and no one really wanted him to leave. Reading between the lines, the subtext was that everyone felt that the longer we stretched everything out, the less likely he was to leave. (Platts, 2001, p. 75)

Meanwhile, Gabriel was sorting through some other difficult personal issues during the composing and rehearsal sessions for *The Lamb*. His wife Jill had an affair with the group's road manager during the US leg of the *Selling England By The Pound* tour—an act she later described as "my pathetic little bid for attention" (Bright, 1988, p. 75)—while she was pregnant with the Gabriels' first child:

> I got very twisted about it all. Very bitter and then I had an affair. It was at the beginning of my first pregnancy, I was feeling really down like you do at the beginning. Every night I would go to the concert and there were always these beautiful girls hanging around … .
>
> My affair caused all sorts of problems. He was a good friend of Peter's and it caused a rift, obviously, between them. I think in Peter's heart he knew what was going on; that's why he was so patient. No one solved it except for me and Peter. It was terrible while it lasted. (Bright, 1988, pp. 75–76)

In May 1974, when Jill was seven months pregnant, she could no longer tour with the group and so she had to live alone in the Gabriels' new home outside Bath (Bright, 1988, p. 76). Gabriel was thus torn between his duties to the band and his need to reconcile with and provide emotional support for his spouse.

By the end of her pregnancy, things had turned difficult. The Gabriels' daughter, Anna, was born on July 26, 1974, in the midst of rehearsals for *The Lamb*; doctors had feared a breech birth, and during delivery she had to be turned twice, resulting in the umbilical cord being coiled around her neck. "What came out was a green lump that was carried away in silver foil like chicken bones," Gabriel recalled. Jill was not permitted to see her daughter until the next day, when the baby had stabilized in an incubator. She had inhaled fluid during the birth, and doctors also suspected meningitis (Bright, 1988, p. 4). She spent two weeks in an incubator with doctors uncertain of her chances for survival (Bowler and Dray, 1993, p. 91). Gabriel describes those first two weeks of his daughter's life as "really traumatic" and his bandmates as "incredibly unsympathetic. They were pissed off I wasn't taking the album as seriously as my child" (Bright, 1988, pp. 4–5).

In August 1974, the group's time at Headley Grange had run out (Platts, 2001, p. 75). With rehearsals completed, the band moved to Glosspant, on the border between Carmarthenshire and Pembrokeshire in Wales. Backing tracks for the album were recorded in about two weeks (Platts, 2001, pp. 75–76), in an old farm house with a cowshed using the Island Mobile Studio, which was equipped with two 3M 24-track recorders, a Helios 30-input mixing desk, Altec monitors and two A62 Studers for mastering (Morse, 1999).

John Burns assisted the group in production and David Hutchins was the engineer. The band remembers Burns as "not only a good engineer, producer and musician, but ... having a good sense of humor and being able to diffuse potentially lethal situations by saying the right thing in a positive way" (Morse, 1999).

Burns assisted Gabriel in experimenting with different vocal effects, recording some tracks in a bathroom and in another cowshed two miles away (Bright, 1988, p. 60). Gabriel was "plagued by ... perennial voice problems," and "could frequently be found standing on his head in the studio control room in the belief that it would help"; he also tried herbal remedies to stop his voice from giving out (Bright, 1988, pp. 60–61).

Because of his slow, exacting method of writing lyrics, Gabriel was still writing and revising lyrics a month after the backing tracks had been finished (Platts, 2001, p. 76). The melodic lines also came later, often improvised over the backing tracks during Gabriel's vocal sessions. "A lot of the melodies were written after the event—after the backing tracks had been put down," Gabriel says (Fielder, 1984, p. 92). Occasionally, Gabriel would record vocals over passages that some band members, such as Steve Hackett, thought would be instrumental. "To me," Hackett said, "it was like taking a painting that I had done, and somebody else painting red all over it" (Gallo, 1980, p. 148). There were also a couple of lyrics Gabriel had written that did not have designated music, and thus needed a song written for them quickly; among these were "The Carpet Crawlers" and "The Grand Parade of Lifeless Packaging" (Fielder, 1984, p. 90).

Gabriel's slow, exacting method of writing and tinkering with his lyrics resulted in the album falling behind schedule. The world tour was scheduled to begin in Newcastle, England, on October 29 (Bowler and Dray, 1993, p. 92; Platts, 2001, p. 77), and of course logic dictated that it would be a more successful tour if there were an album out to promote. Gabriel recalls that at one point the band considered issuing the album in two parts, about six months apart: "I think that would have been a better idea, because there was too much, and it would have also given me a little bit more time to write the lyrics" (Gallo, 1980, p. 155). Instead, the album was finished in a series of marathon mix-down sessions at Island Studios in London. Phil Collins remembers "doing the vocals and mixing the album in shifts. I'd be mixing and overdubbing all night and then Tony and Mike would come in and remix what I'd done because I'd lost all sense of normality by that point" (Fielder, 1984, p. 92).

The album took five months to complete (Bright, 1988, p. 62). "Counting Out Time" was chosen to be the first single, and it was released on November 1, backed with "Riding the Scree" (Bowler and Dray, 1993, p. 93). Robin Platts writes that when *The Lamb Lies Down on Broadway* was finally released on November 18, 1974, it "baffled many listeners":

Even coming from a long-established group of chart-toppers it would have been a risky proposition, but for Genesis, it was a huge gamble. *The Lamb* was difficult to fathom, and the Gabriel-penned story included in the gatefold sleeve didn't really make it much clearer. (Platts, 2001, p. 76)

Steve Hackett describes his role on *The Lamb* as "an innocent bystander ... . It happened despite me, not with me" (Fielder, 1984, p. 92);

> The nightmarishly long sides—everything linked to everything else. I really felt it was very indulgent. I couldn't quite get to grips with it or contribute something great in a guitar sense.
>
> I don't think Tony's ever done a finer album. But I did feel the amount of stuff I was managing to put across was painfully small. (Fielder, 1984, p. 93)

On the other hand, Hackett felt much more comfortable with the tour, once it began. "Playing 'The Lamb' on stage was nothing compared with the emotional experience of putting the thing together. It calmed me down" (Fielder, 1984, p. 93). During the tour, Hackett sounded positively enthusiastic in an interview with *Creem* magazine:

> With this new stage show, we've left a lot of things looser than we ever have before. We're taking a chance that our spontaneous improvisations will create something we haven't had much of as yet. I think we're playing *The Lamb* even better live now than we did on record. (Platts, 2001, p. 77)

Gabriel remarked laconically during the tour, "It's much harder work for us during the period when we're off the road, than when we are actually touring, and that is never appreciated" (Welch, 1975). At the time, of course, fans had no idea that writing and recording *The Lamb Lies Down on Broadway* had been such a draining and arduous experience for all involved. They also had no idea that Gabriel had already decided to leave the band. But first, there was a tour to finish.

Chapter 3
"Counting out time":
The Lamb, song by song

With *The Lamb Lies Down on Broadway*, Genesis made a decisive break from their earlier image of myth and fantasy, nurtured by such albums as *Nursery Cryme* and *Foxtrot*. *Selling England By The Pound* had been a transitional step in that direction; with *The Lamb*, Genesis's music moved into a thoroughly contemporary milieu. The cover signaled the change: color had been replaced by black and white (Hoppe, 1998), and the fanciful script of Paul Whitehead's logo—used for the *Nursery Cryme* and *Foxtrot* albums and a staple of Genesis's merchandising—was replaced by a stark, Art-Deco-influenced logo created by graphic designer George Hardie (who also created the graphics for Pink Floyd's *Dark Side of the Moon*). The group would make further use of Hardie's modernist logo on the *Seconds Out* and ... *And Then There Were Three* albums. Moreover, instead of the paintings that had graced previous Genesis covers there was a series of strikingly surreal photographs, which were "still as unusual as anything that might have been expected from the band during that period" (Hoppe, 1998), laid out as triptychs on the front and back covers. The cover was designed by the British design firm Hipgnosis, who were—along with Roger Dean—the best-known album art designers for the progressive rock genre. Hipgnosis's inscrutable designs were regarded as symbolizing progressive rock's aesthetic of the arcane; even Led Zeppelin made use of Hipgnosis's services on their most "progressive" albums, *Houses of the Holy*, *Physical Graffiti*, and *Presence*. With this album, Genesis joined many of their progressive rock peers—Pink Floyd, ELP, and Renaissance—who had made use of Hipgnosis's services.

The Lamb's unusual cover is comparable to another famous Hipgnosis progressive-rock package: the cover design for Pink Floyd's *Wish You Were Here*, released the following year. Both covers consist of a series of photographs without captions, inviting a narrative interpretation derived from the songs on the album. Accordingly, fans have come up with a number of interpretations of the cover, tying the photos in with specific events in the story. For example, McMahan offers the following interpretation of the photos on the outside:

> On the left hand picture, Rael is clearly in the area of "In The Rapids" and "Riding The Scree", just after he's chased the Raven (in which case this picture would illustrate "It") or just before (in which case it is illustrating the part where his "tube" floats away). As far as Rael, the picture doesn't tie in with the songs/story. He is trying to save the character in the second picture from getting his head sucked through a wall (the intense

discomfort of "The Waiting Room"). The Rael in the first picture perceives the second character to be his brother, John.

If looked at closely, you can tell it is the Rael character again, which ties in with the … debate "Does John exist at all?". It would be reasonable to assume that John was never in this story at all and that Rael originally felt he needed someone to depend on (and who better than a brother?) … .

On the right hand picture [of the back cover], Rael is mouthless whereas everyone else is shouting. "The chamber was in confusion – all of the voices shouting loud" Lilywhite Lilith. He is mouthless because he is less bound (than the "Carpet Crawlers") and so feels less of an urge to shout. I think he also is at this point feeling disheartened (with "townmen" and the "man who does shout what he's found" as in "Chamber Of 32 Doors") and couldn't shout if he wanted to … . (McMahan, 1998, p. 446)

Another fan interpretation of the front cover triptych reads as follows:

The left picture shows Rael being pulled from the rapids, which means he might be John/Rael, or as commented before, the id.

The middle picture shows Rael sitting on a chair (a cold stone throne?) and struggling very hard to pull Rael from the left picture (so to support the Freudian approach, he may be the superego). I think that the one in the left picture isn't really pulling, because his body is bent forward, and he doesn't seem to put much effort in this, while the one in the middle picture seems to be giving all that he's got. (I don't think that Rael's head in the middle picture is stuck in the wall. It's just bent backwards because of the effort).

A third Rael is watching the two of them. That Rael has left the right picture and stands beside the three pictures in *the same* way he stood in the right picture (hands on hips etc.). That may indicate that he really can't move, so he's just watching them. It could be taken from the It scene—Rael looking at Rael, and his spirit moves between the two until it is no longer contained in either, and IT sees them BOTH … .

Someone said that the right picture shows The Chamber Of 32 Doors, but if you'll look closely you'll see it's actually a very long corridor, and there's a leopard lying on the floor near Rael's white figure's legs, so this might be the corridor from The Carpet Crawlers. What bothers me is that there ARE doors in that corridor. If you'll look inside the booklet you'll see Rael in something that looks like a corner of a room, and behind him stands a door, so this might be The Chamber.

Back to the right picture, you'll notice there are more animals in the corridor: there is a goat in the right door, something that looks like a dog walking towards Rael's white figure, something that might be a dog or a lamb to the left and a raven that stands on something that looks a lot like a wooden rail of a staircase (The staircase at the end of the corridor that leads to the chamber of 32 doors?). You'll also notice another white human figure at the end of the corridor. It's a bit hard to place the animals, though, because the crawlers seem to be human. (quoted in McMahan, 1998, p. 447)

Obviously, a cover of this sort invites multiple interpretations, and the detail found in the above readings, as well as others on the web site, is impressive. (It is interesting, for example, that so much interpretation in the above quote is made of the "corridor" pictured on the cover—the location for those shots was the rather prosaic Roundhouse in London, a former rail depot that was converted into a performance stage and used for a number of rock concerts, including some by Genesis, in the late 1960s and early 1970s.) The cover of *The Lamb Lies Down on Broadway* is part of the great tradition of richly nuanced album cover design in the wake of the Beatles' *Sgt. Pepper* album. Its fluid array of meanings is in keeping with the counterculture's value of ambiguity, as discussed in Chapter 1. Allan Moore notes that *The Lamb* "… is normative [among concept albums] in that it is divided up into separate tracks, which pursue the narrative by expanding on certain moments of it (precisely the approach adopted by innumerable eighteenth-century composers of opera)," although Gabriel's story printed on the inside "hardly clarifies the obscurity" (Moore, 2001, p. 97). Certainly its concept album format requires that one would ideally listen to the entire album in one sitting, from beginning to end, while studying the cover and reading the inner-gatefold story—a kind of 1970s hippie *Gesamtkunstwerk*.

In his discussion of *Sgt. Pepper*, Moore points to three musical factors that contribute to building "a unity greater than that of the individual, self-contained utterance" (pp. 94–95): First, the use of a modulating bridge, as found between "Sgt. Pepper's Lonely Hearts Club Band" and "With a Little Help From My Friends," facilitates a transition that "challenges us not to perceive them as separate" (p. 95). Genesis makes use of such transitions, for example, between "Fly on a Windshield" and "Broadway Melody of 1974," and between "Anyway" and "Here Comes The Supernatural Anaesthetist." In other places on the album, however, transitions are more smoothly made by means of studio cross-fades (bringing one mix down while fading another mix in) involving the same key or a common tone between keys. Thus, the opening title track, in E major, fades away as "Fly in a Windshield," in E minor, fades in; and as "Cuckoo Cocoon" fades out on its D major chord Rutherford's bass begins its "heartbeat" pulse on F♯ (the third of D major) to introduce "In the Cage." (The transition between "Cuckoo Cocoon" and "In the Cage" is further discussed below.)

Moore's second criterion of musical unity in a concept album format is the presence of certain recurring motifs. The most obvious example in *Sgt. Pepper*, of course, is the reprise of the opening song as the album's penultimate track; this is most often cited as an example of the album's "unity," and the "reprise technique" was widely imitated. For example, the Moody Blues followed the Beatles' lead to more extensively weave thematic material throughout *Days of Future Passed* (1968), capping the entire project with an orchestral "overture" highlighting the major musical themes of the album (Macan, 1997, p. 21). Genesis, likewise, uses the technique of reprising musical at several key points in *The Lamb Lies Down on Broadway*. For example, the Beatles' reprise of their opening song is echoed here in the song "The Light Dies Down on Broadway." The "reprise" is complicated, however, by the fact that this is not a literal repetition of the opening song, as the Beatles' was; rather, the song is a double reprise, making use of bridge material from "The Lamia" as well as material from "The Lamb Lies Down on Broadway."

Moore's discussion of *Sgt. Pepper* also convincingly cites the use of several descending bass-line models as evidence of unity underlying the musical surface (2001, p. 95). He finds similar "harmonic fingerprints" in *The Lamb*, "particularly the use of ionian I–IV alternations [cf. the introductory opening of 'The Carpet Crawlers'], aeolian $I^{\flat 3}$ – IV – VI – $I^{\flat 3}$ patterns [cf. 'Broadway Melody of 1974'] (both over static bass lines) and descending bass lines, whether diatonic or chromatic" (2001, p. 97). Other musical motives are more subtly reprised at scattered points throughout the album, and these will be discussed later in this chapter.

Moore's third element of unity in *Sgt. Pepper* concerns "the addition of (for instance) sound effects and instruments unfamiliar in rock contexts" (2001, p. 95). Here, the parallels between *Sgt. Pepper* and *The Lamb Lies Down on Broadway* are not so clear. Among Genesis's contemporaries, Pink Floyd, for example, were much more inclined to use sound effects as unifying devices (the famous heartbeat in *Dark Side of the Moon*, for example). Also—perhaps still smarting from the experience of having orchestrations swamp their arrangements for the *From Genesis to Revelation* album—Genesis avoided using additional orchestral instruments on their album, preferring to evoke quasi-symphonic textures with keyboards and guitars. (Gabriel's flute is a notably "non-rock" element in Genesis's overall sound, but from *Trespass* on it had always been an integral part of the group's sound, not an "addition." In fact—perhaps in a nod to Gabriel's desire to avoid "fairyland" pastoral elements with this album—Gabriel's flute makes fewer appearances on *The Lamb Lies Down on Broadway* than it had on previous albums.)

On the other hand, there is a brief and quiet "industrial" passage, lasting nearly a minute, between "In the Cage" and "The Grand Parade of Lifeless Packaging"; although it would appear to function as an introduction to the latter song, the CD tracking for *The Lamb* includes it as the conclusion of the former song. More prominently throughout the album, Genesis did add a new sound element that perhaps could count as unifying "sound effects"—the "Enossification" of Gabriel's vocals by Brian Eno, who Gabriel met working at Island Studios during the mixdown sessions. Phil Collins later mentioned the session work in a 1983 interview for a feature article in *Modern Drummer* magazine:

> For instance, when Genesis was doing *The Lamb*, Eno was upstairs and he met Peter [Gabriel]. Peter wanted to feed his vocals through some of Eno's synthesizers. So, he came down. As payment for that, I was sent upstairs to play on Eno's record, which was a track ["Mother Whale Eyeless"] on *Taking Tiger Mountain (By Strategy)*. We hit it off well, so when he did *Another Green World*, he rang me and Percy [Jones, bass player from Collins's fusion project Brand X] up and I did all the drums on that. (Alexander, 1983, p. 10).

Eno's vocal processing is most obviously heard throughout "The Grand Parade of Lifeless Packaging"—where the treatments are similar to those on Eno's own "The Fat Lady of Limbourg"—but it also occurs at other key points, for example the "porcupine" sections of "Back in N.Y.C." Elsewhere, though not specifically attributable to Eno, Gabriel's vocals are unusually equalized (as on "Back in

N.Y.C.") or distorted through vocal mannerisms such as to suggest some processing was done (the voice of the "Slipperman," for example). Other instruments—such as the guitars in the final verse of "In the Cage"—also appear to be "Enossified" (on "In the Cage," the guitars sound as if they were processed with a VCS3 synthesizer; Eno applied similar modifications to Chris Spedding's guitar on John Cale's "Gun" on Cale's *Fear* album, released the same year as *The Lamb*.)

Some songs on the album came about from improvisations, which had earlier yielded the "Apocalypse in 9/8" section of "Supper's Ready" and the closing section of "Cinema Show"—they were "a conscious effort by the band to move away from the kind of over-rehearsed and over-elaboration of ideas that had marred some of the music on *Selling England By The Pound*" (Bowler and Dray, 1993, p. 91). Banks remembers his earliest compositions as "incredibly complex chordwise, because I was just interested in all the chord changes that no one else had used. Probably, the reason why they hadn't used them was that they didn't sound too good at that stage, so that was really how it started, just trying to write" (Gallo, 1980, p. 125). From time to time, it would appear that Banks attempts to "rein in" his more excessive tendencies through a renewed focus on improvisation and jams; for example, the group returned to an improvisational approach in recording *Abacab*, the album that heralded Genesis's most commercially accessible period. Other improvisations during *The Lamb* sessions yielded "Silent Sorrow in Empty Boats," "Fly on a Windshield," "Ravine," and "Hairless Heart" (Bowler and Dray, 1993, p. 92).

Given Gabriel's lack of direct involvement in the musical aspects of *The Lamb* (as he was focused on Friedkin's film project, Jill's difficult delivery, and the story line and lyrics) and Hackett's alienation from the project, Tony Banks's keyboards take on a greater degree of prominence on this album, and a number of songs bear his harmonic signature. Banks told Armando Gallo:

> I feel that I am probably quite mathematical in the way that I look at things. I always thought that there were two approaches to music, the mathematical approach, and the un-mathematical approach. I always felt that in the Beatles you had the very mathematical approach of Paul McCartney, and the very un-mathematical approach of John Lennon. In certain songs such as "Hello Goodbye" you can see that the format is just perfect, and the way that it happens is so precise. Whereas a song like "Strawberry Fields Forever" is a real hotch-potch of ideas, but it's still really successful. I think that these are the two approaches. (Gallo, 1980, p. 124)

One way in which Banks's "mathematical" approach to musical structure is evident is in his tendency to create chord progressions with small, incremental (often symmetrical) changes in harmony.[1] Figure 3.1a, a harmonic reduction of the toccata-like introduction to the opening title track [0:00–0:35], provides a typical example of this approach. The numbers in angle brackets between chords indicate

---

[1]   For more on Banks's harmonic style, see Holm-Hudson, forthcoming.

the movement of individual voices in the chord, lowest-pitched to highest-pitched, measured in half steps up (a positive number) or down (a negative number). With the exception of the motion between measures 8 and 9, in which two voices move down a half step in parallel motion, all of these chords have a net sum voice motion of zero; that is to say, the positive voice-leading sum in a chord progression is "balanced" or cancelled out by a corresponding negative voice-leading sum. The voice-leading motions from chord to chord comprise almost exclusively an extremely economical half step at a time. Throughout the progression, B features as a common tone and also a boundary tone (highest and lowest pitch) for nearly every chord. When the B finally moves downward to B♭ as part of an E♭ major chord, the rest of the band makes its entrance as if to underscore the dramatic nature of the change. Another example of symmetrical voice leading occurs in the refrain, which first occurs with the entry of voices a few seconds later (Figure 3.1b). "Broadway Melody of 1974" (Figure 3.1c) contains another example of incremental harmonic progression, which returns at the end of "Lilywhite Lilith." Although the voice leading in this example is not strictly symmetrical, the excerpt does show another distinctive Genesis stylistic hallmark, which Mark Spicer calls the "pedal point groove" (Spicer, 2005, p. 4). Beginning with 1972's "Watcher of the Skies" and well into their 1980s period ("Abacab," "Turn it On Again"), Genesis frequently created textures involving changing harmonies over a static, often pulsating bass. Other examples of the "pedal point groove" in *The Lamb* include "Riding the Scree" and "Back in N.Y.C."

Several songs on *The Lamb*, however, also signal a retreat from the formal complexity of much of Genesis's earlier music, reflecting the album's streetwise protagonist. To a greater extent than on their earlier albums, on *The Lamb Lies Down on Broadway* Genesis relies more on expanded versions of song form (AABA) or of simple strophic (verse – chorus or verse with refrain) forms. Among examples of the former are "The Lamb Lies Down on Broadway," "Cuckoo Cocoon," "Back in N.Y.C.," and "Anyway." Examples of strophic form include "The Carpet Crawlers," "The Grand Parade of Lifeless Packaging," "In the Rapids," and much of "Lilywhite Lilith" and "Counting Out Time" (if one considers Hackett's guitar solo to be an "instrumental verse" rather than a separate B section—otherwise it is an example of expanded AABA song form). "The Carpet Crawlers" consists of a simple repetition of verse and chorus, to marvelous effect as Gabriel's vocal ascends in register and expands in range to give the song momentum. "The Grand Parade of Lifeless Packaging," on the other hand, repeats a simple chord vamp in the keys of A major, C major, and E major four times; the chromatic-third key relationships in the song are vintage Banks, but here the key changes merely serve to provide variety amid the repetition. "Counting Out Time" was—at the time of *The Lamb*—the closest Genesis had come to a "typical rock song" with its regular phrasing and easily identifiable chorus, and it was in fact chosen as the first single from the album. The simplicity of "Counting Out Time," its descending bass and chord progression reminiscent of a 1950s doo-wop song, dramatically helps to convey the teenage-romance flashback at which the song occurs in the narrative.

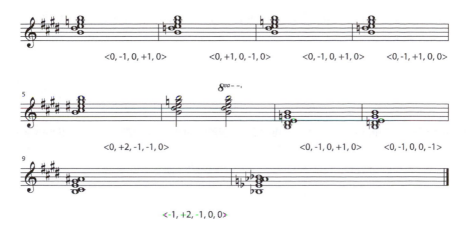

Figure 3.1a   Introduction to "The Lamb Lies Down on Broadway," harmonic reduction

Figure 3.1b   Symmetrical motion in voice parts, "The Lamb Lies Down on Broadway"

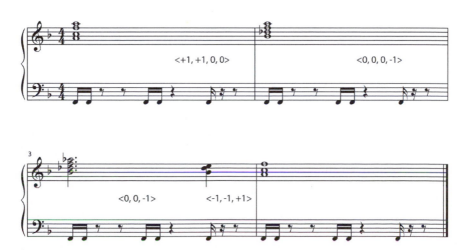

Figure 3.1c   Harmonic progression in "Broadway Melody of 1974"

The formal simplicity of much of *The Lamb* may reflect the strained conditions under which the album was made, both internally because of band frictions and externally because of record company pressures to finish the album and get back on tour. Only "In the Cage" and "The Colony of Slippermen" (and, to a certain extent, "Riding the Scree") have the intricate "organic" formal construction that distinguished much of the group's earlier work ("Dancing with the Moonlit Knight," "The Musical Box," "The Battle of Epping Forest"). At the other extreme, in fact, there are several songs that might be called "proto-ambient" in their reliance on mood and timbre over musical development. "Silent Sorrow in Empty Boats" and "Ravine" functioned as intermezzos on stage, allowing Gabriel to change in and out of his Slipperman costume; other songs, such as "The Waiting Room" and the instrumental coda of "Fly on a Windshield," helped to set a mood while providing an outlet for group jamming.

Regardless of the variety of forms presented on *The Lamb*, however, there does seem to be a guiding principle that unites many of the songs: a threefold division in musical structure or lyrical imagery. One such example, the threefold key structure of "The Grand Parade of Lifeless Packaging," has already been discussed. A similar structure is found in "*it*," although the "A" section originally appears as an instrumental introduction; the "A" section is in F♯ major. The "B" section, beginning with Gabriel's vocal entrance at [0:32], begins in A major. The "C" refrain ("*it* is here …") modulates, via two chords, back to F♯ major and the return of the A section (the overall form of "*it*" is strophic).

The chorus of "Back in N.Y.C." is divided into three thematic ideas: the "porcupine" passage beginning at [2:51], "No time for romantic escape"—itself repeated three times—starting at [3:07], and the repetitions of "off you go"—also threefold—starting at [3:31]. The underlying chord progression of "Broadway Melody of 1974" is divided into a three-part AAB form (listen to the four-bar progressions that begin under Gabriel's "Echoes of the Broadway Everglades," "Lenny Bruce," and "Sirens on the roof tops" lines respectively). The introduction to "Counting Out Time" is a two-chord vamp heard three times, and the Carpet Crawlers say "we've got to get in to get out" three times.

"The Chamber of 32 Doors" consists of three main themes. First is the broadly dramatic opening heard as the introduction and at [2:38]. The "B" section is itself in three sub-sections: First, a double-time passage expressing the confusion in the corridor, followed by a calmer and more sparse passage which presents the dualities of rich man/poor man or mother/father surrounding Rael, and concluding with the refrain "I need someone to believe in, someone to trust." Throughout the B section there is a gradual thinning of texture and decrease of dynamics, effectively depicting Rael's aloneness within the bustle of the crowd. The desolate mood is swept away by the "C" section, a "folksier" bridge where Rael expresses who he would indeed rather trust (first heard at [1:47]). Over the course of the song, since the return of the "C" section at [4:22] is abbreviated, there are three such people: the "countryman," the man "who works with his hands," and the man "who doesn't shout what he's found."

Even the improvised "Waiting Room" can be heard as consisting of three parts, according to prominent or persistent gestures in the ensemble texture. The first section, until about [1:11], includes a rapid high-frequency synthesizer sequencer pattern. This fades out around [1:12], replaced briefly by a similar-sounding bell tree. The second section from [1:12] to about [3:03] features sustained tones, first on heavily chorused guitar and echoed by "meowing" synthesizer sounds, eventually deepening in register. To these sustained tones some more staccato and angular electric guitar responses are added. The third section begins dramatically at [3:04] with the "explosion" that results when Rael throws the rock at the globes of light, followed by the more structured group jam on the octave riff.

The vocal introduction to "Here Comes the Supernatural Anaesthetist" consists of three lines. The likely chorus to "The Lamia" (even though it has different lyrics in its two appearances; the first appearance is at [1:09]) is constructed from three sections, the first two of which feature repeated melodic and harmonic lines and the third of which develops more organically through a series of sequenced cadential patterns (this is discussed in more detail later in the analysis of "The Lamia").

"The Colony of Slippermen" is, of course, explicitly divided into three titled sections. In the "Arrival" section of "The Colony of Slippermen," the verse is divided broadly by its chord progression: I – vi – V (with neighboring vi chords). The verses are followed by a transition, which is itself made up of three ideas: a busier passage (with Gabriel's treated "Slipperman" voice) beginning at about [2:46], a series of cascading synthesizer arpeggios with portamento beginning at [2:57], and a series of ascending staccato synthesizer patterns, beginning at [3:13] and leading into the next section, "A Visit to the Doktor."

"The Lamb Lies Down on Broadway"

The opening song and title track for *The Lamb Lies Down on Broadway* began its life as a Tony Banks toccata-like piano piece (Morse, 1999). For the bulk of the song's backing track, Banks used an RMI electric piano; the grand piano introduction was added later during final overdub sessions at Island Studios in London (Morse, 1999). After the quiet piano introduction, however, comes an energetic rock number dominated by a distinctive bass riff contributed by Mike Rutherford. Riffs, according to Allan Moore, have "connotations of aggressive energy" (Moore, 2001, p. 111), and indeed this song immediately conveys something of Rael's angry and defiant character as the story begins. Rutherford used a Micro Frets six-string bass, which he remembers as "one of those basses that has tons of character, but it's difficult to play. Not only did I find that the strings are closer together, but I also found that the scale length was much shorter" (Morse, 1999). The biting tone in his playing was created by using a Marshall fuzz unit through an Acoustic amplifier (Morse, 1999). Hackett, similarly, played a 1957 Gibson Les Paul through an HH 100-watt amplifier, creating fly sounds in the introduction by hammering notes on the guitar, using the two-handed tapping technique later popularized by Eddie Van Halen, and running the sound into a pair of fuzz boxes (Morse, 1999). Hackett also used an Echoplex tape echo and a volume pedal for the sustained notes during the quieter bridge section (Morse, 1999). Collins played a Gretsch drum kit with a Ludwig snare and Paiste cymbals; the kit was fully miked, and room microphones were also used to capture the ambience of the recording space (Morse, 1999). Gabriel used a Neumann U47 microphone—a widely coveted model among engineers—for his vocals; he continues to use this microphone to this day (Morse, 1999).

This track was one of the few songs from the album to enjoy repeated performances in concert after the *Lamb* tour; it remained in Genesis's set list until around 1978. Peter Gabriel, in his early career as a solo artist, also performed the song; the rock format of this song and "Back in N.Y.C." suited Gabriel's more stripped-down solo approach, so these were virtually the only acknowledgements Gabriel made as a solo artist to the group that he had co-founded. The song has been a favorite cover for later progressive rock bands; the Swedish progressive rock band the Flower Kings covered the song on their live album *Alive on Planet Earth*, and the Italian band Mellonta Tauta included a live version as a bonus track on their 1993 album.

Writing in *Melody Maker*, Chris Welch called *The Lamb* "the first Gabriel Genesis evolution [*sic*] of music and lyrics to have been influenced by contact with America, and the casual observer can find himself totally mystified by its allusions and imagery" (Welch, 1975). This would perhaps be especially true for many of the band's British fans, who may have been as baffled by the album's Americanisms as American fans were by some of the British cultural and historical references in *Selling England by the Pound*. The French philosopher Jean Baudrillard, after a visit to America, wrote:

> nothing could be more intense, electrifying, turbulent, and vital than the streets of New York. They are filled with crowds, bustle, and advertisements, each by turns aggressive or casual. There are millions of people in the streets, wandering, carefree, violent, as if they had nothing better to do—and doubtless they have nothing else to do—than produce the permanent scenario of the city. There is music everywhere .... (Baudrillard, p. 18)

Gabriel, visiting from the relatively placid UK, was no doubt equally captivated by New York's excitement and energy. He made it clear, however, that he made "no claims to be anything other than an observer" after his visits to New York; "we haven't discovered any truths about the place" (Welch, 1975). Gabriel told the *New Musical Express*'s Max Bell, "Americans didn't mind that I was telling them about an American. I didn't pretend to be anything other than an observer there for short periods. I wasn't unleashing the secrets of New York" (Bell, 1975, p. 14).

Nevertheless, in 1973–74 it was difficult not to observe New York; its social problems were hardly secrets. In January 1973, the South Bronx was the subject of a detailed four-part series in the *New York Times*, which noted that 40 per cent of its 400,000 inhabitants were on welfare and that the area had a 30 per cent unemployment rate (Killen, 2006, pp. 204–205). Graffiti—Rael's means of "making a name for himself" as the album opens—first began to appear on New York City's subway trains in the early 1970s (Killen, 2006, pp. 9–10); the South Bronx was the setting for turf battles among "Puerto Rican gangs who made their homes in abandoned and burned-out buildings" (Killen, 2006, p. 205); Rael, of course, was half Puerto Rican. Another interpretation of Rael's "graffiti" act in the song is that Rael's "hidden spraygun" may be a phallic symbol; thus, the image of Rael "wiping his gun" and "forgetting what he did" could refer not to subway vandalism but an act of sexual violence (Currie, 1998). Certainly, this interpretation can be supported by Rael's attitudes toward sex as expressed in both "Back in N.Y.C." and "Counting Out Time," an attitude that ultimately disfigures him through his encounter with the Lamia and his transformation in the colony of Slippermen.

Joseph Campbell has observed that in a number of myths and legends, the hero and/or the world in which he finds himself frequently "suffers from a symbolical deficiency ... in apocalyptic vision the physical and spiritual life of the whole earth can be represented as fallen, or on the point of falling, into ruin" (Campbell, 1968, p. 37). Perhaps this explains Gabriel's choice of New York City, during the "apocalyptic" years of 1973–74, as the location for Rael's gateway into his metaphysical adventures, for it is amid this urban decay that Rael first notices "something moving in the sidewalk steam." Gabriel told a writer for the magazine *Beat International* in 1977, "One of the first things you notice when you go to New York is the steam rising from out of the manhole covers in the streets. It's a very strange sight and it gave me the idea of a vast underground world going on which we are not even aware of as we walk the surface. It all ties in with the conscious and the subconscious mind" (Bowler and Dray, 1993, p. 97). Another gateway, of sorts, to this subconscious realm is the lamb itself, which "seems right out of place" on the busy, dirty street. In spite of its Christian connotations, however, the lamb "isn't a symbol" for Christ, according to Gabriel; rather, it is merely "a catalyst for peculiarities that take place" (Bell, 1975, p. 14).

As the song fades away, we hear the first of several intertextual references to songs of the 1960s in *The Lamb*, here a musical and lyrical quote from the 1963 Drifters hit "On Broadway." Along with the unusual apparition of the lamb lying down on Broadway, the lyrics remind us that all is not as it seems—"there's always magic in the air."

"Fly on a Windshield"

In his book *The Varieties of Religious Experience*, William James noted that most of the accounts of mystical experiences he had collected took place outdoors (James, 1925, p. 394). "Fly on a Windshield" marks Rael's crossing of the portal—in the form of a solid wall-like cloud—that descends onto Times Square and moves toward him, encrusting him and swallowing him, sending him into the *Bardo* realm. "Fly on a Windshield" begins with a delicate recitative-like passage with quiet guitar strumming accompaniment. After a brief pause to let tension build in anticipation of the cloud's impact, the second section begins violently with an electric guitar solo over a heavy drum beat (suggesting the style of Led Zeppelin's John Bonham) and loud bass pedals. Allan Moore sees the way that "the heavy entry of the kit seems to change the music's focus" and thus "beckons us into the whole" as a further parallel with *Sgt. Pepper*, serving a similar function to "With a Little Help from my Friends" (Moore, 2001, p. 97).

"Fly on a Windshield" is an excellent example of how, in Tony Banks's words, "at times things were little more than improvisations on an idea. For instance, Mike would say, 'Pharoahs going down the Nile' and he would just play two chords and instantly the rest of us would conjure up that particular mood" (Fielder, 1984, p. 91). Interestingly, Baudrillard referred to New York as a "city of Pharoahs, all obelisks and needles" (1989, p. 14). Among the demos of *The Lamb* that have surfaced is a 12-minute live-in-the-studio improvisation on "Fly on a Windshield," with wordless vocals by Gabriel; given that so much of the music of *The Lamb* was written and recorded before Gabriel became directly involved, this recording is especially interesting in that it seems to fix the recording of "Fly on a Windshield" at a later date in the sessions. (The topic of *Lamb* bootlegs will be explored in more detail in Chapter 6.) The second part beginning at [1:18] bears the stylistic imprint of Steve Hackett, as it is similar to some of his solo songs (see for example "Shadow of the Hierophant," from *The Voyage of the Acolyte*) (Couture, n.d.). After the *Lamb* tour, "Fly on a Windshield" was only occasionally performed live, as part of a medley with the title track and "Broadway Melody of 1974"; the theatrical film *Genesis in Concert 1976* includes a performance of "Fly on a Windshield" and an instrumental version of "Broadway Melody of 1974." By 1978, Genesis had stopped performing both songs, although the title track survived longer on set lists (it makes a severely truncated appearance as part of the "Old Medley" on 1993's *The Way We Walk, Volume 2: The Longs*).

"Broadway Melody of 1974"

As Rael is sucked into this realm of the subconscious, he witnesses "echoes of the Broadway Everglades"—memories of Broadway's past. In some performances Gabriel would describe the cloud enveloping Rael as becoming "solid, like a screen showing up pictures of what existed around it before on the back side of it"; and as Rael was engulfed he saw himself projected on the cloud alongside these other images (Finegan et al.); "audience and event are locked as one" (Gabriel, 1974). The image is evocative of the *Tibetan Book of the Dead*: "The deceased human being becomes the sole spectator of a marvellous [*sic*] panorama of hallucinatory visions … he, like a wonder-struck child watching moving pictures cast upon a screen, looks on, unaware, unless previously an adept in *yoga*, of the non-reality of what he sees dawn and set" (Evans-Wentz, 1960, p. 33). The lyrics present a cavalcade of these images, prompting Chris Welch to comment that the song had "affinities with John Lennon's 'Walrus'" (Welch, 1974). Gabriel himself likened the effect to "the Victorian reaction to early photography. They were afraid their spirit would be trapped on the plates and they refused to be photographed" (Welch, 1975). (Interestingly, Gabriel would later return to this idea of photography stealing one's spirit, transplanted to an African setting, in "The Rhythm of the Heat" from his *Security* solo album.)

Lenny Bruce (who "declares a truce") was a comedian known for his darkly satirical humor. One of the first to use extreme profanity in his act, he was imprisoned for obscenity in 1961. Following an initial show at the Establishment Club in London in 1963, he was prevented from returning to Britain to do another show (McMahan, 1998, p. 411). Bruce died of a drug overdose in 1966 and was eulogized in songs by Tim Hardin, Simon and Garfunkel, and Phil Ochs. In the same year that *The Lamb* was released, Dustin Hoffman made *Lenny*, a film portrayal of the troubled comic's life. "His lasting significance is that he was among the first comedians whose purpose was to disturb instead of simply amuse through his unique insights and observations about the violence of his time" (McMahan, 1998, pp. 411–412).

Marshall McLuhan ("casual viewin'") was a Canadian sociologist and pop-culture theorist. According to McLuhan, societies are most affected by their fastest mode of communication; they are governed by their most dominant media (McMahan, 1998, p. 412). He is best known for his concept of the "global village." One aspect of McLuhan's theory holds that television is an example of a "cool" medium, in which the viewer passively partakes; this may explain McLuhan's depiction here as "casual viewin'" (Currie, 1998). Groucho Marx is depicted as standing alone "with his punchline failing"; by 1973, Groucho was the last surviving of the three best-known Marx brothers, and he had collaborated with author Richard J. Anobile on a book, *The Groucho Marx Scrapbook*, that revealed a nastier side of the beloved entertainer.

Caryl Chessman was an American criminal who was convicted on 17 charges of kidnapping, robbery and rape. After his conviction, he carried out a successful series of appeals from prison and was granted 8 stays of execution by the Governor of California. After spending 12 years on death row, he was executed in 1960. The phrase "in a scent" might be a pun on the word "innocent" (McMahan, 1998, p. 412). Chessman was one of the first people to die in a gas chamber, under the then newly reinstated death penalty; "peach blossom and bitter almond" is the characteristic smell of cyanide gas. Another connection with the unusual scent reference in this song is that at the 1929 premiere of *The Broadway Melody*, one of the first Hollywood movie musicals, perfume was sprayed from the ceiling onto the audience (Smith and Kiger, 2006, p. 96). By 1973 American millionaire Howard Hughes was an eccentric recluse, the subject of a spurious "autobiography" written by Clifford Irving in 1971. In early 1972, Hughes broke his self-imposed silence and informed journalists by phone that the book was a fake. Irving was found guilty of fraud in June 1972.

The images presented in the "Broadway Melody of 1974" are presented as elements in a topsy-turvy universe. The "Broadway Everglades" may refer to New York before it was settled, as swamps and marshes, a kind of Eden. The historical Lenny Bruce would have never "declared a truce"; here he is deferential and conciliatory. McLuhan, an astute observer in his day of all forms of media culture, is depicted with "head buried in the sand." The Sirens of Greek mythology are singing to no one in particular. Groucho is depicted as a failing, unfunny comic. The Ku Klux Klan serves African-American cuisine (Yesfans.com, n.d.). All of the cultural icons that Gabriel invokes in his "Broadway Melody" are either deceased or in decline (Currie, 1998). Gabriel cites a host of additional characters in his liner notes for this portion of the narrative, and here his words are rich in carefully studied wordplay and assonance, which is curiously mostly threefold: "holla – dollar – collar," "King – sing – ring," "bell, cell, hell," "shoot us, Julius, Brutus," "still – till – bill." Gabriel evidently revised these liner notes as painstakingly as he did the lyrics—this was no stream-of-consciousness rambling.

Like the title track, "Broadway Melody of 1974" ends with an intertextual song reference: "Needles and Pins," written by Sonny Bono and Jack Nitzsche, which had been recorded by Jackie DeShannon in 1963 and was a UK number 1 hit for the Searchers the following year. The four-note melodic contour on Gabriel's last line matches the melodic fragment in the original line. The last line of the song, "The children play at home with needles …', also alludes to heroin use, which is regarded by some fans as the meaning for the following song, "Cuckoo Cocoon" (McMahan, 1998, p. 448). Interestingly, Killen notes that these gangs differed from their 1950s and 1960s predecessors in their rejection of heroin (Killen, 2006, p. 205). A musical segue to "Cuckoo Cocoon" is facilitated by an abrupt change of key on the closing words at [1:38].[2] The soft guitar theme that follows, accompanied by quiet Mellotron, is the first appearance of what I will refer to as the "swoon music." (The "swoon music" is treated in more detail in Chapter 5.)

"Cuckoo Cocoon"

In "Cuckoo Cocoon," Rael awakens to find he is wrapped up in a cocoon. The sound of water drops suggests he might be in some kind of cave, but the reassuring warmth of the cocoon soothes him and he falls asleep. The accompaniment

---

[2]   Many CD copies of *The Lamb Lies Down on Broadway*—including the 1994 "Definitive Edition" remasters—are incorrectly tracked in regard to "Fly on a Windshield" and "Broadway Melody of 1974", attaching the first [1:38] of the true "Broadway Melody" track onto "Fly" and separating the instrumental "swoon music" coda, labeling it as "Broadway Melody." As the lyric sheet indicates, "Broadway Melody of 1974" actually begins with the lyric "Echoes of the Broadway Everglades," which occurs at [2:45] into the "Fly on a Windshield" track on these CDs. My timings here are corrected in accordance with the song divisions provided by the lyric sheet.

emphasizes gentle finger-picked electric guitar processed through a Leslie speaker set at a slow speed, providing a warbling underwater effect. It also provides a rare flute solo on the album; given the pastoral connotations of the flute in most progressive rock (Macan, 1997, p. 37), this may have been one of the few places where it was appropriate. On the *Lamb* tour, Gabriel sang the song partly hidden in the stage floor. It was not performed on subsequent tours, but the country-folk band Hazeldine covered it on their 1998 release *Orphans*.

"In the Cage"

"In the Cage" begins with a modulating introduction. With a nod, perhaps, to the Tin Pan Alley song models that begin with a passage of introductory material before the song "proper," "In the Cage" begins with a musically independent passage ("I've got sunshine in my stomach") in B minor. Rutherford's bass pattern here is evocative of a heartbeat as Gabriel's vocal line slowly traces its way down a B minor scale to end on the phrase "sleep deep in the deep." Interestingly, by this time Gabriel's vocal reaches the low B at [0:37]—which should be the point of greatest stability—Rutherford's bass line has also descended, to F♯. This pitch, originally the third of the "Cuckoo Cocoon" final D major chord, has now returned to be the fifth of B minor. Thus, Rutherford's bass puts the B minor "goal" in its least stable inversion. A low vocal drone on F♯ fades in at [0:42], doubling Rutherford's heartbeat bass pulse, facilitating a key change to the true key of "In the Cage," E♭ minor; by the time the organ begins its ostinato pattern at [0:56], the F♯ has enharmonically become G♭, the third of E♭ minor. Upon this new key change, Rutherford's bass note shifts to B♭ at [1:01], maintaining its "dominant pedal" function now as the fifth of E♭ minor (Figure 3.2); we will come back to this point.

Gabriel has succinctly said that "In the Cage" "deals with fear" (Gallo, 1980, p. 155). Rael has awakened from his comforting cocoon surroundings in a state of great fear and sensory agitation, "in a cold sweat with a strong urge to vomit" (Gabriel, 1974). The water drops that Rael hears in "Cuckoo Cocoon" are revealed to be dripping from the ceiling of a cave in which he is trapped; the water is quickly forming stalactites and stalagmites that have grown together, forming a cage pressing in on him. Moreover, the water drops occasion Rael/Gabriel's third intertextual music reference, an unscripted reference to the Burt Bacharach and Hal David song "Raindrops Keep Falling on my Head" (a hit for B. J. Thomas in 1970) heard at [5:31]. He finds he is not alone; others are also in cave-cages that are "joined to form a star"; each occupant is "tied to their things / ... netted by their strings," indicating that perhaps each is bound by some materialistic karma. Outside the cage, however—and thus implicitly free to leave these intensely uncomfortable surroundings—is Rael's brother John; the moment when Rael sees John is distinguished by a "remarkable change of tempo" (Moore, 2001, p. 97) as well as the highest note in Banks's keyboard solo, a dramatic sustained B♭5 at

"Cuckoo Cocoon"
@ [2:09]   "In the Cage," [0:01-0:07]   [0:37]   [0:42-0:56]

[0:56]

[1:01]

Figure 3.2   Enharmonic common-tone transition from "Cuckoo Cocoon" to "In the Cage"

[4:10].[3] John says nothing in response to Rael's pleas for help, but responds only be shedding a "silent tear of blood."

There is evidently a play on various Biblical symbols throughout this episode. Earlier, in "Cuckoo Cocoon," Rael speculates that he may be "some sort of Jonah shut up inside the whale." Some have speculated that "brother John" is a reference to Jesus' brother John (although Steve Hackett's flute-playing brother is also named John). The "tear of blood" may be a reference to Jesus' sweating "great drops of blood" recounted in Luke 22:44; John's abandonment of Rael—which also happens in "The Colony of Slippermen"—may also refer to Peter's repeated denials of Jesus. This is not to suggest that Rael is a Christ-figure, but it is worth noting here that the ultimate moral outcome of *The Lamb*—when Rael forsakes pursuing the raven in order to save his brother—also echoes Jesus'

---

[3]   In seeming response to Banks's arrival on this note, Rutherford's bass plays the same pitch with an emphatic pattern that indicates the role of the B♭ has temporarily shifted from dominant to tonic; the tone is also distorted, with a timbre reminiscent of the opening title track.

remarks concerning men who have "made themselves eunuchs for the Kingdom of Heaven's sake" (Matthew 19:12), or perhaps more figuratively, "he who loses his life ... will save it" (Mark 8:35).

As John walks away, the cage dissolves and Rael's body begins to spin out of control. The constant queasiness and panic felt by Rael is quite compellingly captured in this track, much of which consists of a two-chord organ vamp and a continual hemiola, or metric interplay, between $\frac{6}{8}$ and $\frac{3}{4}$ time. Special mention should also be made of Tony Banks's continually restless keyboard solo beginning at [3:17] and extending well past the return of Gabriel's vocals at [4:36]. Edward Macan notes that "a definite influence of J. S. Bach's toccata style" is found in progressive rock: "the scalar runs, the sequential spinning out of a particular rhythmic motive, the virtuoso arpeggiation of straightforward chord progressions" (Macan, 1997, p. 36); all of these features are present in this solo.

The uncertainty of Rael's situation is also subtly conveyed in the changing roles that B♭ and E♭ play in Mike Rutherford's bass work throughout the song. In much of the song, Rutherford stays on B♭, the dominant or fifth of E♭ Aeolian minor; this is the "dominant pedal" referred to earlier. Traditionally in "classical" music this would be the least stable inversion for a tonic chord, demanding resolution to the dominant chord (B♭ major) and from there to the tonic. Instead, the chord progression oscillates between second-inversion E♭ minor and B♭ minor; given the structure of the verses, one could also interpret this progression as a series of plagal progressions (second-inversion iv going to i) in B♭ minor. Indeed, this very tonal ambiguity is but one facet of the song's psychological tension. The bass does eventually "resolve" to a tonic (E♭) pedal tone at three key points, in the sections at [1:51], [2:47], and [6:23]; thus, one could hear Rutherford's bass work as a kind of ongoing "struggle for control" between B♭ and E♭. Moreover, in the last verse beginning at [5:46], following Banks's second keyboard solo (an abbreviated version of the first), we hear Rutherford's bass alternating between E♭ and B♭ for the first time rather than doggedly maintaining the B♭ pedal—perhaps the point of greatest "conflict" between the two pitches?

"In the Cage" is one of the best-known tracks from *The Lamb*, as Genesis continued to perform the song well into the 1980s; by the mid-1980s, this song was often the only one from the Gabriel years left in the group's set lists. Phil Collins's performances of the song were more rhythmically charged than Gabriel's, Collins telling an interviewer that the lyrics:

> are almost irrelevant to the backing track. Having not heard the original in such a long time, when we actually came 'round to doing it, I treated each word like a percussive thing so that it all fit in with the percussive track. I think the singing of it has changed to fit in with the drum—with the rhythmic side of it—rather than the other way around. (Alexander, 1983, p. 48)

Beginning in 1980, live performances of the song were often included in a medley with keyboard solos from "The Colony of Slippermen" (or occasionally from other early Genesis songs such as "Cinema Show," as can be heard on 1982's *Three Sides Live*), ending with a complete performance of "Afterglow." This practice eventually developed into more intricate medleys made of shorter song segments, as evidenced on *The Way We Walk, Volume 2: The Longs*.

"The Grand Parade of Lifeless Packaging"

Eventually Rael stops spinning and sits down on a highly polished factory floor until his dizziness stops. He finds a "dreamdoll saleslady" sitting at a reception desk, who shows him around the "Grand Parade of Lifeless Packaging," delivering a smoothly prepared sales pitch. Rael recognizes old members of his gang along with his brother John, who has a number 9 stamped on his forehead; fearing for his safety, he escapes into a corridor. Some have interpreted this detail to be a Gabrielesque pun concerning John Lennon, who referred to the number in "Revolution 9" and "No. 9 Dream" (McMahan, 1998, p. 417). A more plausible interpretation, however—especially given Gabriel's penchant for Biblical imagery—is that the number is a reference to the famous "number of the Beast" in Revelation 13:18; whereas the number in Revelation is a "man's number" of 666, John's number 9 represents divine perfection (3 times 3). At various times in the narrative, John appears as a guide or a symbol of spiritual aspiration for Rael. (In "The Cage," Rael sees John outside the cages; here, he is stamped with a mark of perfection. Later still it will be John who advises Rael of the way to escape his grotesque transformation in the "Colony of Slippermen.")

The "factory floor" setting of the "Grand Parade," and its nightmarish scenario of human beings prepared on a "production line," strongly recalls the opening hatchery sequence of Aldous Huxley's 1932 novel *Brave New World*. Compare, for example, the speeches of Gabriel's "dreamdoll saleslady" and Huxley's Director of Hatcheries and Conditioning:

> "This is the Grand Parade of Lifeless Packaging, those you are about to see are all in for servicing, except for a small quantity of our new product, in the second gallery. It is all the stock required to cover the existing arrangements of the enterprise. Different batches are distributed to area operators, and there are plenty of opportunities for the large investor … . Except for the low market mal-nutritioned, each is provided with a guarantee for a successful birth and trouble free infancy. There is however only a small amount of variable choice potential – not too far from the mean differential … ." (Gabriel, 1974)

> "Essentially," the D.H.C. concluded, "bokanovskification consists of a series of arrests of development. We check the normal growth and, paradoxically enough, the egg responds by budding." …
> He pointed. On a very slowly moving band a rack-full of test tubes was entering a large metal box, another rack full was emerging. Machinery faintly purred. It took eight minutes for the tubes to go through, he told them. Eight minutes of hard X-rays being

about as much as an egg can stand. A few died; of the rest, the least susceptible divided into two; most put out four buds, some eight; all were returned to the incubators, where the buds began to develop; then, after two days, were suddenly chilled, chilled and checked. Two, four, eight, the buds in their turn budded; and having budded were dosed almost to death with alcohol; consequently burgeoned again and having budded—bud out of bud out of bud—were therefore after—further arrest being generally fatal—left to develop in peace. By which time the original egg was in a fair way to becoming anything from eight to ninety-six embryos—a prodigious improvement, you will agree, on nature … .

"Scores," the Director repeated and flung out his arms, as though he were distributing largesse. "Scores."

But one of the students was fool enough to ask where the advantage lay.

"My good boy!" The Director wheeled sharply round on him. "Can't you see? Can't you *see?*" He raised a hand; his expression was solemn. "Bokanovsky's Process is one of the major instruments of social stability!" …

"Ninety-six identical twins working ninety-six identical machines!" The voice was almost tremulous with enthusiasm. "You really know where you are. For the first time in history." (Huxley, 1998, pp. 6–7)

The dystopian theme of technology dominating human life is a recurrent theme of progressive rock (see also ELP's "Karn Evil 9," analyzed in Macan, 2006, pp. 285–310), and Gabriel had earlier touched on the theme of technologically-assisted human genetic engineering in "Get 'Em Out By Friday." The title of the song itself may be another of Gabriel's puns; "Grand Parade" is the name of several prominent streets in British communities (somewhat akin to the proverbial "Main Street" in the US), including the beach resort of Brighton and the town of Bath, near Gabriel's home. This song was performed live only during the *Lamb* tour, and indeed it does appear to be little more than a simple musical scaffold for one of Gabriel's denser lyrics on the album. Musically, the song has a cyclic structure involving three keys—A major, C major, and E major—all of which have E as common tone (in fact, a high E5 is sustained as a drone as the song progresses, from [1:40] onward, and the treated drums at the end of the song have a pitched resonance approximating E2). Fielder (1984, p. 90) points out that the song was quickly written to fit Gabriel's extra lyrics. Perhaps to compensate for the song's musical paucity, there are some novel studio gimmicks, including panning of the introduction from one stereo channel to the other to imply parade-like movement and the continually changing electronic processing of Gabriel's vocals; it is here that Eno's "Enossification" is most pronounced.

The end of "Grand Parade" also represents the first "break" in the narrative, imposed by the limitations of the original vinyl medium (the end of Side 1). Many rock artists took advantage of side endings, using them as a kind of intermission in the story line.[4] The abrupt, drum-saturated ending of "The Grand Parade" thus

---

[4]   To cite just a few examples: Side 1 of Lindsey Buckingham's *Go Insane* (1984) concludes with a loop of music that runs into the wind-off grooves of the record and resumes

acts as the musical equivalent of a theatrical "blackout"—with the opening of Side 2 the scene changes to New York City.

"Back in N.Y.C."

> Such is the whirl of [New York City], so great its centrifugal force, that it would take superhuman strength to envisage living as a couple and sharing someone else's life in New York. Only tribes, gangs, mafia families, secret societies, and perverse communities can survive, not couples. This is the anti-Ark. In the first Ark, the animals came in two by two to save the species from the great flood. Here in this fabulous Ark, each one comes in alone—it's up to him or her each evening to find the last survivors for the last party. (Baudrillard, 1989, pp. 18–19)

The second album side of *The Lamb* begins with an extended flashback in the storyline, consisting of "Back in N.Y.C.," "Hairless Heart," and "Counting Out Time." This flashback occurs as Rael's response to the fear and trauma of "In The Cage" (note the heartbeat-like F♯ bass with which the song begins, identical to the opening of "In The Cage") and the confusion of "Grand Parade"; Rael copes through nostalgia, recalling the power and aggression of his street-gang life in "Back in N.Y.C." and his burgeoning masculinist sexuality in "Counting Out Time." Nostalgia, of course, was a dominant trend in 1970s culture, as can be seen in the success of musicals such as *Annie* and *A Chorus Line*, gangster films such as *The Godfather*, "1930s period pieces" such as *Paper Moon* and *The Sting*, and the television series *Happy Days* (Clecak, 1983, pp. 92–93). Clecak explains this impulse to nostalgia as a response to Americans' loss of "psychological, social, and moral bearings—their sense of time, place, and manner"; nostalgia was appealing because it "sanctioned a tight, or what was more convenient, a loose hold on elements of the past. In the extreme, nostalgia serves as an exercise in primary narcissism, a longing to reverse biographical processes to an infantile state wherein security and wholeness are thought to reign" (Clecak, 1983, p. 93). Rael's nostalgic retreat, then, may be interpreted as symbolic of 1970s American society.

It is here, however, that in his characterization of Rael Gabriel makes some unusual gaffes. Rael's reference to "progressive hypocrites" is one example in which Gabriel's British upbringing manages to penetrate his Puerto-Rican-American persona. The sense in which the term "progressive" is used here is more akin to the American "liberal"; McMahan observes that "Rael would have been very out of character to use this term, or to even be aware of the politics going on at all" (McMahan, 1998, p. 418). Another seeming gaffe concerns the reference

---

at the beginning of Side 2; on The Who's *Tommy* (1969), "Eyesight to the Blind" (the end of Side 1) ends with an unresolved cadence that is resolved by the first chord of "Christmas" (the opening song on Side 2); and on Pink Floyd's *The Wall*, Pink's isolation behind the wall is finally completed at the end of Side 2 (closing the first half of the album).

to Rael's incarceration at Pontiac Reformatory; although McMahan locates the Pontiac Reformatory in New York State, it was actually located in Illinois, southwest of Chicago. If Gabriel chose this facility because of its fame, he must have been unaware of its location (or this could be more wordplay, a reference to the American automobile of the same name). Nevertheless, "Back in N.Y.C." was quite unlike anything else Genesis had recorded before. The "pedal point groove" over an asymmetrical meter had been done before (for example in the "Apocalypse in 9/8" section of "Supper's Ready"), and it was a device to which Genesis would return (as in "Down and Out" from 1978's ... *And Then There Were Three*). The lyrics, however, were a harsh jolt of reality. If Genesis could earlier be accused of having fey or twee lyrics, there was nothing fey about lines such as "I'm not full of shit," which Gabriel spat out with all the venom of a proto-punk-rocker. More than any other song on the album, it is this one that stands as the best example of Gabriel's desire with *The Lamb* to "throw away all that intellectual stuff," and replace it "an aggressive, ballsy character in Rael ... someone who meant something to people who were not necessarily from a middle-class background" (Gallo, 1980, p. 155). The song seethes with violence; during performances on the *Lamb* tour, Gabriel would actually throw a small Molotov cocktail on stage.

In Gabriel's story notes for the song, Rael is depicted returning from a gang raid, "cuddling a sleeping porcupine" (Gabriel, 1974), who counsels him that his heart is "deep in hair / Time to shave, shave it off." In some performances of *The Lamb*, Gabriel would acknowledge that "cuddling the porcupine" was a reference to masturbation (Currie, 1998), but another interpretation holds that the porcupine is "an incredibly vulnerable animal, which is only protected by its sharp quills. No animal dare approach it, or try and devour it, because it will get a painful surprise," in other words a picture of Rael himself; underneath the tough exterior so painstakingly portrayed in the first part of the song is a very vulnerable youth (Yesfans.com, n.d.). The quills of the porcupine are modified hairs that can be up to five inches long, protecting the animal's soft unprotected underbelly; shaving the quills off would make the heart "vulnerable to attack, and ready for violation" (Yesfans.com, n.d.). The porcupine's voice is interior, like Rael's conscience; it is also distorted with Eno's treatments, making its voice a distinctly different persona from the angrily asserted posturing of Rael the street tough. What follows then— "No time for romantic escape, / When your fluffy heart is ready for rape. No!"—is a dialogue; the distorted quality of the repeated "No!"s must be the protests of the heart in anticipation of its violation and subsequent vulnerability. "To now have an audio version, of what was once an image of a defenseless porcupine, is horrific as well as incredibly sad. The pity one feels toward this now tiny, vulnerable creature, would now in fact, break your own heart" (Yesfans.com, n.d.).

"Back in N.Y.C." prefigures the more stripped-down musical direction of Gabriel's first two solo albums; the "porcupine" as well anticipates the unusual sexual imagery that would characterize his later work ("Sledgehammer," "Kiss That Frog," etc.). After Gabriel's departure, Genesis largely stopped performing the song, except for the October 2, 1982 Milton Keynes, UK reunion show with

Gabriel and a handful of early *Duke* tour dates (the *Rare Tapes* bootleg set contains a Collins-era rendition of the song recorded, appropriately enough, at Madison Square Garden, New York). Gabriel, on the other hand, sometimes used the song as an encore on his first two tours; one performance (from the Roxy in Los Angeles on April 9, 1977) has been widely bootlegged.

"Hairless Heart"

This soft instrumental piece was probably composed primarily by Steve Hackett; although Genesis never performed it after the *Lamb* tour, Hackett has revived it in his own live performances (a lovely version, with John Hackett on flute and Roger King on keyboards, can be heard on a bootleg recording made at Carnglaze Caverns in the UK on August 4, 2005). The song's theme, in D minor, is first stated on classical guitar, then on an electric guitar played with a volume pedal. The theme is then developed in an expansive keyboard setting, flirting with a movement to F major before ending on a Db major chord. When the theme is repeated, this creates an unusual "sliding" harmonic effect, the melody's concluding F being the only common tone between Db major and D minor. Upon the end of the second playing, however, the Db chord is revealed to be the subdominant (IV) of Ab major, the key of "Counting Out Time" (Figure 3.3). The keys of D minor and Ab major are as distant as possible from one another, and this—along with the acceleration of tempo going into "Counting Out Time"—would seem to indicate a rather rapid change of scene in the narrative.

Gabriel's story refers to a dream in which Rael "pictured the removal of his hairy heart and to the accompaniment of very romantic music … watched it being shaved smooth by an anonymous stainless steel razor" (Gabriel, 1974). There is an indirect Biblical allusion here, to "circumcision of the heart" (Deuteronomy 30:6), symbolic of spiritual rather than sexual arousal. Rather than prepare Rael's heart for focusing on spiritual things, however, the action leads instead to one of Rael's carnal reminiscences. The image—which recalls the razor incision of a woman's eye in the Luis Buñuel film *Un Chien Andalou* (1929)—portrays Rael's reawakening of "romantic" (sexual) feelings, in the same way that shaving the skin enhances its sensitivity; Gabriel's description of the organ as "cherry-red" (Gabriel, 1974) perhaps also indicates a return to virginity, with the concomitant adolescent desire for sexual initiation.

"Counting Out Time"

The last of the three songs that make up Rael's extended flashback, here he relives his first sexual encounter, for which he has prepared by studying a "how-to" manual (a number of books such as Eric Weber's *How to Pick Up Girls* and *How to Make Love to a Single Girl* were published in the early 1970s). He attempts to apply his

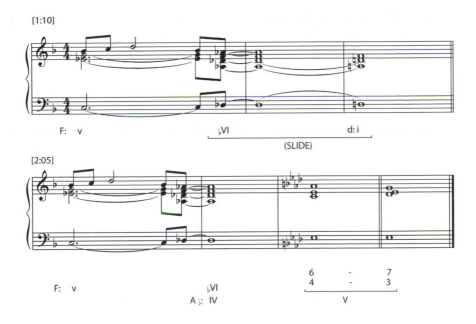

Figure 3.3   "Double duty" of the D♭ major chord in "Hairless Heart"

newfound knowledge ("Look! I've found the hotspots, Figures 1 to 9"), but "going by the book," needless to say, doesn't please his date. Unlike most of the other songs on *The Lamb*—which were, at least musically, group efforts—"Counting Out Time" was written completely by Gabriel (Platts, 2001, p. 75). Gabriel had turned to the theme of sexuality earlier, in *Nursery Cryme*'s opening track "The Musical Box." In that song, the protagonist's sexual frustration had "clear parallels with Gabriel's perceptions of the widespread repression of English society and its accompanying sexual hypocrisy" (Bowler and Dray, 1993, p. 54). In "Counting Out Time," Gabriel is making a similar satirical point—that, for all the supposed "progress" of the Sexual Revolution—and the clinical, biological reduction of the courtship process described, again, in Huxley's *Brave New World*—courtship still amounts to more than an assembly-line-like orderly succession of actions aimed at sexual arousal and consummation. At the same time, he voiced the universal complaint of the adolescent male.

Musically as well as lyrically, this song offers a distinctive contrast from the previous two numbers. A rather bouncy number in (mostly) ⁴⁄₄ time, the song's harmonic progression and descending bass line resembles Procol Harum's 1967 hit "A Whiter Shade of Pale," which in turn borrows much, musically, from Percy Sledge's "When a Man Loves a Woman" (Gillett, 1972, p. 257). "Counting Out Time," then, has all sorts of musical antecedents—it may even be considered to be a somewhat elaborated version of a 1950s doo-wop "make-out" song. The genealogy of this song's musical style offers a useful example for Paul Willis's provocative theory on the development of "progressive" music from earlier "rock 'n' roll":

> We can see rock 'n' roll as a deconstruction and "progressive" music as a reconstruction. The simple expedient of replacing tonality with beat as its main organizing structure let rock 'n' roll out of the constructions of recorded music. It went no further, itself, however, than a primitivistic celebration of the simplicity and timelessness it had rediscovered. The crucial simultaneous development of advanced techniques for recording and reproduction also relieved rock 'n' roll of the constriction of a transposed notation. Progressive music would have been impossible without this stage of regression, and clearing of received convention. Though this risks minimization and ignores its crucial modernity, one way of conceptualizing rock 'n' roll, and its relation to "progressive" music, is to see it as a retracement back through the complex roots of romantic and classical music back to a point where the tonal conventions had not become determining and to a point where the body was still openly in the music as beat. "Progressive" music can be seen as an experimentation with alternate routes—exploiting the new techniques, of course—from this point into a greater complexity. (Willis, 1978, pp. 166–167)

Thus, in "Counting Out Time" we find a simplistic goal-directed chord progression in the verses, reminiscent of earlier rock 'n' roll styles. This backward-looking element is parodied by the phase-shifted electric piano and interspersed with the "progressive" and violent interruptions of fuzz bass and syncopation over asymmetrical meter ($\frac{5}{4}$) in the "erogenous zones" choruses. (The fuzz-tone bass here recalls the similar tone for the "aggressive" riff that characterized "The Lamb Lies Down on Broadway.") Hackett's guitar solo at [2:28] adds another element of humor to the song; he processed his guitar with an EMS Synthi Hi-Fli guitar synthesizer (Platts, 2001, p. 77), an early multi-effects pedal that was introduced in 1973 and included fuzz, ring modulation, a wah-wah pedal and octave-shifting options (Hinton and Wood, 1995–98). Perhaps this solo was one of the "neat, clever tricks" to which Chris Welch of *Melody Maker* referred in his otherwise lukewarm review of *The Lamb* (Welch, 1974).

"Counting Out Time" was chosen to be the first single in advance of the album release, backed with "Riding the Scree," one of the more progressive-styled songs on the album. Taken as a pair, the two songs are sufficiently different in style that a listener would have little indication of the overall content of the album—a more commercial direction for Genesis? Or a continuation of the intricate compositional paths blazed by *Foxtrot* and *Selling England By The Pound*? Unlike *Selling England*'s "I Know What I Like," the new single failed to make a significant impact on the charts. Live performances of the song ended with an extended scat vocal improvisation, sometimes lasting for as long as a minute. The song was only performed on the *Lamb* tour (Couture, n.d.).

"The Carpet Crawlers"

Along with the title track, "The Carpet Crawlers" (also titled on some recordings as "Carpet Crawlers" or "The Carpet Crawl") is perhaps the most beloved song on *The Lamb*. After the relative failure of "Counting Out Time," this song was chosen to be the second single from the album, backed with "Evil Jam" (an early title for "The Waiting Room," discussed below) and released in April 1975. It was a minor hit in the UK.

It is here that the lamb, originally a minor-character "catalyst" in the title track, makes its first musical return. The song begins with a short, seemingly unrelated introductory section, just as "In the Cage" did, functioning much like a recitative in an opera or the introduction to a Tin Pan Alley standard. "There is lamb's wool under my naked feet," Gabriel/Rael sings, as the musical accompaniment reprises the accompaniment to the quiet bridge of the title track in which the lamb seemed "right out of place." The lamb wool at his feet could in fact be analogous to the hair shaved from his heart in "Hairless Heart"; at any rate, the harmonic rhythm in this passage is initially twice as fast as it was for the title track's bridge, and the line "There is lamb's wool under my naked feet" does not scan with the rest of the opening text, implying that Rael has come out of his flashback rather suddenly (perhaps Rael is the one "right out of place" in this scene). He finds himself in a "red-ochre" carpeted corridor, where a procession of crawling people is moving toward a spiral staircase. The crawlers are seemingly drawn toward the staircase, because going into the next chamber is the only way out ("We got to get in to get out").

Like "The Grand Parade," the song is in a simple strophic form developed through increasing dynamics and layers of texture, particularly Hackett's ghostly guitar counter-melody that runs throughout the song, though curiously buried in the mix (the rendition on 1977's live release *Seconds Out* showcases Hackett's playing to better effect). Banks's repetitive cascading arpeggios would later be heard on "Ripples" from *A Trick of the Tail*, Genesis's first post-Gabriel release. Like "Broadway Melody of 1974," the lyrics present a cavalcade of iconic personages—from Superman to the Biblical wise and foolish virgins. The final verse is filled with unusually playful Gabrielesque wordplay, assonances and alliterations.

Genesis kept the song in their set list until about 1980. Divorced of its theatrical context, the introductory "scene-setting" section would often be omitted in live performance, starting directly at the first verse. All five members of the "vintage" Genesis line-up re-united for a new version of the song, which was included on the compilation *Turn it On Again: The Hits*. This version, "The Carpet Crawlers 1999," is particularly interesting in that Gabriel and Collins share lead vocals on the song, ultimately harmonizing toward the end; Collins also contributes some percussion programming that hints at a more contemporary, drum-and-bass influence.

"The Chamber of 32 Doors"

This song marks the emotional high point of *The Lamb*; it is at this point that with Rael's closing admonition to "take me away," his defenses seem to finally have been broken down. Rael has made it to the end of the carpeted corridor and climbed the staircase referred to in "The Carpet Crawlers," finding himself in a large hemispheric chamber with 32 doors around its circumference. He finds the chamber "in confusion," as people dart in and out looking for the only door that provides escape rather than leading back into the chamber. As Rael tries to find the correct door, he must deal with the advice and opinions of those with him (Couture, n.d.); hence, the drama of the piece is broken occasionally with folksy interludes, with an appropriate change of characterization by Gabriel, supported by harmony vocals from Collins: "I'd rather trust a countryman than a townman."

The pervasive dualities in the lyrics are interesting. Aside from the countryman/ townman images, Rael is flanked first by the rich man in front of him and the poor man "behind my back," then by "my father to the left of me" and "my mother to the right." Gabriel's lyric choice of Rael's "father to the left" places Rael at the right side of his father, analogous to the Biblical placement of Christ as "seated at the right hand of God the Father."[5] The placement of these archetypal images— rich man, poor man, mother, father—at the four cardinal directions around Rael is also symbolically laden,[6] as is the pairing of these archetypes as dichotomies that match their directional orientation ("as far as the east is from the west," Psalm 103:12), a concept also found in Kabbalistic philosophy.

Couture remarks that the song's sparse musical arrangement is "what makes it powerful: there is space between each chord and Peter Gabriel's voice echoes in this large room as if lost amidst the crowd, depicting the hero's feelings of solitude in a society he rebels against" (Couture, n.d.). Several musical ingredients contribute to this song's emotional power: Hackett's opening guitar solo (a rarity on this album), selective use of reverb on the vocals and drums (compare the stately beginning and ending, for example, with the "countryman/townman" sections), and Banks's dramatic and colorful use of Mellotron strings and Hammond organ.

Spicer (2001, p. 83) has remarked in his study of "Supper's Ready" that Banks tends to reserve the Mellotron strings for "climactic moments," and its appearance here reminds the listener that, in fact, Banks has not used this element in his timbral arsenal in a soloistic context since "Fly on a Windshield" back on Side 1. In addition, Macan cites progressive rock's use of the "Hammond as a substitute pipe organ" as evidence of the influence of Anglican church music on musicians' stylistic development (1997, p. 32). Macan goes on to say that this is one feature that contributes to progressive rock performances having an almost liturgical aspect for many of its fans (1997, pp. 66–68). Interestingly, although Tony Banks

---

5   McMahan (1998) contains other examples of Rael-Christ topic references in *The Lamb*.

6   Consider, for example, the parallels with Kate Bush's "Lily" from *The Red Shoes* (1990): "Gabriel before me / Raphael behind me / Michael on my right / Uriel on my left side."

uses the Hammond in a *rhythm*-instrument capacity on this album (on "In the Cage," for example, a distant cousin of "The Knife"), he generally does not use it for its *sustaining* qualities, that role being given to the Mellotron instead (as in, for example, "Hairless Heart"). This is in stark contrast to earlier Genesis albums (note the sustaining organ on "Seven Stones" or "Firth of Fifth," for example), and it may be that the avoidance of the sustaining Hammond is tied to a desire to get away from the "liturgical," "English" aspects of Genesis's style and more toward a "secular," "American" style. One rare exception to this rhythm-oriented use of the Hammond on *The Lamb* is found here, in "The Chamber of 32 Doors." If progressive rock musicians' use of the Hammond as "substitute pipe organ" was a *subconscious* reference to their Anglican upbringings, as Macan seems to suggest, here Banks seems to be exploiting the associations of the straight-toned Hammond with high-church liturgy *intentionally*. The sustained organ is virtually the only accompaniment to Rael's admissions of insecurity: "I need someone to believe in, someone to trust"; interestingly, the harmonic progression at this moment is a poignant flat-six to tonic progression in D♭ major. Susan McClary (1983, p. 78) has argued that in nineteenth-century Romantic music the flat-six chord represented "false hope"; if so, Rael, in his resigned surrender, may already have given up hope of leaving the chamber.

Most of the music to "The Chamber of 32 Doors" was written by Gabriel, along with the lyrics (Platts, 2001, p. 75); perhaps because Gabriel had such a major input in writing the song, it was not performed after the *Lamb* tour (Couture, n.d.). "The Chamber of 32 Doors" marks the end of the first half of *The Lamb*; befitting its status as a side-closer in the double album (concluding Side 2), it is also a major turning point in the story. Only after Rael sings, "Take me away," does he meet the guide he needs to lead him out of the confusion—Lilywhite Lilith, his first real guide in his journey thus far.

"Lilywhite Lilith"

While trapped in the confusion of the chamber of 32 doors, Rael hears a blind woman asking for help. If he could guide her to the center of the room, she could feel where the breeze blows, coming from the only door that provides an escape. Once he helps her—the first time in the narrative where Rael shows any inclination of helping another—she leads him through the exiting corridor and into a dark cave. Gabriel told Chris Welch (1975) that the cave was "like the black tank," a reference to the epsom-salt flotation tank sensory deprivation experiments undertaken by scientist John C. Lilly in the 1960s (and described in his book *The Center of the Cyclone*, published in 1973). There, she sits him on what appears to be a jade throne and tells him "They're coming for you / Now don't be afraid" before she leaves. A reprise of the music from "Broadway Melody of 1974" comprises the last one-third of the song (from [1:45] to the end), concluding once again with the "swoon" music, this time a flourish on Mellotron flutes instead of quiet guitar.

McMahan notes that Lilith's cryptic comment "They're coming for you" foreshadows Rael's encounter with the Lamia (p. 427). McMahan also offers a detailed discussion of the Lilith symbol (1998, pp. 424–426), tracing its origins to a female demon in Babylonian mythology (a nocturnal predator, particularly dangerous to children) and from there to an esoteric Jewish cult that survived until about 700 C.E. Johann Wolfgang von Goethe's *Faust Part I* introduces Lilith briefly in the "Walpurgis Night" scene:

> FAUST.
> Who's that there?
> MEPHISTOPHELES.
> Take a good look.
> Lilith.
> FAUST.
> Lilith? Who is that?
> MEPHISTOPHELES.
> Adam's wife, his first. Beware of her.
> Her beauty's one boast is her dangerous hair.
> When Lilith winds it tight around young men
> She doesn't soon let go of them again.
>
> (Goethe, 1992, Greenberg translation,
> lines 4206–4211)

An 1880 translation of *Faust* notes that the name Lilith "occurs in Isaiah (xxxiv. 14); in the Vulgate it is translated Lamia" (Goethe, 1880, p. 310). McMahan's discussion of various translations of Isaiah 34:14 shows that the "night monster" or "night hag" referred to in the verse, thought by some commentators to be a reference to the Babylonian Lilith figure, is translated into the Vulgate Latin as "Lamia." In this way, McMahan connects Lilywhite Lilith to the Lamia, and thus her apparent aid to Rael in leaving the chamber of 32 doors may in fact be construed as a betrayal (McMahan, 1998, pp. 424–426).

"Lilywhite Lilith" was a re-working of an early Genesis song called "The Light" (Bowler and Dray, 1993, p. 94). That early song provided the guitar riff and the verse melody of "Lilywhite Lilith" (Russell, 2004, p. 203). Only one recording of "The Light" is known to exist, from a performance at the La Ferme V club in Woluwe, Belgium on March 7, 1971 (McMahan, 1998, p. 84). In a foreshadowing of future developments, "The Light" was perhaps the first Genesis song to have lyrics by Phil Collins. Banks remembers:

> "The Light" ... arrived when Phil first came in. We asked him if he had anything we could use, and he had this song called "The Light" with a slightly embarrassing lyric about Joe and Mary. It was to do with Jesus and was a bit kind of odd in that sense. It

was quite a good melody so we constructed a big song around it. It had some good bits in the middle, the little triplet section.[7] (Russell, 2004, p. 203)

An example of the sort of short-order musical patchwork the band resorted to as the release deadline loomed, "Lilywhite Lilith" seems like an attempt to fit in too much storyline into a pre-existing musical framework for which it is not a particularly good fit; the narrative "gets very linear ... directly describing the action instead of evoking it or relating to it" (Couture, n.d.). Consequently, the song was dropped after the *Lamb* tour; the only known Collins performance of the song, included on the *Rare Tapes* bootleg set, comes from the first show of the *Wind and Wuthering* tour on New Year's Day 1977. There, the song appears in a medley with a brief "Waiting Room"-like improvisation and the Collins-composed *Wind and Wuthering* instrumental "Wot Gorilla?" (also the only known live performance of that song); medleys of older songs were to become a staple of Genesis's later live performances in the 1980s and 1990s.

"The Waiting Room"

As "Lilywhite Lilith" draws to a close, Rael is left to "face his fear"—the first time he has acknowledged his fear since his experience in the cage. Here, Rael's fear is exacerbated by an approaching, blindingly bright light and a growing succession of fearful sounds—"The Waiting Room."

William James noted in his study of religious experience that the vision of an approaching light—a *photism*—is especially common (1925, p. 251); the light appearing at the end of a long tunnel (or corridor) is also a common element in accounts of near-death experiences. If this is death, we may assume this to be a second (spiritual?) death, since Rael presumably physically died when he was engulfed by the "wall of death" on Times Square ("Fly on a Windshield"). Thus, this episode is best understood as another test—which, once again, Rael fails, in this case by responding with violence (throwing a rock at the light).

"The Waiting Room" remains one of the most unique songs in Genesis's recorded output, because it was a totally "free" group improvisation. Phil Collins recalled that during the Headley Grange rehearsals, the group tried an experiment: "We started to play and the only guidelines were that we should start off with 'nasty' and finish off 'nice' and where we went in between was up to us ..." (Bowler and Dray, 1993, p. 92). According to Tony Banks, "We switched off all the lights and just made noises. And the first time it really was frightening" (Fielder, 1984, p. 92). Collins provides further detail:

---

[7]   The "little triplet section" to which Banks refers also wound up recycled for *The Lamb*, as the "Raven" section of "The Colony of Slippermen."

We were all getting really intense; Peter was blowing his oboe reeds into the microphone and playing his flute with the echoplex [tape-delay echo box] on when suddenly there was this great clap of thunder and it started raining.

We all thought, "We've got in contact with something heavy here." It was about five or six in the evening and we were making all these weird noises when the thunderstorm started and it began to pour down. And then we all shifted gear and got into a really melodic mood.

At moments like that it really was a five-piece thing. We worked well together on "The Lamb"—the two albums gave us the room to do it. (Fielder, 1984, p. 92)

The parallel between Rael's fear and the "frightening" experience of the group's improvisation is interesting, for in this song Genesis—a group of mostly sheltered, quiet public-school-raised musicians used to tightly proscribed musical arrangements—stepped out of their comfort zone (indeed, out of the comfort zone for most musicians!) into the kind of totally structure-less group improvisation pioneered by the likes of the Grateful Dead. In fact, in the same way that a Dead show invariably featured a "space" set for spontaneous improvisation, the *Lamb* shows similarly featured their own "space" set, night after night. Two blinding spotlights—a reference to the "two golden globes" referred to at the end of "Lilywhite Lilith"—accompanied the song in live performances. The group jam "brought magnificent tension to the live show while providing one short moment of uncertainty" (Couture, n.d.). Indeed, for some members of the group—especially Banks and Collins—"The Waiting Room" provided a necessary "release valve," lessening the tedium of playing the same rigidly structured set night after night. A live recording from the first leg of the tour was issued as the B-side to "The Carpet Crawlers" under the title "Evil Jam"; since then, the song has appeared under both titles on bootlegs (Couture, n.d.). Steve Hackett released a similar jam titled "Waiting Room Only" on his CD *Watcher of the Skies: Genesis Revisited.*

"Anyway"

The amount of musical material borrowed from unreleased or unfinished Genesis songs in the second half of *The Lamb* reveals something of the group's desperation to finish the project, even as they began to run out of new musical ideas. Just as "Lilywhite Lilith" made substantial use of an earlier Genesis song, "Anyway" began as a number originally entitled "Frustration," recorded back in January 1970 for a BBC documentary about painter Mick Jackson (Platts, 2001, p. 24). Like some of the songs on *From Genesis to Revelation*, "Anyway" is centered on Tony Banks's piano, providing—along with much of "The Lamia"—an acoustic interlude after the previous electronic numbers. François Couture notes that the "cascading piano arpeggios and thundering bass notes" of the song's middle section prefigure Banks's 1976 song "Ripples" (Couture, n.d.). Once again, the song was not performed again after the *Lamb* tour.

Here, trapped in the cave that has collapsed in rubble around him, Rael awaits death calmly—even philosophically ("How wonderful to be so profound / When everything you are is dying underground"). This quality of philosophical detachment recalls William James's discussion of the "divided self," in which he quotes from the French novelist Alphonse Daudet:

> Homo duplex, homo duplex! The first time that I perceived I was two [selves] was at the death of my brother Henri, when my father cried out so dramatically, "He is dead, he is dead!" While my first self wept, my second self thought, "How truly given was that cry, how fine it would be at the theatre." I was then fourteen years old.
>
> This horrible duality has often given me matter for reflection. Oh, this terrible second me, always seated whilst the other is on foot, acting, living, suffering, bestirring itself. This second me that I have never been able to intoxicate, to make shed tears, or put to sleep. And how it sees into things, and how it mocks! (Quoted in James, 1925, pp. 167–168)

Rael's period of self-contemplation in the collapsed cave is an example of the "belly of the whale" motif found in many myths. "The idea that the passage of the magical threshold is a transit into a sphere of rebirth is symbolized in the worldwide womb image of the belly of the whale. The hero, instead of conquering or conciliating the power of the threshold, is swallowed into the unknown, and would appear to have died" (Campbell, 1968, p. 90).

"Here Comes The Supernatural Anaesthetist"

> This brief song is, like its predecessor, another indication of how thin Genesis's material was stretched as they worked on the second half of *The Lamb*; essentially the song is an instrumental track prepared by Banks, Hackett, Rutherford and Collins, to which Gabriel added a brief vocal introduction. While Rael is entombed in the collapsed cave, he is visited by Death, personified as the "Supernatural Anaesthetist," who releases a puff of gas ("If he wants you to snuff it/All he has to do is puff it," a couplet reminiscent of the appearance of Caryl Chessman in "Broadway Melody of 1974") and disappears, apparently leaving Rael still alive (or at least sentient in some metaphysical sense). The song, which was only performed live on the *Lamb* tour, was accompanied in concert by slides showing a grotesque figure jumping up and down on a pogo stick (Couture, n.d.).

Because of Hackett's prominence in this song (his guitar carries the melodic line for nearly the entire song), François Couture suggests that he had the greatest hand in composing it. The meticulous craftsmanship of Steve Hackett's guitar solo is remarkable; in its avoidance of literal repetition and constant variation of motives it recalls the "Canterbury" progressive rock of groups such as the Soft Machine (the length of the solo and variety of motives in "Here Comes the Supernatural Anaesthetist," in fact, is comparable to that of the "head" melody in the Soft Machine's "Facelift" [1970]). All the same, careful listening reveals that Hackett's solo is also double-tracked, with two solos panned hard left and right in the stereo field; at [0:57–0:58] and at [1:06], one can hear brief moments where the final notes in phrases are held for slightly different lengths!

Even though this song is one of the weakest on *The Lamb*, it precedes one of the strongest songs in Genesis's catalogue. "The Lamia" is the mythological center of the album, the richest both in psychosexual imagery and harmonic complexity. In operatic terms (for, as Allan Moore [2001] has pointed out, *The Lamb* shares certain dramatic affinities with opera), "Here Comes The Supernatural Anaesthetist" may be regarded as a prelude of sorts to "The Lamia"—a recitative to the aria of "The Lamia."

"The Lamia"

"The Lamia," Peter Gabriel told Armando Gallo, "was a dream [from childhood] … . I used to dream of being in a pool of Ribena, and there were all these beautiful girls swimming all around me, nibbling at my buttocks … I think this was probably my first wet dream … . It was in colours and was sensual, all soft, warm colours" (Gallo, 1980, p. 151). Steve Hackett once wryly observed, "Everyone has skeletons in the cupboard. Peter's got more than most. Mine are schoolgirls, his are snakes, Adam and Eve and the destruction of the apple" (Bell, 1975, p. 14).

When *New Musical Express* journalist Max Bell offered an interpretation of "The Lamia" as "an obvious allusion to oral sex," Gabriel responded, "Actually, I'd been reading Jung at that period, so it was deliberate to a certain extent. I think the main thing I was striving for was the contrast between character and fantasy" (Bell, 1975, p. 14). Gabriel told Bell that in "The Lamia," Rael discovers his "hidden personality. He's not as butch as he hoped he would be. There's a masculine and feminine in everybody and that brings out his romantic side" (Bell, 1975, p. 14). As Gabriel has acknowledged the influence of Jung, it is not surprising that we find a similar assertion in Jung's writings:

> It is a well-known fact that sex is determined by a majority of male or female genes, as the case may be. But the minority of genes belonging to the other sex does not simply disappear. A man therefore has in him a feminine side, an unconscious feminine figure—a fact of which he is generally quite unaware. (Jung, 1969, p. 284)

There is, of course, much more to this song, which Couture describes as a blend of "fantastic themes (the sirens), ritualistic initiation, and erotic cannibalism" (Couture, n.d.). Much of its imagery is derived from John Keats's 1819 poem "Lamia," although what Gabriel has gleaned from Keats's poem seems to pertain more to descriptions of the Lamia and their setting rather than of Keats' narrative.[8] In Keats's account, the Lamia convinces Hermes to change her into a woman in order to seduce a young philosopher named Lycius, who had been able to tame all of the passions through philosophy except for love. He falls in love with her, and they hold a splendid banquet, at which among the guests is Apollonius, Lycius's mentor. Apollonius recognizes Lycius's betrothed to be no woman but a Lamia-serpent, and under his gaze she changes back to her original form and vanishes from his arms. Lycius then dies, presumably of grief. Gabriel retains none of this story (although Rael's flesh does become the "feast" for the Lamia); he does, however, describe the Lamia as "three vermillion snakes of female face," an image which is consistent with Keats's descriptions of "a Gordian shape of dazzling hue, / Vermillion-spotted, golden, green, and blue" (Part 1, lines 47–48) whose "head was serpent, but ah, bitter-sweet!" (Part 1, line 59). As for the home where the Lamia brings Lycius, "Sounds Aeolian / Breth'd from the hinges, as the ample span / Of the wide doors disclos'd a place unknown" (Part 1, lines 386–388), and at the location of the feast itself, "Of wealthy luster was the banquet-room" (Part 2, line 173), where "Soft went the music the soft air along" (Part 2, line 198). Such lines can be compared with Gabriel's lyric "muted melodies fill the echoing hall." Finally, as the Lamia in Keats's poem withers under the coldly rational glance of Apollonius, "The myrtle [an herb sacred to Venus, and thus a symbol of love] sicken'd in a thousand wreaths" (Part 2, line 264); and so, as the Lamia die after tasting of Rael's flesh, "a sickly sourness fills the room, / The bitter harvest of a dying bloom."

After the departure of the "Supernatural Anaesthetist," Rael notices a smell of perfume. He works his way out of the rubble and follows the scent to a chandelier-lit room with a pool in its center. In the pool are three small half-snake/half-woman creatures who welcome him. Entering the pool, he swallows some of the water and feels himself losing his life energy as the lamias nibble at and caress his body. Once the lamias make contact with his blood, however, they quickly perish; Rael, out of passion, eats their lifeless bodies. As he leaves the chamber, he looks back to see the scene is back to its initial appearance, awaiting a new visitor (Couture, n.d.).

The musical setting of the song is notable for its subtle support of Gabriel's lyric imagery. Delicate piano arpeggios trace a slowly descending chord sequence that seems to depict Rael's descent into the water (interestingly, descending harmonic progressions are also found in the verses of Genesis's other water-related epics, "Fountain of Salmacis" and "Ripples"). At the same time, each chord in the series has its third, not its root, in the bass, resulting in a lighter or airier feel (Figure 3.4a). The sudden downward leap in the uppermost voice from the fourth chord to the fifth seems almost like a larger step downward in Rael's descent to the pool. The phrase ends on the seventh chord in Figure 3.4a with an unresolved dissonance [0:11–0:15], which arouses an expectation of continuation in the

---

8   The full text of the Keats poem may be found in Abrams et al., 1987, pp. 1852–1869 and in McMahan, 1998, pp. 428–434.

listener. Within this sequence, however, is nestled a series of descending parallel tenths, the upper voice of the dyad alternating between upper and inner voices of the chords (Figure 3.4b). The prevailing descent in the verse is balanced with a surging ascending sequence in the refrain [1:46–1:53] (Figure 3.5).

Figure 3.4a   Descending harmonic progression, "The Lamia" [0:00–0:15]

Figure 3.4b   Descending parallel tenths, "The Lamia"

Figure 3.5   Ascending harmonic sequence, "The Lamia" [1:46–1:53]

Banks's keyboard orchestrations also considerably enhance the effect of the song. For example, as the lamia introduce themselves to Rael and welcome him to the pool's waters, a crescendo of Mellotron strings emerges from the texture [1:46–2:10]. The association of Mellotron strings with the water imagery is a further link with "Fountain of Salmacis." When the same musical passage returns at [4:28–4:54], after the lamia have perished, Rael's quasi-Eucharist is accompanied this time by Mellotron choir. Here, the disembodied voices are evocative of the lamias' departed spirits. A similar transformation of keyboard timbre occurs in the brief mysterious interludes that lead back to the verse; the first time at [2:11–2:42] features piano, but the second, at [4:54–5:25], replicates the piano arabesques on synthesizer (again, this timbre change occurs after the lamia have died). The last two chords of this interlude—a B♭ ninth chord and an G♭ ninth chord—are joined by symmetrical voice leading of the sort that we have already seen in the opening title track (Figure 3.6). The expansion in register as the two voices more outward chromatically gives the passage an "opening" quality leading back into the verse.

Figure 3.6   Final two chords of instrumental interlude, "The Lamia" [2:26–2:41]

The Lamia image is also connected to Lilith, as discussed earlier, and McMahan connects it to the later appearance of the Raven (in "The Colony of Slippermen") as well (McMahan, 1998, pp. 423–424).[9] After the *Lamb* tour, the song was not performed again, but it has had a lasting impact on Genesis fans because of its inventive staging. A tube of multi-colored fabric descended, maelstrom-like, over Gabriel, obscuring him from view. Given that fans had become accustomed to numerous costume changes in a Genesis show (for "Musical Box," "Watcher of the Skies," and "Dancing with the Moonlit Knight," to name a few), live *Lamb* performances were fairly minimalist in the costume-change department; Gabriel had been dressed in his Rael leather street clothes up to this point. Thus, this symbolic depiction of Rael's transformation had considerable dramatic power. It was one of two significant costume changes for Gabriel—the second, as the Slipperman, would have an even more powerful dramatic impact.

"Silent Sorrow in Empty Boats"

This instrumental, showcasing the Mellotron and a "six-note pedal-volume guitar motif" (Couture, n.d.), is a static interlude, closing Side 3 of the original double album. Its sole purpose was to provide an open-ended pause in the narrative, allowing Gabriel to exit the stage in darkness, leaving the empty Lamia costume behind, and change into his Slipperman costume. The unwieldy costume and difficulties in microphone placement inside the costume meant that the rest of the group had to "buy time" to allow the costume change. Because of its obvious function as a dramatic set-piece, the song was not performed again after the *Lamb* tour. Musically, the song bears some interesting similarities to the song "Aguirre" by the German group Popol Vuh, featured in the Werner Herzog film *Aguirre, der Zorn Gottes* (1972). "Aguirre" similarly features a pedal-volume guitar ostinato

---

[9]   For further detail concerning the changing characterizations of Lilith and her connection to the Lamia archetype, see Scerba, 1999. The Jungian symbols in *The Lamb* will be further explored in Chapter 5.

over slowly changing Mellotron-choir pads. It is uncertain whether Genesis was aware of the Herzog film; the song was not released on album until 1974, when a compilation of Popol Vuh's film music was released on the Ohr record label in Germany. It is quite possible that Gabriel, with his wide range of interests including art cinema (he was attracted to the work of Alejandro Jodorowsky, for example), had encountered the Herzog film. The Mellotron theme emphasizes the lower tetrachord of the E Lydian mode (E – F♯ - G♯ - A♯), lending a certain mysterious or exotic mood to the instrumental. This choice of mode also provides a subtle means of preserving continuity between the end of Side 3 and the beginning of Side Four, as the "Arrival" section of "The Colony of Slippermen" is in F♯ major, the organ ostinato again emphasizing F♯ - G♯ - A♯.

"The Colony of Slippermen"

"The Colony of Slippermen" is about "people's attitudes towards sex," Gabriel told Armando Gallo (1980, p. 155)—a theme that would recur through much of Gabriel's solo work ("Sledgehammer," "Steam," "Kiss That Frog"). Its structure is perhaps the most stereotypically "progressive" of the songs on *The Lamb*, being that of a multi-part suite with subtitles for individual sections ("The Arrival," "A Visit to the Doktor," "Raven"). As in "The Lamia," Gabriel derives at least a partial inspiration from English Romantic poetry; the opening stanza parodies William Wordsworth's 1804 poem "Daffodils":

> I wander'd lonely as a cloud
> That floats on high o'er vales and hills,
> When all at once I saw a crowd,
> A host, of golden daffodils;
> Beside the lake, beneath the trees,
> Fluttering and dancing in the breeze.[10]

After leaving the lamias' pool, Rael wanders "lonely as a cloud" until he finds a group of deformed creatures covered with oozing pustules. These are the slippermen, described by Gabriel as "grotesque and totally sensual beings whose entire day is spent gratifying every orifice including nose, mouth and ear" (Welch, 1975). He learns every member of the colony has lived the same experience with the lamias as he did and that he is now one of them. The setting is reminiscent of a leper colony; its individuals' ailments and circumstances of contagion imply the more modern-day scourge of venereal disease. Uwe Hoppe comments that "like the protagonist in Franz Kafka's famous tale 'Die Verwandlung' Rael and his fellow-sufferers have turned into (slimy) monsters. The irony, however, lies in the

---

[10]   The full text of the Wordsworth poem can be found in Abrams et al., 1987, p. 1426.

fact that Rael only realizes his own mutation when he is welcomed as a newcomer to the colony ('Me ? Like you? Like that!')" (Hoppe, 1998).

Among the group Rael recognizes his brother John, who tells him that the only way to cure his condition and escape the colony is to undergo castration, a service provided by Doktor Dyper. After the procedure, Doktor Dyper gives them their organs back in yellow plastic tubes, but a large raven snatches Rael's tube away from him. Rael asks for his brother's help, but John deserts him a second time (see "In the Cage"). Rael pursues the raven to a ravine, where he sees the bird drop the tube in the water. Rael helplessly watches the tube float away as the song fades.

Doktor Dyper is another potent symbol in the narrative. According to myth scholar Joseph Campbell, the doctor is "the modern master of the mythological realm, the knower of all the secret ways and words of potency. His role is precisely that of the Wise Old Man of the myths and fairy tales whose words assist the hero through the trials and terrors of the weird adventure" (Campbell, 1968, p. 9). The purpose of ritual actions such as castration was:

> to conduct people across those difficult thresholds of transformation that demand a change in the patterns not only of conscious but also of unconscious life. The so-called rites of passage … are distinguished by formal, and usually very severe, exercises of severance, whereby the mind is radically cut away from the attitudes, attachments, and life patterns of the stage being left behind. (Campbell, 1968, p. 10)

The ascetic aspects of castration call to mind Jesus" remarks about "casting away" parts of the body that cause one to sin (Mark 9:43–47), a scripture that was taken literally through the voluntary castration practiced by the Heaven's Gate cult, which came to public attention through a mass suicide in 1997. The German spelling of "Doctor" also evokes the cruel quackery of Nazi doctors such as Josef Mengele.

Like "Lilywhite Lilith," parts of "The Colony of Slippermen" came from the unreleased song "The Light." Couture calls the song "the most memorable moment of both the album and the live show," and this is no doubt because of the elaborate costume Gabriel used for the song. During the introduction Gabriel slowly emerged from a translucent reddish cocoon, an emergence clearly meant to symbolize birth. The Slipperman outfit, covering Gabriel head to toe in grotesque latex bumps, had two testicles made of balloons that could be inflated and deflated by a roadie. Unfortunately, the suit's oversized head didn't allow Gabriel's vocals to be heard clearly, because the microphone was too far from his mouth; Gabriel had to re-record the vocals on this song for the complete live version of *The Lamb* included on the *Genesis Archive 1967–75* box set.

"The Colony of Slippermen" was one of the few *Lamb* songs to outlive the tour, if only in truncated form. Along with "In the Cage," the keyboard solo from the "Raven" part of the song survived as part of a medley well into the 1980s.

"Ravine"

A duet of sorts for Banks's eerie synthesizer and Hackett's ultra-rapid chord tremolos, this is, like "Silent Sorrow in Empty Boats," a static instrumental interlude. Like that piece, it served a strictly utilitarian function in concert, allowing Gabriel sufficient time to change out of his Slipperman costume. Both this song and "Silent Sorrow" were added to the album late in the recording sessions when it became apparent that they would need interlude music to allow for the elaborate costume changes.

"The Light Dies Down on Broadway"

With this song, Genesis borrows a trick from The Beatles' *Sgt. Pepper* and arguably goes one step further. In the same way that *Sgt. Pepper* included a reprise of the opening title track toward its conclusion, this song is also a reprise—not only of the album's opening but part of "The Lamia" as well (thereby cementing that song's importance in the narrative). It occurs at the climax of the story, when Rael sees a way out of this nether world—a skylight-like passage, apparently built into the cliff of the ravine, leading back to his old life and surroundings on Broadway. The slower pace of the music, however, suggests that Rael's feelings about that former life are not so enthusiastic now—instead he seems reflective, pondering.

As noted in Chapter 2, the lyrics for this song were written not by Gabriel, but by Banks and Rutherford. The difference in tone is immediately apparent; nevertheless, if there had to be one song on the album with lyrics not by Gabriel this would perhaps be the ideal choice. Most of the lyrics are in the third-person voice of an omniscient narrator, in contrast to the largely first-person voice of the rest of the album.

The song's two musical antecedents—"The Lamb Lies Down on Broadway" and "The Lamia"—represent the two worlds of Rael's journey, respectively the mundane world of modern-day New York City and the subconscious world through which Rael has been traveling. Likewise, in the narrative, Rael is presented with a choice between one world and the other, for just as he starts to head for the portal back to Broadway he hears the voice of his brother John, struggling for life in the rapids. For a moment he hesitates—John has failed to come to his aid in the past, and the open portal at last represents escape from staying "forever in this forsaken place." He decides to save John, and as he does the gateway back to Broadway disappears. McMahan offers the following interpretation of Rael's decision:

> Had Rael decided to exit through the sky-light and return back to New York City, he would have simply reappeared right where and when he was when he started, and the whole thing would have begun again. By making this final correct spiritual decision to save his brother, in spite of the many times John had refused him aid, he allows himself

to leave this purgatory into the true afterlife. Seeing his own face from the outside may represent his spirit being reborn into another body. (McMahan, 1998, p. 440)

McMahan notes that the notion of purgatory is found in Anglican as well as Catholic theology; moreover, the concept of "being reborn into another body" ties this passage in with the Book of Revelation (1998, p. 440). It also, however, connects this moment with concepts of reincarnation found in the *Tibetan Book of the Dead*; this will be examined in more detail in Chapter 5.

"Riding the Scree"

Mark Spicer (2005) notes that the irregular metric division of this song—$\frac{9}{8}$ ("Brother John is number nine") divided into $2 + 2 + 2 + 3$—is identical to the meter of the "Apocalypse in 9/8" ostinato in "Supper's Ready" (p. 4). Like the "Apocalypse," "Riding the Scree" begins with an extended keyboard solo—in this case on an ARP Pro-Soloist synthesizer—before the entry of Gabriel's vocal at [2:10]. Banks even relies on similar musical devices in his keyboard solo here; for example, the way that he develops arpeggios in a kind of *fortspinnung* to impose a polymeter over the $\frac{9}{8}$ groove at [1:48–2:05] in "Riding the Scree" closely resembles the portion of his "Apocalypse" solo at [16:37–17:02]. Spicer describes "Riding the Scree" as driven by "a relentless pedal-point groove" in which Collins's drums "propel the groove forward" against Mike Rutherford's riff, creating an "ever-changing syncopated dialog"; Spicer wryly adds that "this is about as close to funk as any British progressive rock group would get" (2005, p. 5). In an ironic recognition, perhaps, of this song's lop-sided funkiness, the American duo 310, consisting of Joseph Dierker and Tim Donovan, sampled the groove for "The Voice of Britain," a track from their 1999 "plunderphonic" remix EP *Prague Rock*. The unlikely groove is layered with other Genesis samples, including one of Gabriel's concert introductions to "Dancing with the Moonlit Knight" ("I am the voice of Britain …") and a Mellotron chord from "Watcher of the Skies."

Before diving in, Rael mutters "Evel Knievel, you got nothing on me … Here I go!" This line almost certainly dates the lyrics to "Riding the Scree," at least, late in the recording sessions. Motorcycle daredevil Evel Knievel, one of the more colorful celebrities of the early 1970s, attempted to jump across the Snake River Canyon in a special rocket-propelled cycle on September 8, 1974. The jump was a highly publicized media event, and a spectacular failure. Seldom in Genesis's music (or in progressive rock in general, for that matter) does one find such a transparent reference to an "external" historical event. Its inclusion here is further evidence of Gabriel's desire to distance this project from previous Genesis albums, even if the result is further dated than it otherwise would be.

"In the Rapids"

This climactic moment in the rapids—when Rael rescues John and finds his own face, not John's, staring back at him—is another illustration of the "divided self" or "homo duplex" referred to in the discussion of "Anyway." Here, Rael is at last made conscious of his divided nature—and, in encountering himself face to face, at last achieves psychic reunification. The song ends with a dramatic upward swoop on synthesizer, leading directly into "*it*."

"*it*"

In the 1960s and early 1970s, organized religion went into something of a decline and was largely supplanted by individual, eclectic approaches to spirituality. Early in the twentieth century, however, a colleague of William James prefigured the spiritual outlook of the 1960s with his conception of an "Absolute Reality" behind all phenomena, recounted as follows:

> although I had ceased my childish prayers to God, and never prayed to *It* in a formal manner, yet my more recent experience shows me to have been in a relation to *It* which practically was the same thing as prayer. Whenever I had any trouble, especially when I had conflict with other people, either domestically or in the way of business, or when I was depressed in spirits or anxious about affairs, I now recognize that I used to fall back for support upon this curious relation I felt myself to be in to this fundamental cosmic *It*. (James, 1925, p. 64, emphasis in original)

Jung writes that when "the summit of life" is reached:

> "One becomes Two," and the greater figure, which one always was but which remained invisible, appears to the lesser personality with the force of a revelation ... . The long expected friend of his soul, the immortal one, has now really come ... to seize hold of him by whom this immortal had always been confined and held prisoner, and to make his life flow into that greater life. (Jung, 1969, p. 121)

Such a moment occurs when Rael brings John to the water's surface and sees his own face on John's body. This event recalls William James's discussion of the resolution of what he called the "divided self":

> ["Reunification"] may come gradually, or it may occur abruptly; it may come through altered feelings, or through altered powers of action; or it may come through new intellectual insights, or through experiences which we shall later have to designate as "mystical." However it come, it brings a characteristic sort of relief; and never such extreme relief as when it is cast into the religious mould. Happiness! happiness! religion is only one of the ways in which men gain that gift. Easily, permanently, and

successfully, it often transforms the most intolerable misery into the profoundest and most enduring happiness. (James, 1925, p. 175)

According to Joseph Campbell, the conclusion of the hero's "successful adventure" is characterized by "the unlocking and release again of the flow of life into the body of the world" (Campbell, 1968, p. 40). At the conclusion of "*it*," it is unclear what will happen to Rael beyond the obvious feeling of cosmic exultation. As Gabriel put it, "I don't think he's dead, just going through the cosmic juice"; Gabriel described the song as "an attempt to force substance from negatives" (Bell, 1975, p. 14):

> You know how they approach drama in good suspense movies. You never see what's so terrifying because they leave it up in the air without moulding or labeling [*sic*] it. (Bell, 1975, p. 14)

If, however, *The Lamb* is, in Gabriel's words, "really a series of events that could happen to somebody who doesn't even know his subconscious exists" (Welch, 1975), then it can be surmised that "*it*" is that moment when Rael at last acknowledges and unites with his subconscious self, for even his brother "turns out to be another illusion" (ibid.). It is that Lennonesque moment when "you are me and we are all together."

One intriguing musical link can be made with Genesis's earlier "Watcher of the Skies," the introduction of which opens with the same two-chord vamp. "Watcher" was sometimes an encore choice during the *Lamb* tour; in the first tour after Gabriel's departure, Genesis would occasionally close concerts with a medley, "*it*" segueing seamlessly into an abbreviated version of "Watcher of the Skies." It is thus possible to interpret the chord sequence in "*it*" as a musical symbol of the extraterrestrial intelligence portrayed in the earlier song, even if the musical connection, pointed out in the medley, was most likely an afterthought.

The closing line, "It's only knock and knowall, but I like it," is a punning reference to the Rolling Stones' 1974 hit "It's Only Rock and Roll." Gabriel told Max Bell that the line was "partly aimed at the Press and ... partly a throwaway in story terms ... . While it's fun to be pompous and sermonise it's still an illusion, a grand illusion. If you can retain your sense of humour and be cynical, it's better. I go right inside my lyrics and laugh at them at the same time" (Bell, 1975, p. 14).

There has been much speculation and interpretation of the allegory and subconscious symbols in *The Lamb*, and fans continue to provide their own exegeses. This chapter presents only a gloss of the prevalent interpretations. Like the Book of Revelation or the *Tibetan Book of the Dead*, which will be discussed in Chapter 5, there are so many layers of meaning that it would be impossible to completely "get" everything. Gabriel himself has been notoriously elusive about some of the specific details. Perhaps in the end it is therefore best to consider the closing words from the *Tibetan Book of the Dead*:

Those who meet with this [doctrine] are indeed fortunate. Save for them who have accumulated much merit and absolved many obscurations, difficult it is to meet with it. Even when met with, difficult it is to comprehend it. Liberation will be won simply through not disbelieving it upon hearing it. (Evans-Wentz, 1960, p. 152)

In Chapter 5, we will revisit the topic of interpreting *The Lamb*; first, however, we need to examine how the album was presented to live audiences, and the reception to the album and tour from both critics and fans. It is to the tour, then, that we turn in the next chapter.

Chapter 4

"The Lamb seems right out of place": In the press and on tour

[Rock band] Status Quo are just as cultural as Wagner's Ring Cycle. As to the pleasure people derive from the two I don't know, but in terms of entertainment they are the same.

—Peter Gabriel[1]

The Lamb Lies Down on Broadway was released in the UK on November 18, 1974 and reached number 10 in the UK charts the following month, a few spots lower than *Selling England By The Pound*'s peak position. In America the album only reached number 41 in the charts, but still this was their highest charting entry yet in the US (Platts, 2001, p. 79). The first leg of the world tour to promote the album—three weeks of British dates—had to be cancelled when Steve Hackett severed a tendon and a nerve in his thumb by crushing a wine glass in his hand at a reception following an Alex Harvey concert, a mishap attributed to "an involuntary surge of adrenalin due to stress" (Bright, 1988, p. 62). The delay turned out to be fortuitously timed; canceling the first three weeks bought the band extra time to rehearse. As Hackett had already completed all his overdubs, the release of the album itself was not affected (Bright, 1988, p. 62).

The Lamb received decidedly mixed reviews. While critics such as Barbara Charone wrote in the November 23, 1974 issue of *Sounds* that the *Lamb* "sticks out of the present vinyl rubble like a polished diamond" (Bowler and Dray, 1993, p. 94), other critics asserted that Genesis had simply overreached this time. Chris Welch, normally an enthusiast of the band, wrote in *Melody Maker* that the band needed to "take heed of the adage that 'small is beautiful'"; amid this "vast amount of music to wade through" there were only a few songs "worthy of such interminable development" (1974).

As much as the album remains beloved by fans and is an acknowledged touchstone of the progressive rock genre, Welch's opinion is the one that has persisted among critics, even among those inclined to appreciate progressive rock. Paul Stump, for example, asserts that much of the album consisted of "ramshackle and discrete songs constructed unpretentiously but originally around hastily arranged melodic fragments … to tell, or (to put it more succinctly and accurately) *intimate* a story" (Stump, 1997, p. 179). Even aficionados of the album concede

---

[1]   Quoted in Bell, 1975, p. 14.

that the album's obscure story line hinders full appreciation of the group's efforts; for example, Genesis biographers Bowler and Dray write that "any weakness that the album showed was in its storyline. Peter's tale of Rael had to fail simply because of the immense wealth of detail that he tried to get across" (Bowler and Dray, 1993, p. 95). Tony Banks, discussing the idea of turning the album into a film (to which we will return in Chapter 6), "pointed out that there was enough going on in the story to make ten films: 'There was too much information—some of the lyrics were too cumbersome'" (Bowler and Dray, 1993, p. 95).[2] Mike Rutherford concurred, somewhat more diplomatically, with Banks's opinion; *The Lamb* was "a perfect example of conflict between the music and the lyrics. Pete's lyrics and melody are great, brilliant, and the music is brilliant, but put the two together, disaster! The backing track by itself sounded so strong; there was a clash really" (Gallo, 1980, p. 56). Perhaps in recognition of the dense wordplay and obscurity of his finished narrative, Gabriel saw to it that his story was also included in the inner gatefold sleeve of the album, "because it was too encompassing for all the songs to contain the action"; the story became "a clothesline on which you can hang up the songs" (Bowler and Dray, 1993, pp. 95–96). For hardcore fans, however, the obscurity of the story and accompanying songs is part of its enduring appeal; its arcane symbolism imparts a gnostic quality to the package, entirely in keeping with Paul Willis's observations of the cultural values of the hippie culture and the progressive rock aesthetic that sprang from it. As Andy Bennett (2004) has shown in his study of the "virtual scene" centered on the Canterbury subgenre of progressive rock, the Internet has dramatically facilitated bringing together disparate progressive rock taste publics around the world. In the case of the ongoing discussion concerning *The Lamb*, Scott McMahan, Jason Finegan and the editors and contributors of the Genesis online fanzine *Paperlate* went so far as to compile an "Annotated *Lamb Lies Down on Broadway*" (Finegan, McMahan et al., 1994; see also McMahan 1998). This document is essentially a line-by-line parallel exegesis combining the lyrics, the corresponding passages in Gabriel's inner-sleeve story, and interpretations by various fans, many of whom appear to be as well educated and eclectic as Gabriel (certainly, catching the obscure references to Jung, Keats and Babylonian mythology, among other things, refutes the conventional stereotype of rock fans being uneducated!). Other writers, of course, have in turn offered their own interpretations on various fan sites across the Web. *The Lamb Lies Down on Broadway*, in fact, has joined a select pantheon of rock recordings—from the Beatles' *Sgt. Pepper's Lonely Hearts Club Band* to Radiohead's *OK Computer*—that have been analyzed, line by line, in often excruciating detail. (This book, of course, serves as further evidence of that status.)

---

[2]   This was not the first time that Banks had harbored issues with the density of Gabriel's lyrics. Earlier, discussing "The Battle of Epping Forest" with Armando Gallo, he said that the vocals "completely ruin the song because there's too much happening—a complete battle between the vocals and the music all the way through" (Gallo, 1980, p. 56).

Gabriel's story, then, clearly seemed to be too obscure for mass consumption. At the precise point in the band's career when success in the US at least seemed within its grasp, Gabriel's bizarre story seemed to militate against such mass appeal. Certainly Tony Banks, in several interviews, has not seemed completely supportive of Gabriel's lyric-writing style:

> one criticism I do have is that the lyrics have a kind of sameness to them, they are all of one kind, because Pete tends to do a certain things [*sic*] with words ... he is always playing with them, playing with the actual construction. While Mike and I tend to be more specifically into the language, and the meaning of the words. It is just a different sort of approach, and you get a different quality. Also, I tend to write lyrics much faster than Peter does, which gives a different kind of flow to them, and I just felt that it was a shame on that album because there were some ideas I really could have got inside. (Gallo, 1980, p. 68)

As noted in Chapter 3, Mike and Tony did, in the end, contribute lyrics—for "The Light Dies Down on Broadway." Bowler and Dray observe that their lyrics for that one song are "more linear," giving the song "a more approachable, understandable slant which could have greatly benefited the album" (1993, p. 95). Additional input from the rest of the band could have given the album more variety, making it less obtuse in the process; it also, perhaps, could have saved the "vintage" Gabriel-era lineup.

As songwriting royalties are counted as distinctively different from "mechanical" recording royalties, there is an obvious economic incentive to having one's songs heartily represented on a group's recording; this issue had led to the breakup of bands in the past. (In the latter years of the Beatles, for example, George Harrison came to resent his lack of representation on Beatles records—most of his first solo album *All Things Must Pass* was made up of songs the Beatles had passed up.) Genesis had solved this problem by giving all songs group compositional credit, musically as well as lyrically. Prior to *The Lamb*, lyrics were often group efforts, or at least contributions from various band members (usually Gabriel, Banks, and Rutherford) were given equal consideration. This communal approach to song writing helped to mitigate the attention lavished on Gabriel as the group's flamboyant front man, at least from *Foxtrot* onward (when Gabriel began adding costumes, unusual make-up and hair, and elaborate stories to the group's performances). With *The Lamb*, however, not only had Gabriel insisted on writing all of the lyrics himself, but he had also copyrighted the inner-sleeve story in his name alone. Lacking equality in lyrical contributions to *The Lamb*, Gabriel's band mates became increasingly resentful of the inordinate attention lavished on Gabriel as the group's front man during the *Lamb* tour. In interviews, Gabriel appeared to be designated as the sole member capable of commenting on the story, the other band members often relegated to responding to questions about what it was like "playing behind" Gabriel's story. Some of their responses are telling; Steve Hackett told Max Bell that "it's true—we choose to make ourselves anonymous" on stage. "But it annoys me when people think Peter did everything right down to writing all the songs and designing the stage." On *The Lamb*, Hackett said, Gabriel "wrote less of the music than us" (Bell, 1975, p. 14). On the other hand, it should be pointed out that Gabriel feels he was never properly credited for his contributions to the music (Bright, 1988, p. 61).

The tour in support of *The Lamb* consisted of 102 shows in the US, Canada and Europe (Gallo, 1980, p. 68); 41 of these shows were in the US, compared with 14 shows in their native UK. The UK was saved for nearly five months into the tour, after the road show had been thoroughly tested (Welch, 1975).

Analysis of the tour itinerary—provided in the appendix to this volume—reveals some interesting patterns of market demographics as well as the still-occasionally-haphazard aspects of tour management in the early 1970s. Macan (2006, p. 770) points out that the US accounted for some 50 per cent of world album sales during progressive rock's heyday; accordingly, US shows account for about 40 per cent of the tour locations. The cities on the American itinerary, moreover, reflect the prevailing regional market patterns for progressive rock; Macan (1997, p. 154) observes that the genre's strongest markets were in the Midwest, Northeast and Mid-Atlantic regions, and to a lesser extent the West coast. Cities in these regions, not surprisingly, formed the bulk of the US tour, which began at the Auditorium Theatre in Chicago on November 20, 1974. Of the 41 US shows, 15 shows (approximately 37 per cent) were in the Midwest; aside from this concentration, the remaining shows were fairly evenly distributed by region, with eight shows (approximately 20 per cent) in the Mid-Atlantic region and six shows (15 per cent) each in the Northeast, South, and West. The tour included two shows in Canada, one each in Montreal and Toronto; a planned performance in Vancouver was cancelled.

Closer study of the tour itinerary reveals some unusual detours. For example, the group performed at the Indiana Convention Center in Indianapolis on November 22, only to return to Indianapolis to play at the Market Square Arena on December 14, just three weeks later. In light of progressive rock's early roots in the university and college circuit, it is telling that throughout the entire US *Lamb* tour there were only two performances in university venues. The European leg of the tour shows some changes of priorities as well. For example, while there were 14 shows in the UK, there were 17 in Germany and 12 in France. It is unclear whether Germany and France had substantial contingents of Genesis fans at the time, especially compared to the group's homeland, or whether these represented new markets on which the band was concentrating its efforts. A more baffling and unfortunate statistic concerns the Italian portion of the itinerary. Even though the Italian audience was pivotal in establishing Genesis's live reputation in 1970–71 while they were a struggling outfit—a fact repeatedly acknowledged by biographers of the group as well as the band members themselves—Italy was graced with only one appearance during the *Lamb* tour, a Turin show on March 24 that was fortunately preserved for posterity on the bootleg *The Real Last Time* (Stonehenge STCD 2004/2005).

In spite of Banks's recollections that a number of shows on the tour were cancelled, there were only four cancellations—Dallas and Berkeley in the US, Vancouver in Canada, and Toulouse in France. Some of these can be readily explained, even as they also highlight some of the haphazard conditions of tour planning. The Vancouver show was apparently double-booked with a show in Kansas City, or perhaps the Kansas City appearance was arranged to replace the Vancouver cancellation. If the latter reason is correct, then the Vancouver show would have been an inconvenient and ill-advised detour between shows in San Diego, California and Grand Rapids, Michigan. The January 26 Berkeley show was probably cancelled because of a lack of ticket sales, perhaps not surprising as there had been a Berkeley performance (in the same venue) just four days before. Some sources indicate a final show in Toulouse, France had also been cancelled because of a lack of ticket sales; Banks remembers there was such a cancellation (Russell, 2004, p. 208).

When the tour began in Chicago, Hackett's hand had still not fully healed from its tendon injury; he later recalled, "I went to a hospital and had electric shock treatment on my hand, to set it working. I swear the guy who was giving me the so-called physical therapy was a sado-masochist, who was turning the juice up much too high and getting off on it" (Platts, 2001, p. 78). It was a rather inauspicious beginning. The album was not released in America until several dates into the tour, which meant that, for the first few shows at least, fans were presented with virtually an entire show of songs they had never heard before (Platts, 2001, p. 77). "You had an audience who were coming along to listen to old favorites," Hackett recalled about the Chicago show, "who were not exactly thrilled to see this English band playing a concept album based on the idea of a New Yorker who hails from Puerto Rico. It was one of those days when life throws everything at you" (Platts, 2001, p. 79).

Recognizing that the American audience would likely need a "refresher" introduction to the band and its history as well as to the new conceptual theatre piece they were about to witness, Genesis's management saw to it that the *Lamb* tour program booklet contained extensive notes:

> Back in the late 60's progressive music seemed all but dead, barely kept alive by the faint spark of a lingering mellotron. Rock audiences had overdosed on loud psychedelic riffs and gentle acoustic flower-power tunes, wondering all the time if there was anything more to progressive music than strobe lights, incense and the odd synthesizer. Just when adventurous rock seemed forever moving backwards, Genesis began flirting with multi-media concepts … .
>
> From their earliest concerts and records, the group stubbornly insisted on doing everything their own way, an individuality that today separates them from other "progressive" groups. Genesis were the naive rockers who brought tea and toast to sleazy backstage concerts as Gabriel began miming to some of the more story-book lyrics in a last ditch attempt to reach the audience. Record companies demanded traditional single releases that they refused to create. Genesis headlined before they reached headlining status as a problem quickly evolved, what kind of band could they possibly open for?

The same problem was to plague them during their first few American visits, where a relatively unknown group found themselves in the unique position of headlining concerts. Whether there were 400 or 4000 people in the audience, Genesis worked hard, hypnotically pulling the listener into their own formless world. As the lyrics began to take on a more animated form, as the music became a soundtrack for a film that was happening onstage, a clear direction evolved for the group, merging theatrical stage visuals with the music. 70's rock was at last moving forward. After *Trespass*, drummer John Mayhew and guitarist/songwriter Anthony Phillips left the group.

Phil Collins arrived at a time when Genesis badly needed a healthy injection of fresh blood and revitalized energy. His musical adeptness and percussive proficiency on drums made it that much easier for Genesis to create the time changes so integral to their world. Enter also Steve Hackett, a guitarist capable of colouring various passages and textures instead of only being able to play the archetypal guitar solo. With Rutherford on bass and acoustic guitars, Banks on keyboards, mellotrons and synthesizers and Gabriel onstage an occasional flute, Genesis had gone through a necessary transformation, emerging unscarred as one of the few 70's bands moving towards tomorrow instead of being merely content to recall what was once yesterday. From this transitional 1971 period, Genesis began moving closer to bridging the gap between theatre and music both onstage and record. Yet the band's visual attempts at clearing up lyrical discrepancies created some dire misconceptions which followed the group like the plague, and begged for clarification ... . And it came to pass that people wrongly assumed that Genesis bore a strong resemblance to bands like Yes, ELP musically and people like Alice Cooper and David Bowie visually. Musically all that bound those groups together was the keyboard based instruments used to colour different sounds. Time changes, chord structures, song construction, vocals and lyrics differ between them so much so that no obvious similarities exist. Visually Genesis share no bonds with other popular rock posers of our time.

Unlike his contemporaries, Gabriel's stage movements bear a direct one to one relationship to the lyrics. From the start Genesis have operated on the basic principle that the visuals, while often entertaining are merely a vehicle to make the songs themselves more easily understood and accessible. To this day the band insist that they are primarily songwriters who play at being musicians and then only later play at being presenters. The songs are most important, the visuals only an aid in emphasizing the songs themselves ... . "We're closer to cartoons than the conventional rock band", Gabriel once said. "As far as other bands go, I think we're in a little puddle all by ourselves". Genesis are working towards something closer to the Red Buddha Theatre than the rock bands they are so often compared with ... . Both lyrics and music began to take on unique qualities; the stories were slightly vague and subtly weird while the music added to the uneasy eeriness of the tune. The group was progressing both as songwriters and musicians.

Not content to remain stationary, the *Foxtrot* album made fanatics out of fans and friends out of disbelievers ... . The band's following quickly spread to the Continent and across the Atlantic where Americans were particularly fascinated with their peculiar English surrealism. A transitional period followed, allowing the group to catch their breath and further develop the technical side of production and musical adeptness. Albums were months in the making, as they were a product of not one mind but five, and group equality was always stressed. *Selling England By The Pound* confirmed suspicions that Genesis were becoming a self-contained unit, capable of creating and sustaining musical imagery both visually onstage and lyrically on record with the musical accompaniment integrated into the proceedings so that the whole equalled a solid, animated fantasy … . With the release of the album and the subsequent stage show that followed, lighting and sound systems took a giant leap forward and one excitedly wondered what futuristic delights lay ahead … .

Which brings us presently up to autumn 1974 and a new Genesis stage show based around their new double album "Lamb lies down on Broadway". Not a terribly wealthy band, Genesis continually feed profits back into the stage show. To convey the complex story line of the new album, visual aids will be used on three backdrop screens, hinting at three dimensional illusions, slowed down slides will also add to an animated feel. As always, these new technical improvements will serve as painted landscapes adding to the fantasy and clarifying the story line. While the emphasis remains on the music and players the show will be theatrical and exciting, the music and imagery will not be separate, but whole, working together to pull the listener into the Genesis fantasy and out of everyday street realities. What Genesis are working towards is the future and their present flirtation with multi-media concepts is only the beginning of a whole new world. Welcome. (McMahan, 1998, pp. 396–399)

The uncredited notes are interesting for their aggressively modernist tone, seeking to distance Genesis from their progressive- and glam-rock contemporaries both musically and theatrically. Concert program notes often hyperbolically trumpet the accomplishments of their subject; even so, it is intriguing to read how "progressive" music "seemed all but dead" by the end of the 60s, when King Crimson's *In the Court of the Crimson King*—widely regarded as the first true "progressive rock" album and a key influence on the emerging Genesis—was released in 1969. Similarly, the phrase "70's rock was *at last* moving forward" seems premature given the vantage point in the decade, and in Genesis's history (1971!). It is as if Genesis was responsible not only for "saving" progressive rock from its end-of-the-60s demise (over before it had even begun, as it were), but for rescuing 70s music in general. At the same time, the program notes also reveal how the group, and sympathetic journalists, proactively defended the value of their theatrical enterprise. Gabriel's remark that a Status Quo show was "just as cultural" as a Wagner opera, in this chapter's epigraph, is one instance of this; Max Bell similarly declared to his readers that Genesis's variety of rock theater was "mostly as legit as any other breed of rock being toted for the public's edification" (Bell, 1975, p. 14). A feature on the tour for the American rock magazine *Circus* in March 1975 offered further insights on Gabriel's theatrical goals for the production:

I like to keep visuals in mind at the same time as lyrics and music. In the near future, I expect to see groups and artists work more closely together. I think the time is nearly ripe for the first visual artist to become a pop star. There will be situations in which the band itself becomes much less important, and there will be less of an ego thing. If one can build the visual image stronger, one can make the fantasy situation more real and involve an audience more deeply. (Ross, 1975, p. 68)

Because the storyline and the music for *The Lamb*, as new as it was (and, early in the tour, as-yet-unreleased), were likely to be completely unfamiliar for the American audiences, Gabriel, of course, had to introduce the performance with one of his stories to set the *mise-en-scène*. Early in the tour, the introductions were brief, as this transcript from the third performance of the tour, at the Indiana Convention Center in Indianapolis on November 22, 1974, shows:

> The thing is a story concerning a guy off the streets of New York by the name of Rael. A large wall is lowered into Times Square and sinks across 47th Street until it eventually wipes off the entire Manhattan Island, the wall hits our hero and knocks him unconscious. He regains consciousness in a cocoon-like situation, which in turn becomes a rock-like cave which causes a claustrophobic fear.
>
> He removes himself from this at the sight of his brother John, and is taken into a place called The Grand Parade of Lifeless Packaging which is an inanimate building filled with motionless bodies.
>
> We have divided it up roughly as we have on the record, which is four sides and this is the first section of the story of Rael, thank you. (Russell, 2004, p. 102)

As the tour continued and Gabriel became more self-assured, the introductions became more elaborate, as this story introducing the second section, taken from the February 4, 1975 show at the Arie Crown Theatre in Chicago, indicates:

> And at this point our hero is moving into an almost perfect reconstruction of the streets of New York, and he begins to recollect his childhood adventures particularly his romantic adventures. He purchased a discount book entitled "Erogenous Zones and Overcoming the Difficulties in Finding Them" [*applause*]. I understand there are a few fanatics of the book in here tonight.
>
> He spent many months studying this miraculous piece of literary accomplishment, until he mastered his sexual motions by numbers. The day of judgment arrived, and complete performance from initial arousal to completion, he came to the end, was a mere 78 seconds. This miraculous feat of masculine achievement failed to even remotely titillate his opposite partner.
>
> He was left cuddling a rather large prickly porcupine, which he took onto a soft carpeted corridor with thousands of other people, small people, little people crawling obsessively towards a large wooden door, which in turn led them up a spiral staircase into a chamber with 32 other doors, only one of which was capable of getting any of them out. (Russell, 2004, p. 103)

The last and most elaborate story below comes from the April 27, 1975 performance at the Manchester Palace Theatre in the UK. Note the change of person in the narrative, as Gabriel is now recounting the events of the narrative *as* Rael:

> This chamber with hundreds of doors and a woman who was as pink and pale as all the little beetles and creatures that I had seen crawling around the floor of the caves, approached me and she said, "Can you help me?" How could I resist a proposition

like that? So we held sweaty hands and she led me through one of the doors down a passageway that I hadn't seen before, into a series of tunnels entering a large dark cave, and she left me on a cold wet stone throne.

This wasn't comfortable and being on my own I began to hear funny things and there was this strange noise on my left, a whirring sound and these two golden globes hovered in filling the cave with this amazingly bright, white, light. [*high-pitched matronly voice*] "I was amazed at the whiteness," Mrs. J.H. of Bournemouth. [*laughter and applause*] "It was the whitest I've ever seen," Mrs. P.W. of Bognor Regis. [*applause*]

I know this is getting boring but I too was astonished at the whiteness so I picked up this little pebble, hurtled it at the centre of it and smashed it, I hit it right in the middle in fact, and the whole ceiling collapsed on my head. This was a little painful, I escaped like all good heroes and went into the small rescue area, where the delightful shattering, shimmering, spectre, [*game-show announcer voice*] your friend and mine better known to all of us here tonight as Death that's D-E-A-T-H! [*applause*]

Mmm this lovely man is wearing one of his delightful costumes he designed so painfully himself, this particular number is his snuff puff outfit, one little puff and you snuff it, mm love it, get it. I escaped again, like all good heroes, only to be sensually and erotically assaulted by three half-woman, half-snake creatures with very long tongues beginning to coil on my body, licking the strange blue liquid that was emanating from my pores. This had the effect of giving these creatures indigestion.

All of a sudden I heard a huge roar to my right [*gestures for cheers from a section of the crowd*], thank you. Shall we try it again? A roar! [*louder cheers*] A huge express rain hurtled in carrying a packet of R-E-N-N-I-E-S[3] but alas it was too late as they had shriveled up and died. I ate all that was left of their horrible bodies, lovely bodies and this turned me, changed me, into a ugly, lumpy, humpy—wait for it—bumpy species of humanity not totally dissimilar to Mr. Philip Collins on my left [*more applause, cheers*].

The only way of getting rid of all these horrible lumps and bumps was the severing of the sexual organs [*cheers*]. Rael—that's me—and John's organs were placed in a fully sterilized yellow plastic tubes [*sic*], by Doktor Dyper notorious sniper, who for a very small fee is guaranteed to cut off very neatly our very own windscreen wipers. The tubes, the yellow plastic tubes. But all of a sudden a huge black bird called Raven zoomed out of the air—zoom zoom zoom—grabbed the yellow plastic tube with my deceased sexual organ in it and flew off. [*very high voice*] "Christ," I said. [*applause, cheers*] So I hurtled off in hot pursuit, and just as I was about to catch the tail of this Raven, it dropped it in a huge area of gushing water with R-A-V-I-N-E in blue watery letters. "A ravine," I thought.

I watched the yellow tube disappearing, bobbing away, bob bob bob, and I saw my drowning brother John also in the water. Oh dear. (Russell, 2004, pp. 103–104)

The full-length presentation of *The Lamb*, then, made up the entire show. Afterward, there was a rotating pool of three other songs used for encores: "The Musical Box," "Watcher of the Skies," and—toward the end of the European leg of the tour—"The Knife" (Russell, 2004, pp. 105–180). (It is interesting that the

---

3   "Rennies" are a British brand of antacid, similar to the American "Tums."

The dramatic effect was immediate, beginning with the shock of Gabriel's "new look." As Banks began his intro to "The Lamb Lies Down on Broadway" and slides of early morning Manhattan were projected onto the screen behind the stage, "Gabriel soon appeared, almost unrecognizable at first, in his Rael gear: short hair, make-up, leather jacket and jeans" (Platts, 2001, p. 79). Gabriel noted that the leather jacket "has given us a more raunchy appearance, and we can sense a change in the audiences" (Welch, 1975). It was indeed "a far cry from his Britannia and Narcissus guises, just as the music contrasted sharply with Genesis' earlier work" (Platts, 2001, p. 79). Gabriel's skin was even darkened to resemble a Puerto Rican punk (Bowler and Dray, 1993, p. 100). Further clues to the visual impact of the show can be found in a profile of the group that appeared in the American rock magazine *Circus* in March 1975:

> While Genesis play through their most extended built-in jam ever on "Fly On A Windscreen [*sic*]," Shaw's slides super-realistically smash a greatly magnified and grotesque insect against a stolid fifties Ford. The plot, the music, and the visuals become even more disturbingly surreal once Rael is sucked body and soul into Genesis' harrowing halfworld. As the band plays "The Hairless Heart" Shaw's slides show a snowy white feathered heart nestled in crimson satin drapery. A rubber-gloved hand begins to shave the heart with cruel precision; the combined impact of the music and the visuals makes for one of the show's strongest emotional moments. (Ross, 1975, p. 70)

During "The Lamia," Gabriel would become "engulfed by a cone which revolved around him" (Bowler and Dray, 1993, p. 101); the cone represented the *tourbillon*, "the wheel that catapaults beings into the mystical world" (Bright, 1988, p. 62). Upon entering the colony of Slippermen, Gabriel emerged wearing a "grotesque yellow body stocking, covered, in Peter's words, with 'lumps and bumps and slimy humps' coupled with one vital extra for all aspiring rock stars, inflatable genitalia" (Bowler and Dray, 1993, p. 101). Although Bowler and Dray call this outfit "probably the most extraordinary costume of his entire tenure as lead singer" (1993, p. 101), the design presented difficulties with Gabriel's vocals, muffling them and making them more difficult to hear. As Tony Banks later reflected, "That's when we thought that the balance had gone the other way. I mean we were all involved with the slides and that was great fun, although the technology at that time was very limited so we couldn't always realize what we wanted to do" (Russell, 2004, p. 208).

One final dramatic effect was saved for "In the Rapids," at the climactic moment when Rael recognizes himself as two selves. A life-size dummy of Gabriel's Rael character was made, revealed under a spotlight at the end of the song, so that for a moment two Raels appeared on stage facing each other. Gabriel even underwent the experience of having a life mask made for the dummy to provide even more realism to the mannequin, telling Chris Welch:

I had pipes up my nostrils to breathe and was totally encased in plaster. A lot of people hallucinate in that state … . It feels like you are trapped, and I had a strong urge to breathe through my mouth. Very claustrophobic. The plaster gets very hot, and as it changes from liquid to solid, that adds to the delight.

Now I have to take the dummy with me to the hairdressers to match up my hair to the dummy's. It caused a few scenes in San Francisco when I took the top of the torso into an elevator. A lady screamed in fear when she saw the legs were missing. (Welch, 1975)

The dummy was the object of occasional mischief on the road. On one gig roadies stuck a banana out of the zipper in the dummy's pants, and on the last show of the tour the dummy was replaced by a naked roadie (Bright, 1988, p. 62). The lighting cues for the final song, "*it*," reveal the need for precise timing. The dummy had to be taken off stage while Gabriel had to "make a blind jump in the darkness from the rostrum to get back to the centre of the set before the lights go up" (Welch, 1975). As Gabriel told Chris Welch: "If the spotlight goes on too soon, then the audience sees me sprawling on the floor" (Welch, 1975).

Gabriel was justifiably proud of how his story translated to live performance. "We've been really lucky to be able to put on the album as a show, in its entirety," he said, perhaps recalling Yes's earlier unsuccessful attempt to keep their audiences' full attention during their complete renditions of *Tales From Topographic Oceans*, "because it makes huge demands on audiences with so much entirely new material" (Welch, 1975). His band mates, however, apparently did not share his enthusiasm. Phil Collins said that playing the entire album was "pretty grueling, especially in America, because the album wasn't out there when we started touring. We played two hours of completely new music and a couple of tunes which they knew at the end but by then it was too late" (Fielder, 1984, p. 93). Mike Rutherford had an even more direct opinion: "It was a big mistake. We tired of 'The Lamb' tour much earlier than the others because we were tied down to playing the whole album—we were stuck with some sections that weren't great live, just because they were part of the story" (Fielder, 1984, p. 93). He said in another interview that playing entire album night after night was "a bit of an effort" (Russell, 2004, p. 207).

Perhaps the most persistently negative remarks about *The Lamb* tour have come from Tony Banks, who called it "the least enjoyable of all the shows we've ever had to play. It was a very rigid show. You couldn't change the set … . The first half of the show was better which meant you had the weaker half to finish with" (Fielder, 1984, p. 94). Even the group's road manager, Nick Blythe, told *Melody Maker*'s Brian Harrigan, "all the roadies are bored with it! I mix the monitors when they're playing and if they threw in a new song tonight it'd probably be about half an hour before I woke up enough to notice it" (Harrigan, 1975). Because of the fixed set list from show to show, Banks, Rutherford, and Collins looked forward each night to the total improvisation on "The Waiting Room," the only time the group was freed from strict constraints on their playing. For them, it was the highlight of the show. Banks told *Melody Maker*, "some nights it's great, some nights it's awful, which is nice, really, because it means there's a challenge to it" (Platts, 2001, p. 77).

In fact, a comparative analysis of different performances of "The Waiting Room" shows how the group adjusted to the challenges of live group improvisation, keeping ideas that worked and reusing them in future performances. Unlike a King Crimson improvisation of 1972–74, which was often spontaneously creating improvisations *ex nihilo*, a performance of "The Waiting Room" relied on certain gestures and cues as "landmarks" in the group composition. Comparing performances[4] reveals a consistency of order in which new gestures were introduced, often with a time variance of as little as five to ten seconds between performances recorded weeks apart from one another. A performance of "The Waiting Room" would usually begin with high-frequency sounds—bell tree, wind chimes, high-pitched synthesizer sequences—against which Hackett would play a series of descending gestures using a whole-tone scale,[5] fading in each note quickly with his volume pedal to enhance the amorphous effect. He would usually conclude this series of guitar patterns with a few augmented triads,[6] also faded in. Around 30 to 40 seconds into the improvisation, Banks would initiate his series of "cat" sounds on synthesizer that are heard so prominently on the studio version, the first usually somewhere within the octave above middle C and each subsequent "meow" at a lower pitch. Often Rutherford would continue these gestures with faded-in and bent fuzz bass notes. Next, at around 38–55 seconds into the performance, Hackett would begin a series of fast, angular bursts of notes from his guitar, often answered by similarly fast percussive outbursts from Collins; Banks often entered atop these bursts of sound with wobbly Mellotron chords, the pitch manipulated with the tuning knob. Beginning at around [1:10–1:20] into the improvisation Banks would suddenly break into what I call the "tonal moment," a baldly conventional chord sequence of I – ii[6] – V – I (the keys varying from night to night) on Mellotron (usually in the choir setting). The last chord in the

---

[4]   Recordings used for this comparative analysis—all bootlegs—were from performances in: Providence, Rhode Island, December 8, 1974 (Hogweed Project 14); West Palm Beach, Florida, January 10, 1975 (*The Lamb Descends on Waterbury*); Los Angeles, California, January 24, 1975 (BURP 019); Turin, Italy, March 24, 1975 (*The Real Last Time*); London, April 15, 1975 (*Lamb Stew*); Manchester, UK, April 27, 1975 (Hogweed Project 02); and Birmingham, UK, May 2, 1975 (*Swelled and Spent*). Details of these and other recordings can be found in the appendix to this volume.

[5]   The whole-tone scale, made famous by Impressionist composers such as Claude Debussy (1862–1918), is a scale made up entirely of whole steps rather than the mixture of whole and half steps found in the traditional major or minor scale. An example of a whole-tone scale is: C – D – E – F♯ - G♯ (A♭) – B♭ – C.

[6]   An augmented triad is a chord consisting of notes from the whole-tone scale, a major third apart, for example, F – A – C♯. Hackett's concluding chordal gesture usually involved a given chord, its transposition a major third up (resulting in a reordering of the chord), and then a final chord a whole step down from the previous chord, for example: F – A – C♯ / A – C♯ – F / G – B – D♯.

progression, however, was invariably "distorted" in pitch, either by wobbling "out of control" or abruptly gliding upward, again manipulated with the tuning knob. (By early 1975, the "tonal" moment was frequently given a decidedly pastoral mood with bird call noises contributed by Collins.) The distorted last chord was often met with frenzied bursts of drums or drums and guitar; by late in the tour this had evolved into a kind of clichéd high-speed boogie (often with stop-on-a-dime endings). Early in the tour Gabriel would also contribute oboe at this point in the improvisation, the oboe generally adding to the din with increasingly shrill squeaks; frequently he would follow this with a brief bit of flute as well to bring things down. Later in the tour, Hackett and others would store bits of sound in their analog echo boxes by setting the regeneration settings high, then manipulate the speed of the delay to create whooshing, cascading waves of feedback—an effect pioneered earlier by Pink Floyd. In some mid- and late-tour performances there would also be a brief, solo-like moment of fast vibraphone playing from Collins. In some later performances (such as Birmingham, UK, at [1:02]), Hackett can also be heard quoting his riff from "Dancing with the Moonlit Knight"; Russell (2004) traces the earliest instance of this quotation to the January 28, 1975 show in Phoenix, pointing out that he had hinted at quoting this figure in some earlier improvisations (p. 133).

At some point, the chaos needed to be led into a conventional "jam" pattern. The studio recording achieved this by a simple cross-fade of the improvised disorder into a $\frac{6}{8}$ jam, with a skipping octave riff contributed by Rutherford, that was already well under way at the point at which it was faded in. In live performance, the riff portion of the improvisation would be gradually introduced by either Collins (who would simply start a groove at his kit) or, more commonly, by Rutherford. Usually Rutherford would quietly begin his octave riff and fade in the volume, with Collins acknowledging the introduction of the riff and reinforcing the tempo—with cymbals or high hats—a few seconds later. Full drum-kit playing would soon follow. In the Los Angeles performance, however, Rutherford can be heard tentatively introducing fragments of the riff to come, with plenty of space in between fragments, starting at about [1:59] in, completing the riff at last about 15 seconds later. The Turin performance of this moment is amusing in that Gabriel contributes some very lyrical flute over the $\frac{6}{8}$ jam, making it sound like a jig. Invariably, Banks would be the last band member to concede to the structure of the jam, often sustaining dissonant organ chords well after the others had joined into the riff. Once Banks changed to a consonant chord, it seemed that was the signal that the "chaos" had at last passed.

Sometimes the "song" that would emerge from the jam would be entirely different from the $\frac{6}{8}$ jam heard on the studio recording. In some UK performances late in the tour (Wembley, Manchester, Birmingham), the jam that emerged from the chaos would be in the key of E minor and in $\frac{4}{4}$ time. (The Manchester version, in fact, is prescient of the sinister jam that led to Genesis's hit "Mama" in the early 1980s; Gabriel also adds to the edge of this moment by improvising some unhinged scat singing with plenty of delay feedback.) Russell (2004) notes that the

March 30, 1975 show in Saarbrucken, Germany, marked the first time the group chose to come out of the chaotic section with a jam altogether different from the studio version, as Hackett began a different riff that Collins picked up on and the rest of the group followed suit (p. 154).

The different performances of "The Waiting Room" reveal how much the Genesis group members were willing to experiment in improvisations, but also how many constraints they maintained, probably to rein in the duration of the performance. The performances of "The Waiting Room" are remarkably consistent in length, most lasting around five and a half minutes and only occasionally approaching six minutes in length, although the Wembley performance—in which the group seems to have stumbled upon its "new" groove coming out of the improvisation—is over nine minutes in length.

Summarizing the tour experience in an interview with Paul Russell in 2004, Banks and Rutherford made the following observations:

> BANKS: It was ambitious and it didn't really work in lots of ways. People remember it being this glorious show, but for a start, technically, we were trying to be too adventurous and most of the time all the slides we had didn't work and that used to depress us. And we knew Pete was leaving and it was pretty awful.
>
> RUTHERFORD: I'm sure the punters enjoyed it.
>
> BANKS: It was my least enjoyable period in the group, some of the songs are great— some good writing. The Evil Jam (The Waiting Room) was the best thing, "Carpet Crawl" had a sought [sic] of feel about it. A few good things, but a bit laboured.
>
> (Russell, 2004, p. 207)

As a result of the set-list constraints, Genesis's "homecoming" concerts at the Empire Pool Wembley on April 14 and 15, 1975, trimmed some of *The Lamb* (for example, only the "arrival" section of "The Colony of Slippermen" was played) in favor of including a few additional older songs. Gabriel told Chris Welch, "We will try and play more old numbers in England and we want to do something special there" (Welch, 1975). The Wembley shows received a review in the London *Times*, not known for its coverage of "pop" events. Michael Wale noted that "the screen could have been tauter, as at times it gave the images a scratched effect. Often, I found Gabriel's words indistinct because I was too near the amplifiers." Overall, though, Wale concluded that Genesis's success was proof that "British youth is ready to grapple with music much more complicated than that provided by the Bay City Rollers" (Platts, 2001, p. 82).

Genesis seemed to have made a triumphant arrival. Most fans did not know, however, that the group was barely holding together. Gabriel, in particular, was experiencing severe professional and personal stress concerning his future options with the group. "I was saying to myself, 'OK, we get successful in America. We get rich. What then? Do we become like the other bands who've made it?' There were things about those groups that I didn't like, and I didn't want to become part of a supergroup. I was beginning to dislike myself for doing what I was doing" (Fielder, 1984, p. 94).

The tour had barely begun, it seemed, when, while in Cleveland for a two-concert engagement at the Allen Theatre on November 25 and 26, 1974, Gabriel made his decision to leave Genesis. Characteristically, he told the band's manager, Tony Smith, before telling his band mates (Platts, 2001, p. 80); this may be indicative of his overall shyness, or it could be an indicator of strained communications within the band at the time. Smith persuaded Gabriel to stay long enough to complete the tour because "there was a good chance the band could pay off their debts to Charisma, which had become considerable in the preceding three years" (Bright, 1988, pp. 63–64). Even so, the group was still about £160,000 in debt when Gabriel did finally leave (Bright, 1988, p. 64).

The decision to stay with the group to finish the tour, when it had only just begun (Genesis had just completed the first week of shows in a tour that ultimately would last another six months), took its toll on Gabriel. His wife Jill noticed the change:

> He was angry, and it was a very powerful performance. He totally opened himself and put himself on the line to the world, but he wasn't in his relationship with me. I would say to him, "Why can't you be like that for me?" I remember sitting in the audience and feeling completely turned on by this guy who I was married to. But he was not able to be that person outside the stage. And that is what has slowly broken down over the years, being able to take that part of himself into his everyday life. (Bright, 1988, p. 63)

Gabriel later shared the immense professional and personal pressures leading up to his decision to go solo:

> I wanted a career where I had the opportunity to take on other projects but the band had this army-like attitude. There was no room to be flexible—if you were in the band, you were in it 100 percent, or you were out.
>
> A lot of the friction towards the end arose because I wanted to follow up those opportunities and also, I was the first one to have kids. My first child spent three weeks in an incubator, and the doctors didn't think she was going to live.
>
> Although there was sympathy, it held up recording schedules. The band didn't understand that. For me there was absolutely no question of priorities in a situation like that.
>
> Now [that] the others have kids they understand. This was one of the factors which helped me think, "This is not a lifestyle that I wish to continue."
>
> I had no idea what I wanted to do, but I knew I was sick of rock, the business, and everything about it. I just wanted to get out. (Fielder, 1984, p. 94)

Perhaps because Gabriel had decided months before to leave the group, his peace at having arrived at this decision led to *Melody Maker*'s Chris Welch's observation that Gabriel seemed to possess "a marked degree of confidence," being "a much more relaxed and communicative weaver of fantasies than he was in the early days of this most extraordinary group" (Welch, 1975). The Wembley shows aside, however, the European leg of the tour could hardly be described as triumphant. The March 25, 1975 show at the Turin Sports Palace in Italy was marred by an altercation between police and fans outside the venue (Platts, 2001, p. 82), and according to some accounts (including Banks's own recollections), more than one show had been cancelled because of a lack of ticket sales (Russell, 2004, p. 208). The last *Lamb* performance took place at the Palais des Sports in Besancon, St. Etienne, France, on May 27, 1975 (Russell, 2004, p. 221).

News of Gabriel's departure was eventually leaked to the *New Musical Express* in July 1975. Charisma Records at first denied the rumors, but six weeks later Genesis finally admitted that Gabriel had left. The next week Gabriel issued his own press statement, with the stipulation that the press should publish it in full or not at all (Bright, 1988, pp. 64–65). Gabriel's statement read as follows:

I had a dream, eye's dream. Then I had another dream with the body and soul of a rock star. When it didn't feel good I packed it in. Looking back for the musical and non-musical reasons, this is what I came up with:

OUT, ANGELS OUT—an investigation.

The vehicle we had built as a co-op to serve our songwriting became our master and had cooped us up inside the success we had wanted. It affected the attitudes and the spirit of the whole band. The music had not dried up and I still respect the other musicians, but our roles had set in hard. To get an idea through "Genesis the Big" meant shifting a lot more concrete than before. For any band, transferring the heart from idealistic enthusiasm to professionalism is a difficult operation.

I believe the use of sound and visual images can be developed to do much more than we have done. But on a large scale it needs one clear and coherent direction, which our pseudo-democratic committee system could not provide.

As an artist, I need to absorb a wide variety of experiences. It is difficult to respond to intuition and impulse within the long-term planning that the band needed. I felt I should look at/learn about/develop myself, my creative bits and pieces and pick up on a lot of work going on outside music. Even the hidden delights of vegetable growing and community living are beginning to reveal their secrets. I could not expect the band to tie in their schedules with my bondage to cabbages. The increase in money and power, if I had stayed, would have anchored me to the spotlights. It was important to me to give space to my family, which I wanted to hold together, and to liberate the daddy in me.

Although I have seen and learnt a great deal in the last seven years, I found I had begun to look at things as the famous Gabriel, despite hiding my occupation whenever possible, hitching lifts, etc. I had begun to think in business terms; very useful for an often bitten once shy musician, but treating records and audiences as money was taking me away from them. When performing, there were less shivers up and down the spine.

I believe the world has soon to go through a difficult period of changes. I'm excited by some of the areas coming through to the surface which seem to have been hidden away in people's minds. I want to explore and be prepared to be open and flexible enough to respond, not tied in to the old hierarchy.

Much of my psyche's ambitions as "Gabriel archetypal rock star" have been fulfilled—a lot of the ego-gratification and the need to attract young ladies, perhaps the result of frequent rejection as "Gabriel acne-struck public school boy". However, I can still get off playing the star game once in a while.

My future within music, if it exists, will be in as many situations as possible. It's good to see a growing number of artists breaking down the pigeonholes. This is the difference between the profitable, compartmentalized, battery chicken and the free-range. Why did the chicken cross the road anyway?

There is no animosity between myself and the band or management. The decision had been made some time ago and we have talked about our new direction. The reason why my leaving was not announced earlier was because I had been asked to delay until they had found a replacement to plug up the hole. It is not impossible that some of them might work with me on other projects.

The following guesswork has little in common with truth:

Gabriel left Genesis

1) To work in theatre.
2) To make more money as a solo artist.
3) To do a "Bowie".
4) To do a "Ferry".
5) To do a "Furry Boa round my neck and hang myself with it".
6) To go see an institution.
7) To go senile in the sticks.

I do not express myself adequately in interviews and I felt I owed it to the people who have put a lot of love and energy supporting the band to give an accurate picture of my reasons. So I ask that you print all or none of this. (Platts, 2001, pp. 85–86)

Genesis biographers Bowler and Dray find clues to Gabriel's unhappiness in various passages from *The Lamb*:

"Cuckoo Cocoon" seemed to intimate that [Gabriel] was becoming too comfortable inside the trappings of rock stardom—"I feel so secure, that I know this can't be real"—and did the "cushioned strait-jacket" of "In The Cage" refer to his internal battle between financial security and his need for artistic freedom, a freedom he felt denied within a group structure? Was the production line indicating individual profit potential in "The Grand Parade of Lifeless Packaging" a symbol of his disgust for the music industry? "The Chamber of 32 Doors" his cynical view of all the business suits who claimed to have his best interests at heart while cynically protecting their own? The lyrics point to a man unhappy with the way events had gone. (Bowler and Dray, 1993, p. 97)

Mike Rutherford sees *The Lamb* as a "point of no return" for Gabriel's songwriting. "I think that having written all the lyrics on 'The Lamb', he would not have found it easy to go back to our previous method of songwriting. Perhaps he felt that 'The Lamb' was a good, final statement on which to leave" (Fielder, 1984, p. 94). Perhaps the rest of the band would not have found it easy to go back to their previous method of songwriting either, at least as far as credits were concerned. The group's next release, *A Trick of the Tail*, was their first with individual songwriting credits. The rest of the band, *sans* Gabriel, had already been rehearsing material for the next album for over a month when Gabriel issued the press release confirming his departure (Platts, 2001, p. 85). Tony Banks, already seen to be the most critical band mate concerning Gabriel's artistic heavy-handedness in the making of *The Lamb*, later claimed, "I knew we could write good music without Peter. Any one of us could have left and the rest would still have written good music" (Fielder, 1984, p. 97).

Chapter 5
"*it*": Interpreting *The Lamb*

The Lamb, described by Gabriel's biographer Spencer Bright as "a surreal tale of sex, violence and death" (Bright, 1988, p. 124), is, even today, a polarizing album. For many fans it represents the group's zenith, as well as one of the finest recordings of the progressive rock genre. Nevertheless, some writers consider Genesis's music during the Gabriel years to be weird and disturbing, especially when compared to the generally Utopian progressive vision of other bands such as Yes. Davin Seay, for example, credits Genesis with "some of the strangest, most viscerally unsettling music of all time" (Seay with Neely, 1986, p. 272), singling out *The Lamb* as an "astonishingly unpleasant" double album of "inpenetrable [*sic*] density" (p. 273).

Similarly, David Sinclair called *The Lamb* "the weightiest monument" to Genesis's "earnest and unnecessarily convoluted formula" of progressive rock: "Depending on your viewpoint, it stands either as a masterpiece or as one of the most fatuous releases of the decade" (Sinclair, 1992, p. 129). "Listening to it now," Sinclair writes,

> it sounds as if the idea was for each of the contributors to try and cram as much of their own bits as possible into every nook and cranny of every song. In reaching for such unwieldy extremes of inventiveness, they betrayed their immaturity as much as they demonstrated their grasp of advanced musical technique. (Sinclair, 1992, p. 129)

The Lamb, however, is obviously a product of the early 1970s, during which complexity was seen as a virtue. Such complexity (which was not limited to music—in literature, for example, one could just as easily cite Thomas Pynchon's novel *Gravity's Rainbow*) is an example of what John Covach has called the "hippie aesthetic"—the notion that "the rock musician is an artist who has a responsibility to produce sophisticated music using whatever means are at his or her disposal. The music should stand up to repeated listening and the lyrics should deal with important issues or themes" (Covach, 2006, p. 306).

Viewed through a broader historical lens, however, one could also compare this tendency to complexity in early-1970s rock with the *fin-de-siècle* aesthetics of pre-World War I Europe. For example, the late nineteenth-century Romantic style of Gustav Mahler and early Arnold Schoenberg was characterized by the expansion of chromatic harmony until tonality itself was threatened; the neo-classicism of Igor Stravinsky and the impressionism of Claude Debussy heralded a new "simpler" direction in concert music by turning away from the chromatic complexities of late Romanticism. In the same way that the complexity of such music represented the swan song of the old European order (one is reminded of Debussy's famous remark that Wagner's music was "a beautiful sunset mistaken for a dawn"), the complexity of 1970s progressive rock may be seen not only as an extension of 1960s psychedelia but as expressing the demise of the counterculture that spawned it. Like neo-classicism in the years after World War I, disco and punk rock helped to usher in a stripped-down aesthetic in music that accompanied the mid-1970s implosion of the counterculture; this stylistic change was hastened by a recession-strapped industry only too eager to promote simpler and more financially efficient product.

Therefore, listening with a more historically informed ear—a 1970s ear, as it were—will better reveal *The Lamb*'s deep riches. For example, the nostalgia motif that is scattered through the album—in "Broadway Melody of 1974," the musical structure of "Counting Out Time," and the quotes from earlier pop songs in "In the Cage"—is better understood when considering Andy Warhol associate Bob Colacello's comment that nostalgia was "all over New York in 1973 and 1974" (Killen, 2006, p. 140). Another aspect of 1970s pop culture reflected in *The Lamb* was its prominent "anti-hero"; examples in literature and movies of the era include *Catch 22*, *Taxi Driver*, and *The Godfather*. Gabriel's protagonist Rael is, like Travis Bickle or Don Corleone, hardly noble or even very likeable as the story begins; he is a social "outsider." Gabriel describes Rael as "an outcast in a totally alien situation. I identify with him to a certain extent" (Bowler and Dray, 1993, p. 96). Compounding the alienation of Rael's social status as a street delinquent is his uncertain racial status as half-Puerto Rican (the other "half" of Rael's racial lineage is not specified). Rael's "outsider" racial status is in fact ironically confirmed by the racial stereotyping found in Chris Welch's review of the album:

> "Rael," a Puerto Rican resident of New York searching for freedom ... [attempts] to establish his identity by spraying his name on walls with an aerosol. He would probably achieve greater satisfaction by forming a voluntary association of citizens devoted to wiping clean the city walls from graffiti, thus rendering them pleasant to behold, and removing some of the oppressive characteristics of big city life.
>
> The Puerto Rican could also form a close harmony vocal group, and cut some top selling albums thus making him popular, and rich. (Welch, 1974)

Welch's review—the above racial essentialism notwithstanding—was typical of the muted critical response to *The Lamb*; as Sinclair put it, "the fans loved it while the critics gave it a panning" (p. 129). For many critics—if not the fans—the rococo excesses of progressive rock were largely played out by 1975, thanks to such leaden leviathans as Yes's *Tales from Topographic Oceans* and Jethro Tull's *A Passion Play* (1973 and 1974, respectively). Although punk rock would not be seen as a viable corrective for another year, certainly many critics thought that progressive rock had worn out its welcome and that some sort of change was overdue. In comparing recordings of *The Lamb* tour (such as the Los Angeles Shrine Auditorium show on January 24, 1975 released in the *Genesis Archive*

1967–75 box set) with the bootleg recording made of their famous appearance at the Roxy in Los Angeles in 1973, it is evident that their American audience had grown considerably in the intervening year or so, largely through word of mouth. (The Roxy recordings are interesting to hear, if only because the epic sound of "Watcher of the Skies," "Firth of Fifth," and "Supper's Ready" seems almost wasted on a small club crowd. By 1975, however, the group was at last playing venues appropriate to the larger-than-life scale of their music—the sound is more reverberant, the audience larger and more vocally appreciative.)

If, even now, *The Lamb Lies Down on Broadway* remains one of Genesis's most beloved albums, fans are by no means united in their interpretation of the album. What, exactly, does *The Lamb* mean? Is it merely a weird flight of fancy for Gabriel's imagination, a vessel for his gifted wordplay? Is it an allegory of some sort? Is it autobiographical? In this book I make no claim to having "solved" *The Lamb*—for any interpretations I offer, there will certainly be disagreement among the album's legions of devoted listeners. Therefore, I merely offer a summary of various interpretations of *The Lamb* that have been given by fans over the years, along with some interpretations of my own. It is by no means exhaustive or comprehensive; in fact, it is precisely *because* so many alternate readings can be posited that *The Lamb* emerges as one of the richest creative works of the 1970s. Nevertheless, one way of grasping *The Lamb*'s complexity is to parse its various elements according to three thematic threads. I begin with an overview of psychological aspects of *The Lamb*; certainly much of its imagery may be traced to Gabriel's reading of Carl Gustav Jung, and the entire album can be read as a kind of psychological allegory, tracing a path from psychotic break to individuation. The very title of the album, on the other hand, as well as its overall trajectory of death, tests of moral character, and implied resurrection (or *satori*?), suggests that one can also interpret *The Lamb* as a religious fable, a kind of prog-rock *Pilgrim's Progress*. Thus, the second thread of interpretation considers the religious symbolism in *The Lamb*, which draws upon both Christianity and eastern religions (especially Buddhism).[1] Finally, I examine *The Lamb*'s musical references. Before *The Lamb*, Genesis was unusual among the major progressive rock bands in that they avoided overt musical quotations (their prog-rock contemporaries ELP, in contrast, not only "adapted" entire classical pieces verbatim but keyboardist Keith

---

[1]   Such eclecticism is not surprising, as the early 1970s were a time of spiritual seeking; both the "Jesus Freak" movement and the New Age movement grew rapidly during this time, and popular music and literature displayed both religious syncretism and an interest in alternative religious traditions. For example, the pop-music charts featured songs such as George Harrison's "My Sweet Lord" (with its "Hallelujah"s and "Hare Krishna"s in happy coexistence!), Norman Greenbaum's "Spirit in the Sky," and the "rock opera" *Jesus Christ Superstar*. In popular literature, one can point to examples such as Richard Bach's spiritual allegory *Jonathan Livingston Seagull*, Ram Dass's do-it-yourself manual of yoga and meditation *Be Here Now*, and Carlos Castaneda's series of *Don Juan* books that allegedly detailed the teachings of a Yaqui Indian shaman.

Emerson also incorporated quotations in his solos from musical sources as diverse as jazz pianist Bill Evans and the American folk tune "Turkey in the Straw"). *The Lamb* is unique among Genesis's albums in that it contains several strategically placed quotations from other songs—not only pop songs of the early 1960s, but also of their own music. Some fans cite this self-referential content as evidence that parts of *The Lamb* may be autobiographical.

Psychological aspects of *The Lamb*

Historian Andreas Killen observes that the "generational and oedipal conflicts" of the 1960s "were, for the most part, politically stillborn" in the 1970s; but the 1960s' "cultural revolutions" in "music, film, sensibilities, and lifestyles" continued to play itself out through the decade (Killen, 2006, p. 4). In spite of the "passing of sixties utopianism" that was widely observed, even by contemporary writers, Killen notes that "the seventies revolution of everyday life … was not without its own genuinely visionary aspects" (2006, p. 4). As Paul Stump observes, by the 1960s and early 1970s, given the hippie counterculture's interest in other states of consciousness and so-called "non-ordinary reality," it was not surprising that elements of soul and psyche became "viable artistic [and commercial] commodities" in the popular culture of the 1960s and early 1970s (Stump, 1997, p. 42).

If *The Lamb Lies Down on Broadway* must be regarded as one of the most "visionary" products of the 1970s, it also fits squarely within the Romantic-era narrative paradigm in which "the individual passes through introspection, dream and reflection and emerges transformed" (Rothstein, 1995, p. 222). This pattern, in turn, has its counterparts in the universal structural patterns of the world's mythologies, as outlined by the comparative mythology and religion scholar Joseph Campbell. Campbell was in turn influenced by the psychological theory of C. G. Jung concerning humanity's "collective unconscious," the contents of which Jung called *archetypes*.

Jung's theory was influenced by the work of the early twentieth-century psychologist William James, especially by James's groundbreaking work *The Varieties of Religious Experience*, first published in 1902. James wrote that "our normal waking consciousness, rational consciousness as we call it, is but one special type of consciousness, whilst all about it, parted from it by the filmiest of screens, there lie potential forms of consciousness entirely different" (James, 1925, p. 388).

> We may go through life without suspecting their existence; but apply the requisite stimulus, and at a touch they are there in all their completeness, definite types of mentality which probably somewhere have their application and adaptation. No account of the universe in its totality can be final which leaves these other forms of consciousness quite disregarded. (James, 1925, p. 388)

Jung, elaborating upon James's ideas, posited a *collective* unconscious that is innately biological, as he described it in his 1927 essay "The Structure of the Psyche":

> The collective unconscious contains the whole spiritual heritage of mankind's evolution, born anew in the brain structure of every individual. His conscious mind is an ephemeral phenomenon that accomplishes all provisional adaptations and orientations, for which reason one can best compare its function to orientation in space. The unconscious, on the other hand, is the source of the instinctual forces of the psyche and of the forms or categories that regulate them, namely the archetypes. All the most powerful ideas in history go back to archetypes. (Jung, 1971, p. 45)

Jung carefully distinguished the archetypes from their specific forms as they appeared in myths and fairytales, which he called "forms that have received a specific stamp and have been handed down through long periods of time." By contrast, the archetypes themselves refer to "only those psychic contents which have not yet been submitted to conscious elaboration and therefore an immediate datum of psychic experience" (Jung, 1969, p. 5). The archetype is "essentially an unconscious content that is altered by becoming conscious and by being perceived, and it takes its colour from the individual consciousness in which it happens to appear" (Jung, 1969, p. 5). As a result, the "immediate manifestation" of the archetype, as encountered in dreams, is "much more individual" and thus less understandable (Jung, 1969, p. 5).

In a conversation with longtime Genesis photographer Armando Gallo, Gabriel called dreams "a very rich source of inspiration for me. Not only are they a means of handling and storing information gained during waking hours but they are also a means of observing patterns in what has gone on and what is about to happen … . In one sense dreams are real experiences, requiring the activity of the brain even if they only appear to be experiences of other experiences … . We should be careful what we dream" (Gallo, 1986, p. 36). Joseph Campbell calls dreams "the personalized myth" (Campbell, 1968, p. 19); breaking through to "the undistorted, direct experience and assimilation" of the archetypal images is, according to Campbell, "the first work of the hero" (Campbell, 1968, pp. 17–18). Jung notes that dreams are the primary source for archetypes, having the advantage of being "involuntary, spontaneous products of nature not falsified by any conscious purpose" (Jung, 1971, p. 67).

This perhaps accounts for the obscurity of *The Lamb*'s narrative, a frequent target for criticism; it also perhaps accounts for Gabriel's reluctance to give a precise explanation of its lyrics (Bright, 1988, p. 62). Bright contends that "there would be no point because much of it did not have a direct meaning other than the interplay, feel and sound of words. The understanding was largely in the feeling of the performance rather than the literal examination of the words" (1988, p. 62). Such an open interpretation is certainly consistent with the overriding aesthetics of the hippie counterculture, which "*wanted* conventional meaning to be undercut" in its music (Willis, 1978, p. 159, emphasis in original): "It was the very lack of clarity—the multi-codedness—of their preferred music which allowed it to suggest a multitude of suggestive meanings" (Willis, 1978, p. 160).

The Lamb Lies Down on Broadway, to a degree unrivalled by other narrative-structured concept albums, closely follows the "monomyth" of the hero's adventure, which may be summarized as *separation, initiation*, and *return* (Campbell, 1968, p. 30): "a separation from the world, a penetration to some source of power, and a life-enhancing return" (1968, p. 35). The "really creative acts," Campbell writes, "are represented as those deriving from some sort of dying to the world; and what happens in the interval of the hero's nonentity, so that he comes back as one reborn, made great and filled with creative power, mankind is also unanimous in declaring" (Campbell, 1968, pp. 35–36).

The first stage of the hero's journey is what Campbell calls the "call to adventure." This may begin with "a blunder—apparently the merest chance," which "reveals an unsuspected world, and the individual is drawn into a relationship with forces that are not rightly understood .... The blunder may amount to the opening of a destiny" (Campbell, 1968, p. 51). The apparently random appearance of the lamb, lying down on Broadway, might be seen as the "merest chance" that begins Rael's adventure. Not infrequently, the saga begins with "the call unanswered," or the refusal of the call. "Refusal of the summons converts the adventure into its negative" (Campbell, 1968, p. 59). Thus, for example, Jonah refuses God's call to go to Nineveh, resulting in God's sending a storm upon Jonah's vessel and a great fish to swallow him. In the same way, Rael's defiant, self-asserting shout "Don't look at me, I'm not your kind / I'm Rael!" sets in motion this "negative" form of the adventure's catalyst—the solid wall that swallows up Rael from Times Square. Thus, "whether small or great ... the call rings up the curtain, always, on a mystery of transfiguration ... which, when complete, amounts to a dying and a birth" (Campbell, 1968, p. 51). Indeed, rebirth (or *renovatio*) is itself one of the Jungian archetypes (Jung, 1969, p. 114).

Within each stage of Rael's journey, several of his experiences and the characters he encounters correspond to the archetypes in Jung's psychological theory. For example, the Lamia is an example of Jung's *anima* archetype, which often appears personified in dreams (Jung, 1969, p. 284). The anima can be "a siren, *melusina* (mermaid), wood-nymph, Grace, or Erlking's daughter, or a lamia or succubus, who infatuates young men and sucks the life out of them" (Jung, 1969, p. 25):

> Although it seems as if the whole of our unconscious psychic life could be ascribed to the anima, she is yet only one archetype among many .... What is not-I, not masculine, is most probably feminine, and because the not-I is felt as not belonging to me and therefore as outside me, the anima-image is usually projected upon women. Either sex is inhabited by the opposite sex up to a point, for, biologically speaking, it is simply the greater number of masculine genes that tips the scales in favor of masculinity ....
>
> Everything the anima touches becomes numinous—unconditional, dangerous, taboo, magical. She is the serpent in the paradise .... (Jung, 1969, pp. 27–28)

Jung also notes that in instances of "anima-possession," the patient will "want to change himself into a woman through self-castration" (Jung, 1969, p. 39); an example of this played out in *The Lamb* may be seen in Rael's and John's visit to Doktor Dyper in the Colony of Slippermen. Jung, according to Joseph Campbell:

> emphasized the crises ... when, in order to advance, the shining sphere must submit to descend and disappear, at last, into the night-womb of the grave. The normal symbols of our desires and fears become converted, in this afternoon of the biography, into their opposites; for it is then no longer life but death that is the challenge. What is difficult to leave, then, is not the womb but the phallus ... . (Campbell, 1968, p. 12)

Rael's psychological adventures may be seen as an example of what authors Flo Conway and Jim Siegelman (1978) have termed *snapping*, which Killen defines as "the sudden and complete transformation of the self" under the pressure of the teachings and coercion techniques of religious and political cults (Killen, 2006, p. 113). While there is no "cult" group in *The Lamb* (although the voluntary castration episode in "Slippermen" prefigures the Heaven's Gate cult of the 1990s), Rael does undergo a "sudden personality change" as a result of the extraordinary pressures brought about by his ordeal.

"The idea of the multiple personality has always seemed correct to me," Gabriel told Armando Gallo; "each of us is composed of many parts and in order to achieve some sort of integration they all need to be allowed through to the surface" (Gallo, 1986, p. 88). Certainly by the 1980s, Gabriel was thoroughly aware of Jungian concepts such as the *shadow* (or personal unconscious; "a part of their personality which might not otherwise see daylight") and the bringing together of one's conscious and unconscious through the process of *individuation* ("some sort of integration"). *The Lamb* was evidently Gabriel's first application of those concepts to his songwriting.

Another archetype scattered throughout *The Lamb* is the symbolism of water. "Water," Jung reminds us:

> is the commonest symbol for the unconscious. The lake in the valley is the unconscious, which lies, as it were, underneath consciousness ... . Water is the "valley spirit," the water dragon of Tao, whose nature resembles water—a *yang* embraced in the *yin*. Psychologically, therefore, water means spirit that has become unconscious.... *The descent into the depths always seems to precede the ascent.* (Jung, 1969, pp. 18–19, emphasis added).

In *The Lamb*, one of Rael's immediate sensory impressions upon awakening in the Cuckoo Cocoon is that "the only sound is water drops." Water is later the backdrop for two critical points of the narrative—the pool where Rael has his encounter with the Lamia and the rapids where he rescues his brother John. Water is a recurrent image in Genesis's music, both during and after the Gabriel years; notable examples include "Stagnation," "The Fountain of Salmacis," the "How

Dare I Be So Beautiful?" section of "Supper's Ready," "Firth of Fifth," "Ripples," and "One for the Vine," among others.

The opening sentence of Gabriel's story—"keep your fingers out of my eye"—has been interpreted by some to refer to the placement of a picture of Rael inside the gatefold sleeve, in such a way that the listener's fingers are over his face when holding the album (McMahan, 1998, p. 407). In fact, it would appear to be one of Gabriel's more arcane literary allusions, a reference to the unveiling of the mysterious stranger in H. G. Wells's novel *The Invisible Man*:

> "Why!" said Huxter, suddenly, "that's not a man at all. It's just empty clothes. Look! You can see down his collar and the linings of his clothes. I could put my arm—"
>
> He extended his hand; it seemed to meet something in mid-air, and he drew it back with a sharp exclamation. "I wish you'd *keep your fingers out of my eye*," said the aerial voice, in a tone of savage expostulation. "The fact is, I'm all here; head, hands, legs, and all the rest of it, but it happens I'm invisible. It's a confounded nuisance, but I am. That's no reason I should be poked to pieces by every stupid bumpkin in Iping, is it?" (Wells, 1897, p. 68, emphasis added)

Wells's titular image was adapted by the African American novelist Ralph Ellison in his 1952 novel of the same name. Like Ellison's unnamed protagonist, Rael is also "invisible" to the passers-by of Manhattan, where we find him in the opening title track. He strives to "make a name for himself" and render himself visible to the cabman, the working woman Suzanne, and the "wonder women" looking out their windows, by writing his name in graffiti ("Rael Imperial Aerosol Kid"), shouting out his name ("I'm not your kind—I'm Rael!"), and so forth. He seems to be met with indifference by society around him, however.

Like the protagonist of Ellison's novel, Rael's invisibility is at least in part because of his racial identity—half Puerto Rican. Gabriel does not tell us what the other half of this racial mix is; from the information we are given it is plausible that Rael's mother was Puerto Rican, and that (as is the case in so many poor urban families) Rael grew up with an absent father. The lack of a father figure in Rael's life is played out psychologically in Rael's journeys throughout *The Lamb*. Rael does not encounter a wise father figure who can help him face the challenges of this strange parallel world, akin to Obi-Wan Kenobi in *Star Wars* or Gandalf in *The Lord of the Rings*. The major characters he counters—the saleslady in "The Grand Parade of Lifeless Packaging," Lilywhite Lilith, the Lamia—are all female, or are grotesquely deformed males (the Slippermen). Only John seems to be there as a male guide in his journey—but, as Rael's brother, John is also a fatherless character.

Religious aspects of *The Lamb*

Along with *The Lamb*'s psychological connotations, however, one should also consider its religious dimensions, for as William James reminds us, "the notion of a subconscious self certainly ought not… to be held to *exclude* all notion of a higher penetration. If there be higher powers able to impress us, they may get access to us only through the subliminal door" (James, 1925, p. 243, emphasis in original). James defines *religion* as "the feelings, acts, and experiences of individual men in their solitude, so far as they apprehend themselves to stand in relation to whatever they may consider the divine" (James, 1925, p. 31). Such experiences are by definition solemn (James, 1925, p. 38); one is reminded of Macan's (1997) remarks regarding the "quasi-liturgical" function of progressive rock recordings and shows, discussed in Chapter 1.

The Gabriel children were brought up in the Church of England, but their parents were not regular churchgoers. Peter's mother Irene remembers that "prayers and Bible stories were a part of our lives, but Peter and Anne didn't see it genuinely lived by us" (Bright, 1988, p. 17). The church music that was a part of the regular chapel services at Charterhouse was certainly a formative influence: Gabriel has said that "on the few good hymns, which were anthem-like in some ways, I think it's the closest that the white man gets to soul music" (Bowler and Dray, 1993, p. 6).

Christian imagery suffuses much of Genesis's early output. The group's debut album *From Genesis to Revelation*, of course, was a loose concept album based on the Bible, although credit for the concept goes to their producer Jonathan King (Bowler and Dray, 1993, p. 19). One song that did not make the cut was Anthony Phillips's "Visions of Angels," which was reportedly inspired by Peter's future wife Jill (Bright, 1988, p. 37) and later appeared on *Trespass*. "For Absent Friends," which appeared on 1971's *Nursery Cryme*, is a touching portrayal of an elderly couple going to church. "Supper's Ready," of course, culminates in a Gabrielesque vision of the battle of Armageddon and the second coming of Christ. In his post-Genesis solo career, Gabriel has continued to show an interest in Christian imagery, as in for example "Blood of Eden" and his soundtrack for Martin Scorsese's film *The Last Temptation of Christ*.

Listeners who bring their familiarity with the Christian faith to *The Lamb* will note its many Christian images: the Lamb lying down on Broadway, for example, could be seen as a symbol of Christ "laying down" His life to redeem humanity, and the overall narrative as a kind of *Pilgrim's Progress*-style moral fable ending in resurrection. One of Gabriel's introductory stories would seem to point to a resurrection theme as well, albeit in typically bizarre Gabriel fashion; at the Milton Keynes Reunion Concert in 1982 Peter introduced "The Lamb Lies Down on Broadway" with a story about an old man who:

> used to collect everything that he had in his life: bus tickets, paper bags, all sorts .... So his room was full of junk, and every time he got more and more stuff, he had to build his house a little bit bigger and bigger and bigger.
>
> Eventually, disaster struck when his dog Renaldo died. So he took Renaldo to the place where all dead dogs should go: to the taxidermist. Renaldo was back in his room within a week. He first of all sat him in his chair but he didn't look quite right, didn't look quite comfortable, and he tried him by the fireplace where he usually sat, and then

he lifted him up in his full glory and put him on the table, and just then, the glass eyes began to wink a little. He saw a sign of life return to the dog, and his tail wagged. As that happened, the table began sprouting branches and leaves, and everything started moving backwards into life, ... and there was a strange rug in front of the fire made out of lamb's wool, and the rug slowly returned to life, and there was a little lamb... (Hoppe, 1998)[2]

Other Christian references are scattered throughout *The Lamb*. For example, "The Carpet Crawlers" refers to "the needle's eye … winking, closing on the poor," a reference to Christ's teaching that "it is easier for a camel to pass through the eye of a needle than for a rich man to enter the Kingdom of God" (Luke 18:25). Here, however, Gabriel inverts the meaning of the passage; in the song not even a poor person can pass through, though it may be argued in a Christian context that the "crawlers" are attempting to earn salvation through their own human efforts (or "works") rather than God's grace. The pool encounter in "The Lamia" similarly inverts the Christian concepts of the Eucharist (Rael's flesh and blood become the host for the Lamia) and baptism (rather than emerging spiritually cleansed or "dead to sin" through baptism, Rael emerges with his sinful nature repulsively visible as one of the Slippermen). In "In the Cage," John's "tear of blood" when he looks at Rael recalls Christ's "sweat like great drops of blood" in Luke 22:44. John's two-time denial of Rael—when Rael asks for help in "In the Cage" and when the Raven snatches Rael's tube away in "The Colony of Slippermen"—is analogous to Peter's three-fold denial of Christ. Of course, Rael at last achieves redemption when he forgoes returning through the portal to his old life in New York and instead dives into the ravine to save John from drowning after those denials—a gesture that parallels Christ "emptying Himself" and undergoing His redeeming self-sacrifice rather than simply returning to reclaim His glory in Heaven (Philippians 2:6–8). This is not to argue that Rael is a Christ figure, although that has been the conclusion of some fans of the album. Rather, as it has already been pointed out, Christian imagery in general is a recurrent theme of Genesis's music; here is a case where such imagery is scattered rather liberally throughout the entire album as opposed to being found in one or two songs.

Of course, there is non-Christian religious imagery in Genesis's early music as well. The song "White Mountain" (*Trespass*), for example, has a strongly shamanic character, and the group drew upon Classical mythology in songs such as "The Fountain of Salmacis" and "The Cinema Show." Peter Gabriel was first introduced to other spiritual traditions through his father's library (Bright, 1988, p. 17). Gabriel had always been a voracious reader; in the early 1970s he became close friends with a poet named Martin Hall, who later described their friendship as "like a late schoolboy relationship. One of us would say, you must see this film, or must read that book" (Bright, 1988, p. 9). In 1973–74, during which *The Lamb* was conceived and recorded, Gabriel's reading included Carlos Castaneda's

---

²   A real audio file of this introduction can be heard at <http://members.aol.com/ VWTiresias/sound.htm>, accessed April 11, 2006.

Journey to Ixtlan, books on Zen Buddhism, and *The Tibetan Book of the Dead* (Bright, 1988, p. 9), as well as the writings of Jung. Gabriel has directly linked his reading of Jung with at least "The Lamia" (Bell, 1975, p. 14); subconsciously, *The Tibetan Book of the Dead* may also have influenced the overall structure of *The Lamb Lies Down on Broadway*. Although a direct causal relationship cannot be established, especially in light of Gabriel's reticence to "explain" *The Lamb*, the parallels are worth exploring.

The Tibetan Book of the Dead (or *Bardo Thödol*) is, in psychological terms, a 49-day "prolonged dream-like state, in what may be called the fourth dimension of space, filled with hallucinatory visions directly resultant from the mental-content of the percipient, happy and heaven-like if the *karma* be good, miserable and hell-like if the *karma* be bad" (Evans-Wentz, 1960, pp. 66–67). The manuscript consists of three parts. The first, *Chikhai Bardo*, deals with psychic events at the moment of physical death; the second, *Chönyid Bardo*, deals with the soul's journey immediately after death, a series of episodes involving "karmic illusions." Finally, the third part, *Sidpa Bardo*, occurs with the soul's gravitation toward and preparation for rebirth (Evans-Wentz, 1960, p. xxxvi). The deceased is repeatedly advised that the visions are transitory and illusory, and is exhorted to "be not daunted thereby, nor terrified, nor awed" (Evans-Wentz, 1960, p. 104). The *Tibetan Book of the Dead* instructs that "perseverance in the reading ... for forty-nine days is of the utmost importance. Even if not liberated at one setting face-to-face, one ought to be liberated at another: this is why so many different settings-face-to-face are necessary" (Evans-Wentz, 1960, p. 183). Likewise, the narrative of Rael's journey is largely episodic and in the first-person.

The ultimate goal of the *Bardo* is "illumination or higher consciousness, by means of which the initial situation is overcome on a higher level" (Jung, 1969, p. 39). Broadly speaking, then, we can consider Rael's situation at the beginning of *The Lamb* as one of sociopathic alienation (expressed particularly in the title track and "Back in N.Y.C."); by the end ("*it*"), he has achieved oneness with the universe (individuation in psychological terms, *satori* or enlightenment in the language of the *Bardo*). Below is a possible breakdown of the album according to the three parts of the *Bardo Thödol*:

- *Chikhai Bardo*: "The Lamb Lies Down on Broadway," "Fly on a Windshield," "Broadway Melody of 1974"
- *Chönyid Bardo*: "Cuckoo Cocoon," "In the Cage," "The Grand Parade of Lifeless Packaging," "Back in N.Y.C.," "Hairless Heart," "Counting Out Time," "Carpet Crawlers," "Chamber of 32 Doors," "Lilywhite Lilith"
- *Sidpa Bardo*: "The Waiting Room," "Anyway," "Here Comes The Supernatural Anaesthetist," "The Lamia," "Silent Sorrow in Empty Boats," "The Colony of Slippermen," "The Light Dies Down on Broadway," "Riding the Scree," "Ravine," "In the Rapids," "*it*"

William James writes that transitions in the religious experience may be gradual, "yet when you place the typical extremes beside each other for comparison, you feel that two discontinuous psychological universes confront you, and that in passing from one to the other a "critical point" has been overcome" (James, 1925, pp. 41–42). Accordingly, the division points in *The Lamb* are somewhat porous. For example, Rael's "death" in the cave, coinciding with the arrival of the Supernatural Anaesthetist, is a major turning point in the story; accordingly, the *Sidpa Bardo* could begin with "The Lamia" rather than "The Waiting Room." My own division above is based partly on the two appearances of transitional music that occur at the end of "Broadway Melody of 1974" (on electric guitar) and "Lilywhite Lilith" (on Mellotron), which henceforth will be referred to as "swoon" music (Figure 5.1). This brief theme represents the moment when Rael passes from one *Bardo* to the next through a kind of swoon or momentary loss of consciousness.

Figure 5.1   "Swoon music" from first appearance in "Broadway Melody of 1974"

The *Bardo*'s episodic structure makes it an example of a Jungian "symbolic process"; it is an "experience in images and of images" (Jung, 1969, p. 38). The specific images involved in a symbolic process, as well as the time scale involved in their experience, may vary enormously from case to case (Jung, 1969, p. 39)— 49 days for the reading of the *Bardo Thödol*, about 90 minutes for *The Lamb*. Nevertheless, the beginning of such a symbolic process "is almost invariably characterized by one's getting stuck in a blind alley or in some impossible situation" (Jung, 1969, pp. 38–39); Rael's envelopment by the solid cloud that descends upon Broadway, trapping him like a "fly on a windshield," would certainly fit such a description. The *Chikhai Bardo* is, for the departed soul, a period of profound disorientation, the reader of the *Bardo Thödol* continually reminding the departed that the sights and sounds they experience are but karmic illusions. Likewise, Rael is flooded with a disconnected series of images from Broadway's—and, indeed, America's—past in "Broadway Melody of 1974." Afterward, his first response to his new surroundings, in "Cuckoo Cocoon," is one of trying to make sense of where he is. "Cuckoo Cocoon" in fact marks the beginning of the *Chönyid Bardo*, and his time of testing begins—the visceral fear of "In The Cage," the nightmarish *Brave New World* scenario of "The Grand Parade of Lifeless Packaging," and the series of regressive past-life memories that are replayed beginning with "Back in N.Y.C."

In Campbell's monomyth paradigm, there is often a supernatural guide, a figure of "irresistible fascination" that "appears suddenly … marking a new period, a new stage, in the biography" (Campbell, 1968, p. 55). In *The Lamb*, Lilywhite Lilith is one such guide. Campbell points out that "the hero to whom such a helper appears is typically one who has responded to the call … . But even to those who apparently have hardened their hearts"—as Rael apparently has—"the supernatural guardian may appear" (Campbell, 1968, pp. 73–74). She suddenly appears, precisely at the time that Rael despairs of ever leaving the Chamber of 32 Doors and penitently asks, "Take me away." This marks the first time Rael acknowledges his dependence on someone or something outside himself—compare this moment with the defiant self-reliance expressed in the opening title track ("Don't look at me, I'm not your kind / I'm Rael!") or "Back in N.Y.C," for example. It is Lilywhite Lilith—the blind seer—who leads Rael into the *Sidpa Bardo*.

In his introduction to Evans-Wentz's translation of the *Tibetan Book of the Dead*, Jung describes the *Sidpa Bardo* as the "lowest region of the *Bardo*," in which "the dead man, unable to profit by the teachings of the *Chikhai* and *Chönyid Bardo*, begins to fall prey to sexual fantasies and is attracted by the vision of mating couples. Eventually he is caught by a womb and born into the earthly world again" (Evans-Wentz, 1960, p. xli). The *Sidpa Bardo* portion of *The Lamb* at least initially parallels Campbell's description of "the Road of Trials" that begins the Initiation sequence of the monomyth. "Once having traversed the threshold," through the assistance of the Supernatural Anaesthetist, "the hero moves in a dream landscape of curiously fluid, ambiguous forms, where he must survive a succession of trials." (Campbell, 1968, p. 97) Among the "fluid, ambiguous forms" Rael encounters are the Lamia and the Slippermen.

The Lamia exemplify the "woman as temptress" archetype that Campbell finds in many hero narratives (Campbell, 1968, pp. 120–126). Campbell's explanation of this archetype illuminates the "Lamia – Silent Sorrow – Slippermen" triptych of *The Lamb*:

> every failure to cope with a life situation must be laid, in the end, to a restriction of consciousness … . The whole sense of the ubiquitous myth of the hero's passage is that it shall serve as a general pattern for men and women, wherever they may stand along the scale … .
>
> The crux of the curious difficulty lies in the fact that our conscious views of what life ought to be seldom correspond to what life really is. Generally we refuse to admit within ourselves, or within our friends, the fullness of that pushing, self-protective, malodorous, carnivorous, lecherous fever which is the very nature of the organic cell … .
>
> But when it suddenly dawns on us, or is forced to our attention, that everything we think or do is necessarily tainted with the odor of the flesh, then, not uncommonly, there is experienced a moment of revulsion: life, the acts of life, the organs of life, woman in particular as the great symbol of life, become intolerable to the pure, the pure, pure soul. (Campbell, 1968, pp. 121–122)

The Lamia also evoke the "blood-drinking" wrathful deities referred to in the *Tibetan Book of the Dead*, who are "only the former Peaceful Deities in changed aspect" (Evans-Wentz, 1960, p. 131). The blood, according to Evans-Wentz:

represents *sangsaric* existence; the blood-drinking, the thirsting for, the drinking of, and the quenching of the thirst for, *sangsaric* existence. For the devotee who—even at this stage—can be made to realize that these deities are thus but the *karmic* personifications of his own propensities, born from having lived and drunken life, and who has, in addition, the supreme power to face them unswervingly ... meeting them like old acquaintances, and then losing his personality in them, enlightenment as to the true nature of *sangsaric* existence dawns, and with it, the All-Perfect Illumination called Buddhahood. (Evans-Wentz, 1960, pp. 132–133, n. 3)

In "discovering his hidden personality," Rael receives enlightenment of the true nature of *sangsaric* existence, manifested in his physical transformation in the colony of Slippermen; his enlightenment comes not with the severing of his sexual organ, but ultimately through discarding it, forsaking the pursuit of the flesh (literally) in favor of a moment of self-sacrifice. The moment he sees his face on brother John ("That's not your face—it's mine!") is the moment of *satori*.

Musical References in *The Lamb*

Unlike some of their progressive rock contemporaries, such as ELP, Rick Wakeman, or Yes, Genesis tended to eschew direct quotations of other music, tending instead to construct songs that alluded to "classical" music by virtue of their intricate formal construction or harmonic sophistication, especially in their use of modulation. This is not to say, of course, that such quotations are entirely absent in the early music; for example, the coda of "The Return of the Giant Hogweed" contains a fairly evident reference to the Gregorian *Dies Irae* chant (initially in the piano ostinato beginning at [4:54] and subsequently in the organ at [6:31]), and the introduction to "The Battle of Epping Forest" is a stylistic reference to "Mars, The Bringer of War" from Gustav Holst's orchestral suite *The Planets* (1914–17).

In *The Lamb*, however, several quotations prominently appear, and they are all from popular songs. The first three songs quoted were all hits in the US (and the UK) during the first half of the 1960s. At the end of the opening title track, Gabriel sings the opening lines of the song "On Broadway," which was written by the prolific songwriting team of Jerry Leiber and Mike Stoller and which was a hit for The Drifters in 1963. The closing line of "Broadway Melody of 1974," with its drug-oriented reference to children playing at home "with needles—needles and pins," closes with a melodic and lyric reference to the song "Needles and Pins," written by Jack Nitzsche and Sonny Bono and originally recorded by Jackie DeShannon in 1963; a version by the British band The Searchers was a major hit in both the US and UK in 1964. The third early-1960s song quoted, "Runaway," makes its appearance in "In the Cage." "Runaway" was a 1961 hit for Del Shannon, an American singer known for his moody material and distinctive falsetto (in fact, Gabriel slips into a falsetto voice on this line). Subsequent song references slip out of the early-1960s time frame. For example, "Raindrops Keep

Falling on My Head," also found in "In the Cage," was a Burt Bacharach – Hal David song featured in the 1969 film *Butch Cassidy and the Sundance Kid*; the version in the film, by American singer B. J. Thomas, reached the top of the charts in January 1970.

It is important to note, however, that all four of these songs serve to act as reflections or commentary upon the narrative. Gabriel's choice of songs (and lyric excerpts therein) effectively comment upon either the narrative or *mise-en-scène*. For example, the line on which "The Lamb Lies Down on Broadway" fades, "They say there's always magic in the air," effectively introduces the supernatural experience that will engulf Rael in the following track, "Fly on a Windshield." Rael-Gabriel sings the Del Shannon line "my little runaway" at the point when Rael's brother John deserts him for the first time. The quote from "Raindrops Keep Falling on My Head" is a reference to the water drops that Rael first notices in "Cuckoo Cocoon" and that turn out to be the dripping of stalactites in "In the Cage." Thus, the quotations are not offhand references for the sake of cleverness—a charge that might be leveled against ELP, for example—but are integral amplifications of the story line.

More offhand, playful references, however, may be found in the song "*it*," which marks Rael's celebration of individuation and Gabriel's own "easing" the audience back to its everyday mundane reality. This is the one Gabriel-composed lyric wherein Gabriel steps out of his Rael persona and into the role of omniscient narrator ("The Light Dies Down on Broadway," with lyrics by Rutherford and Banks, is another); consequently, it is at this time that Gabriel indulges in the sort of playful allusions found aplenty in his original *Lamb* story. As part of Gabriel's intent in "*it*" is to demythologize the story just heard (Bell, 1975, p. 14)—a denouement that is also characteristic of Alejandro Jodorowsky's 1973 film *The Holy Mountain*[3]—here Gabriel inserts a couple of more contemporary song references, in his lyrics rather than as musical quotes. We are told, for example, that "*it* is purple haze," a reference to Jimi Hendrix's 1967 hit. The entire epic ends, however, with the casual line "*it*'s only knock and know-all, but I like it." This is a clear reference to the then-current (1974) hit by the Rolling Stones, "It's Only Rock & Roll (But I Like It)"; it is also, admittedly, Gabriel's subtle dig at all-knowing critics whom, he knew, would be dissecting and commenting upon (maybe even "knocking") his latest creative work. In this regard, then, the closing line—in fact, the entire song—is similar to John Lennon's "Glass Onion" ("the Walrus was Paul") as a collection of images designed to be critical red herrings. Most intriguingly, Gabriel's litany of obscure, teasing, potentially self-referential images is set to a chord progression strikingly evocative of "Watcher of the Skies," with which this song was sometimes performed as a medley on the first post-

---

[3] The possible influence of Jodorowsky's style of cinema on *The Lamb*—and the aborted film project of *The Lamb* which was to be directed by Jodorowsky—is discussed in the next chapter.

Gabriel tours. Thus, this most personal of Gabriel creations closes with musical references to the band that, in fact, he was soon to leave.

Again, it should be emphasized here that the very preponderance of quotation in *The Lamb* sets it apart from earlier entries in the Genesis discography. This too may be the result of Gabriel's insistence on creating something that would be a striking departure from the style and subject matter of earlier Genesis albums.

Conclusion

The Lamb is an album of paradoxes, wherein high-minded philosophical conceits co-exist with Rolling Stones references ("*it*"), gang violence ("Back in N.Y.C.") segues to delicate open-hairless-heart surgery, and where there is room for references to highbrow literature and disposable pop tunes (William Wordsworth and Burt Bacharach). Uwe Hoppe writes that the album's title itself embodies a contradiction:

> between pastoral peacefulness and innocence (the lamb) and the din of modern society where it has become very difficult to even survive (Broadway).
>
> Of course, the lamb does not belong there at all just like old Tess in "Aisle of Plenty" [*Selling England By the Pound*, 1973] doesn't belong in modern society or even Harold the Barrel [*Nursery Cryme*, 1971] but it reminds us that after all there is much more to life than money and fame. (Hoppe, 1998)

Certainly Gabriel was grappling with this very conviction as his time with Genesis came to a close. As his band was at last poised to reach the upper-echelon status of the progressive rock "supergroups," Gabriel was having second thoughts about the whole enterprise. The personal difficulties with Jill's pregnancy and her later infidelity, his ambivalent feelings about being seen as the "front man" for what had always been a very democratic group, and his suspicion of the rapid growth of the music business and the "star making machinery" that accompanied it (feelings also harbored by Robert Fripp, who broke up King Crimson in the fall of 1974 for that very reason) all caused Gabriel to re-examine his personal and musical direction. Some of the songs on his first couple of solo albums are the result of this period of introspection. In "Solsbury Hill," for example, which some interpret to be about Gabriel's feeling of freedom after leaving Genesis, Gabriel sings, "I walked right out of the machinery." The song "D.I.Y." (Do-it-yourself) sums up Gabriel's credo of the time: "When things get so big, I can't trust them at all / You want some control, you've got to keep it small."

In the next chapter, we will see what happened to *The Lamb Lies Down on Broadway* in the years after Gabriel left Genesis.

Chapter 6

"And the light dies down on Broadway": Genesis and Gabriel after *The Lamb*, and *The Lamb* after Genesis

As this book opened with an account of one *Lamb* performance, so it closes with another. The event is ProgFest 1994, held at the Variety Arts Centre in Los Angeles, and a band named Giraffe is about to perform *The Lamb* live. Gabriel's Rael role is reprised by Kevin Gilbert, a songwriter who was perhaps best known for his work with Sheryl Crow on her *Tuesday Night Music Club* CD. The audience, of course, exemplifies what Edward Macan has called the progressive rock "taste public" (1997, pp. 200–201); they are fervently devoted to this music and they know it well. The introduction to the performance, preserved on the bootleg recording *The Lamb Lies Down at ProgFest*, is a telling illustration of *The Lamb*'s longevity and prestige as a touchstone recording of the progressive rock era. The show began with a recorded collage of radio excerpts, as if someone were changing stations, eventually settling on the voice of *American Top 40* DJ Casey Kasem and one of his famous "long distance dedications." "We're going to go back in time and dust off all the old records, and pull out a real classic," Kasem's voice informs the audience. "The band: Genesis. And the song—a golden oldie—'Invisible Touch.'" The audience responds with boos, which turn to ecstatic cheers as soon as the familiar piano to *The Lamb* begins.

The two recordings—and the sharply differing responses accorded to them—illustrate opposite poles in Genesis's career. "Invisible Touch" represents Genesis at its most commercial, and, as such, is regarded by the loyal progressive-rock aficionado as a betrayal. *The Lamb*, on the other hand, is—along with the 26-minute epic "Supper's Ready"— regarded as the apex of Genesis's progressive ambitions. To perform *The Lamb* is to re-enact an almost sacred ritual. Certainly the ProgFest audience seems to be very familiar with the performing rituals associated with *The Lamb*. When Gilbert, during his spoken interlude after "Lilywhite Lilith," tells his audience, "it is at this point in our story ... that Rael skips the next three songs for time considerations," the response is one of knowing amusement. The narration is itself part of the performance ritual of *The Lamb*, coming at a point in the performance when Gabriel would usually introduce the events of "The Lamia" and "The Colony of Slippermen." Gilbert's story—complete with references to the "slipperman" condition afflicting percussionist Nicholas DiVirgilio—is patterned after similar stories that Gabriel shared with his audiences (pointing out Collins, or occasionally Rutherford) on the *Lamb* tour (one such story is detailed later in this chapter).

If, during the long tour presenting *The Lamb Lies Down on Broadway* live, Gabriel's bandmates came to resent the attention lavished on Gabriel as the perceived "front man," so one of the factors in Gabriel's departure was in fact his similar "strong desire to prove that behind the flamboyant front man was a talented quartet of musicians who could—and did—succeed by themselves" (Gallo, 1986, p. 5). Indeed, Genesis without Gabriel was far more commercially successful than they were with him; under the apparent musical leadership of Phil Collins, the group at last succeeded in cracking the American market, aided by shorter, simple pop songs and even adding such "American" touches as the Earth, Wind and Fire horns (on "No Reply at All"). Unlike many other bands who suffer acrimonious partings with members, Gabriel and the members of Genesis kept in friendly contact with one another; the band even agreed to reunite for a one-off reunion concert to benefit Gabriel's financially troubled world-music organization, WOMAD (World of Music and Dance), in 1982.[1] Gabriel also recorded a new version of "The Carpet Crawlers," entitled "The Carpet Crawlers 1999," released on the Genesis compilation CD *Turn It On Again—The Hits*. Reuniting the 1971–75 line-up and featuring lead vocals shared by both Phil Collins and Peter Gabriel, the recording was completed in May 1999. The remake was slammed by the *New Musical Express*, which surprisingly made the retrospective concession that the original *Lamb* album was "quite splendid in parts actually" (Platts, 2001, p. 156).

The fact that "The Carpet Crawlers" (as opposed to, say, "Watcher of the Skies" or "I Know What I Like") was selected for re-recording as a "special bonus track" is indicative of the enduring affection that Genesis fans continue to have for *The Lamb Lies Down on Broadway*. Nonetheless, it is clear that *The Lamb* was a source of tension within the band, nearly breaking it up, and so most numbers from the album—with the exception of the title track and "In The Cage"— were quickly dropped from set lists after Gabriel's departure. For Gabriel's part, he kept the title track and "Back in N.Y.C." in his live performances, but after the change of musical direction that occurred with his third solo album (informally called "Melt" because of the "melting face" cover)—including its pioneering use of the Fairlight Computer Musical Instrument (one of the first keyboards to employ digital sampling) and the introduction of world-music elements (the African chorus in "Biko")—he too seemed to leave *The Lamb* behind.

This does not mean that *The Lamb* was altogether dead, however. Writing in December 1979, Armando Gallo revealed that during the next year Peter Gabriel would be "totally absorbed by the film production of *The Lamb Lies Down on Broadway*" (Gallo, 1980, p. 156). The news appeared to be a surprise to many fans, yet not unexpected given Gabriel's previous interest in film-making. Reportedly the director for the project was to be the Mexican filmmaker Alejandro Jodorowsky, best known for the film *El Topo* (The Mole), a surreal Zen Western allegory that was a midnight movie cult favorite in the early 1970s.

---

[1]   The performance was preserved on the bootleg recording *The Lamb Woke Up Again* (Stonehenge STCD 2008/09, 1990).

Jodorowsky certainly seems to share Gabriel's singularity of vision when it comes to art. In the same way that Gabriel conceived, wrote the story and most of the lyrics to, and played the central character in *The Lamb*, so Jodorowsky not only directed, wrote, and starred in *El Topo*, but he also wrote the musical score. Jodorowsky plays the gunfighter El Topo ("The Mole") who with his young son Brontis (played by the director's real-life son of the same name) encounters a desert village whose inhabitants have been massacred. The bandits responsible have holed up at a nearby Franciscan mission, torturing and mocking the monks. El Topo finds and kills the bandits, rescuing a woman, Mara, whom they had taken captive; she leads him on a mission to find and defeat the "four master gunmen of the desert" in order to prove his love. Leaving his son with the monks, El Topo and Mara complete their mission, accompanied by a mysterious woman in black who has joined them. The woman in black shoots El Topo in the desert, leaving wounds in his hands, feet and side (reminiscent of the wounds of Christ) and rides off with Mara. El Topo awakens years later to find that he has been cared for by a clan of deformed people in a remote cavern deep within a mountain. He learns that they were imprisoned there years ago by the residents of a nearby town; the town is run by a cruel sheriff and home to a bizarre religious cult. El Topo's son, now an adult, is a monk in the town. El Topo promises to dig a tunnel through which they can escape; he finances this project by performing as a street entertainer in the town with a dwarf woman from the cave colony. Upon completion of the tunnel, the cave dwellers escape into the town before El Topo can stop them; they are quickly massacred by the townspeople. El Topo rides into town after them and exacts a bloody revenge on the town's inhabitants before immolating himself, an action reminiscent of the Buddhist monks who protested the Vietnam War. Although the film's combination of the styles of Sergio Leone, Luis Buñuel and Sam Peckinpah hasn't dated well—and its impact over the years has also been blunted by a decades-long feud between Jodorowsky and producer Allen Klein that hamstrung its availability until 2007—in its day *El Topo* enjoyed a countercultural cachet on the order of Tolkien's *Lord of the Rings* books, *2001: A Space Odyssey*, and the Don Juan books of Carlos Castaneda. The success of *El Topo* led to a contract with Apple Films' Allen Klein, who financed Jodorowsky's even more ambitious and bizarre follow-up *The Holy Mountain*, released in 1973.

When Gabriel saw *El Topo* it gave him the idea that *The Lamb* could be adapted into a screenplay; "I knew that [Jodorowsky] was the right man to film *The Lamb*" (Gallo, 1980, p. 157). (Interestingly, the "Colony of Slippermen" has parallels with the cave colony in which El Topo awakens, and *The Holy Mountain* contains a scene of castration, with the sex organ placed in a container, much like Rael's castration at the office of Doktor Dyper.) Gabriel sought out and contacted Jodorowsky in Paris in early 1979 (Bright, 1988, p. 124), later telling Gallo that the director "liked *The Lamb* story very much, and we got on very well … . He cleaned up the storyline to make it more viable for a movie, and unfortunately some parts had to go, but the story is still very much the same" (Gallo, 1980, p. 157).

They worked on the project together, developing the script, for about four to six weeks during the summer of 1979 (Bright, 1988, p. 124).

Some of the special effects technicians who had worked on *Star Wars* and *Alien* reportedly showed an interest in the project (Gallo, 1980, p. 157); Gabriel even told Gallo that plans had been made for Gabriel to screen-test for the role of Rael in the spring of 1980, with Gabriel auditioning for the part of Rael. "He wants me to lose some weight and go to dance classes," Gabriel told Gallo, "so I started to jog the two miles to Solsbury Hill every morning, and go to dance classes a couple of times a week" (Gallo, 1980, p. 157). Ultimately, however, it appears that Jodorowsky convinced Gabriel not to play Rael but stay on as co-writer for the project, a decision the director later regretted: "At the time I only knew his songs, I had never seen him on stage. I said he should not play Rael, but now I would say yes because I know how he performs" (Bright, 1988, p. 124). For his part, Gabriel enthused that Jodorowsky was "an incredible character" who "has been a breath of fresh air in helping me re-evaluate my own career .... He's the master and I am the apprentice" (Bright, 1988, p. 124). Gabriel later summed up his time developing the screenplay with Jodorowsky as "great ... a very exciting time" (Bright, 1988, p. 124).

Gabriel had hoped that filming could begin in the summer of 1981 (Bright, 1988, p. 125). Unfortunately, the film was never made. Over the years, conflicting accounts have been given as to the reasons for abandoning the project. He told his biographer Spencer Bright, "I had an original story, it wasn't very long, about twelve pages or something. Alejandro then did his own version of that. I don't think my thing was very strong in the first place, I certainly didn't like it, where it had gone, so I sort of killed it off" (1988, p. 124). A couple of years before, however, he related a different story to Armando Gallo: "Charisma Films, with whom we were dealing, were unable to raise the necessary finance. I was very disappointed at the time but it could have been complicated in that some of Genesis were reluctant to have it resurrected" (Gallo, 1986, p. 13). Even if Bright's account differs from Gallo's, Bright does expand upon the financing details: Gabriel had been dropped by Atlantic Records (the US distributor for his recordings, which were issued by Charisma in the UK) in 1980, because having heard the advance tapes for his third release they found it too commercially risky. (The third album was eventually released by Mercury, giving Gabriel the distinction of having each of his first three solo albums released on a different label in the US—Atco, Atlantic, and Mercury. His fourth release, *Security*, was released on still another label—Geffen Records. This kind of track record hardly inspired confidence from American investors.) As a result, Charisma Films had difficulty finding American backers to commit to the film project. Gabriel kept faith in the project for several years, but the project withered because of his former bandmates' reluctance to involve themselves in the soundtrack.

Genesis's resistance to getting involved in a re-recording of *The Lamb* indicates the long-term psychic wounds that had yet to heal over the project. These wounds were certainly exacerbated by Gabriel's possessive nature toward the story. Since Gabriel had been responsible for the story and nearly all of the lyrics, he had copyrighted the story without consulting the rest of the band. That caused another rift because the group had always operated on "democratic" creative principles. Genesis, however, still collectively "owned" the songwriting credits to the music; consequently, Gabriel had to ask his former bandmates to re-record the soundtrack for the film (Bright, 1988, p. 123). When they turned down the opportunity, Gabriel considered re-creating the musical soundtrack himself: "I think I could have legally recorded my own version … . But that would have been a somewhat dumb thing to do" (Bright, 1988, p. 123).

The Lamb was not Gabriel's last film-related project. He also created a story, during his self-imposed "sabbatical" from the music industry in 1975–76, involving a "mercurial stranger" named Mozo. "He was partly based on Moses, but he was a fictional character who came from nowhere, disrupting people's lives and causing changes and then disappearing" (Bright, 1988, p. 126).[2] In retrospect, even if none of these projects had secured funding, they nonetheless provided Gabriel with important experience in creating music for film that would ultimately reach fruition in the 1980s and beyond with his acclaimed soundtracks for *Birdy* (1984), *The Last Temptation of Christ* (1988), and *Rabbit Proof Fence* (2002), among others.

Gabriel's desire to prepare a movie version of *The Lamb* could be interpreted as an attempt to redress an earlier oversight. Given that *The Lamb* was Genesis's most theatrically ambitious tour, it is unfortunate that no one in the band's entourage made arrangements to have a performance properly filmed. The lack of visual documentation is especially curious given that earlier concerts in promotion of *Foxtrot* and *Selling England by the Pound* were professionally filmed, either by the BBC or an analogous television network elsewhere in Europe.[3] It may be that Gabriel was too consumed with the necessary theatrical logistics at each venue— ensuring completely black stage sets and so forth—whereas his band mates, lacking his enthusiasm, were merely endeavoring to get through another performance on the itinerary. One tantalizing snippet of professionally filmed footage with sound—an excerpt from "In the Cage"— was inadvertently preserved as part of a German television feature about American promoter Bill Graham. Other than that,

---

[2]   According to Bright, "Mozo was inspired was inspired by *Aurora Consurgens*, a medieval alchemical treatise based on The Song of Solomon. It was brought to light by Carl Jung, who thought it the work of St. Thomas Aquinas. The text is full of alchemical and religious symbolism and apocalyptic imagery" (Bright, 1988, p. 126). For more information on Mozo, see Bright, 1988, pp. 126–128.

[3]   Among the videos in circulation are performances for the Belgian "Pop Shop" TV show on March 20, 1972; a Parisian show at the Club Bataclan on January 10, 1973; a full-length concert filmed at the Shepperton Studios in Borehamwood, UK on October 30, 1973; a performance of "Watcher of the Skies" and "The Musical Box" for the American NBC network *Midnight Special* program on December 20, 1973; and the French ORTF TV studios *Melody Programme* on December 10, 1974. Many of these clips can now be seen on video hosting sites such as YouTube.com.

what has survived—aside from a good deal of still photos—has been fragmentary silent 35mm footage filmed surreptitiously by fans from the audience in Chicago and Grand Rapids (US), Hamburg (Germany), and Liverpool (UK). These scraps of footage have something of a home-movie quality about them, and they serve as a reminder of the important function that bootleggers—whatever their financial motivations—serve in preserving rock history.

The music industry conveniently and inaccurately considers bootlegs synonymous with pirate recordings. A pirate recording is a counterfeit of a commercially available product, usually much cheaper than the real thing. The packaging of a pirate recording is usually substandard, frequently employing low-resolution scans of the original cover art. Pirate DVDs are also common, especially of films not yet released for the home video market. Pirate CDs and DVDs are a particularly severe problem in Southeast Asia and China. Bootleg recordings, on the other hand, are generally defined as recordings that have not been commercially released. Sometimes these are recordings of concert performances, taped by a fan from the audience or occasionally directly from the soundboard. Sometimes bootlegs are radio broadcasts. Some bootlegs are also demo recordings or rough mixes of songs that eventually saw release in a more polished form. This last category of bootlegs is especially important, because such recordings—not intended for public perusal—often reveal fascinating details about a song's creation, in the same way that Beethoven's sketchbooks contain valuable forensic information for musicologists.[4] It is generally accepted that the first rock bootleg was Bob Dylan's *Great White Wonder*, consisting of some of the "basement tapes" Dylan made with The Band in 1966–67 and surfacing in underground record stores around 1969. The album's name came from the fact that it was packaged in a plain white sleeve.

Occasionally, the widespread availability of certain bootlegs leads to their legitimate commercial release—Dylan's *The Basement Tapes*, for example, released by Columbia in 1975, may never have seen release were it not for *The Great White Wonder*. A number of the recordings featured in the Beatles' *Anthology* recordings, also, had been widely available in bootleg form, most notably in the *Ultra Rare Trax* series. The *Anthology* recordings, however, are typical of many "official bootleg" recordings in that they were doctored after the fact; certain tracks are often the composite of several takes. Bootleg recordings, by contrast, are often as unaltered as possible; later bootlegs are even "pitch corrected" to undo the effect of multiple tape dubs on improperly calibrated tape recorders. Thus,

---

[4] For example, the earliest demo recordings of the Beatles' "Strawberry Fields Forever"— recorded by John Lennon in a hotel room in Santa Isabella, Spain in 1966— reveal that the second verse of the song was the first part completed, and that the third line ("that is you can't, you know, tune in but it's alright") was the first line of lyric conceived. The hotel recordings can be heard on a Beatles bootleg entitled *It's Not Too Bad* (Pegboy 1008, 1997).

some bootleg recordings provide a documentation of the recording process that is as pure as possible without having direct access to the original master tapes.

The rapid rise of the Internet in the 1990s led to a new era in bootlegging. Copies of bootleg recordings could now be traded on file-sharing forums and blogs. This has led to a greater distribution of bootlegs, many of which have been cleaned up by digital technology so that certain recordings now sound much better than their vinyl counterparts of 30 years ago. In addition, digitized copies of videos are also bootlegged, providing a unique glimpse into a band's history. In the case of Genesis, no complete-concert video footage from the Gabriel era has as of this writing (2007) been released by the band,[5] yet videos of full performances from the *Foxtrot* and *Selling England by the Pound* tours are freely, if illegally, circulated on the Internet, facilitated by such file-hosting services as Rapidshare.com. In 1993, the six-CD collection *In the Beginning* (Extremely Rare EXR 005, 006, 013, 014, 018, 022) was released, a treasure trove of demos and outtakes, including demos and rough mixes from the *Selling England* and *Lamb* sessions, that were apparently at some point stolen from archives at Island Studios (McMahan, 1998, p. 87). Another bootleg of *Lamb* demos, *The Demo Mix Down on Broadway* (Highland 199/200, 1998), followed. Comparing the sessions of the *Selling England* and *Lamb* albums is instructive; most of the *Lamb* demos seem to focus on nuances of mixing rather than experimenting with arrangements or rehearsing sections, whereas the sessions for *Selling England* were much more sectionalized (for example, "The Battle of Epping Forest" was arduously pieced together over some 28 takes). Such recordings and videos offer a glimpse into a band's work that is unmediated by after-the-fact sanitizing, and as such they are historically important and valuable for fans and scholars alike. With few exceptions (such as Frank Zappa's "Beat the Boots" series), it would seem that some artists cannot resist the opportunity to give such recordings some post-production polish (the Beatles' *Anthology* series comes to mind).

The continuing allure of *The Lamb*—and the fact that, aside from the rather poorly recorded *Genesis Live* (1973), there were no legitimately available live recordings of Gabriel-era Genesis—led to the release of *Genesis Archive 1967–75* in 1998. This four-disc boxed set—the first of two—had been in the planning stages since 1994; Virgin Records had initially planned for a November 1995 release, but it was delayed because of licensing issues (Platts, 2001, p. 154). Significantly, the historical survey covered by the boxed set was presented in reverse chronological order, so that the first two discs were given over to the complete live performance of *The Lamb* from the Shrine Auditorium in Los Angeles, then working backward to end rather anticlimactically with a couple of home-recorded demos from the Charterhouse years. The intent of the boxed set was, at least in part, to counteract

---

[5]   Excerpts of video footage may be seen on the video *Genesis: A History* (Virgin, 1992, originally broadcast by the BBC in 1990), as well as *Inside Genesis: A Critical Review, Volume 2 – The Gabriel Years, 1970–1975* (Classic Rock Legends, 2005).

the effect of bootlegs on Genesis's profits; included in the set was most of a widely bootlegged 1973 performance from London's Rainbow Theatre.

Because *The Lamb* was evidently, from the beginning, the commercial focal point of the boxed set, the original concert recording was subjected to a number of post-production "enhancements." For example, "Gabriel was often out of breath from running around the stage, or had to sing from inside a mask" (Platts, 2001, p. 155), and these theatrical elements often compromised the original vocals, a fact readily verifiable from bootleg recordings of *Lamb* performances. As a remedy, Gabriel re-recorded all of *The Lamb* vocals at his Real World Studio in Bath in 1995; these were then inserted where necessary in place of the original vocals (Platts, 2001, p. 155). Steve Hackett also re-recorded several guitar solos, including those on "The Lamia" and "Anyway," because he felt his hand injury still hadn't completely healed by the time of the Shrine performance. The last track, "*It*," was completely re-recorded, as the original tape machine had apparently run out during the last song of the performance; a new version was assembled from a remix of the studio version backing track and a newly recorded vocal by Gabriel (Platts, 2001, p. 155). The official reason provided for the wholesale substitution of "*It*" has never been satisfactory to Genesis bootleg collectors; a recording of the Shrine Auditorium "*It*" does exist in bootleg form (for example, it is included in the *Rare Tapes* bootleg set [MIL Productions 616, 1999]), and the timbre of the aged Gabriel voice is noticeably different from that of the younger one, making the re-recorded passages easy to pick out.

Track-by-track comparison of the original Shrine Auditorium tapes and the *Genesis Archive 1967–75* version reveals that in fact most of Gabriel's vocals are re-recorded. Occasionally this was because of balance problems; for example, on the Shrine tapes, the vocals are rather persistently buried in the mix during "Fly on a Windshield" and "Cuckoo Cocoon," as well as sporadically throughout the first half of the show (the balance does improve as the show progresses, further illustrating how much of a "work in progress" live sound production was even in the mid-1970s). At other times, the mix is faulty as a consequence of Gabriel's very much in-the-moment characterization of Rael, which caused him to weave off- and on-mike, bringing his voice in and out of the sound field. An example of this can be heard on the Shrine tapes during the first verse of the opening title track, as well as the first two verses of "Back in N.Y.C." The only track on the boxed-set release that appears to leave Gabriel's vocals in their original state without any substitutions is "The Chamber of 32 Doors," a wise choice as it is one of Gabriel's most affecting performances (Hackett's guitar solo was re-recorded, however—an audible splice can be heard at the end of the climactic high note at [0:30]).

More dishonestly, however, the re-packaging of the Shrine performance enabled various band members to "correct" mistakes made in live performance after the fact. For example, in the Shrine performance, Hackett momentarily flubbed a difficult sequence of chords in the opening classical guitar solo on "Hairless Heart." The offending passage has been corrected on the *Genesis Archive 1967–75* version, and in fact the entire classical guitar solo was re-done, with some beautiful (though acoustically inaccurate) reverberation added. Just before Banks's lengthy synthesizer solo on "In the Cage," Rutherford botched the first of his two angular bass riffs that introduce the solo; that passage has also been corrected. A brief sloppy transition of chords in Banks's arpeggio filigree supporting the introduction to "The Carpet Crawlers" has similarly been repaired. Finally, a few unwelcome moments of microphone feedback have either been covered considerably in the mix or eliminated altogether.

No one can blame the members of Genesis for wanting to present themselves at their very best to a paying consumer. Something is lost, however, when the final product is so polished—the very immediacy and rawness, ironically, that Gabriel was aiming for in his construction of Rael and his story. There is no question that several of the songs on *The Lamb Lies Down on Broadway* are among the most vocally difficult songs that Gabriel has ever recorded. "In the Cage" and "Back in N.Y.C.," for example, are real tests of endurance and registral extremes. Listening to the Shrine tapes, it is evident that on these songs Gabriel is pushing his considerable vocal strengths to their limits; what results, in the case of "In the Cage," is a very believable picture of panic, while the characterization in "Back in N.Y.C."—in particular the "porcupine / rape" sections—amounts to a sarcastic, deranged cackle. Gabriel's re-recordings of these vocals are technically "better," but they lose something in the immediacy of the characterizations. Similarly, Gabriel is clearly winded at the end of "The Colony of Slippermen," which is the point in the narrative where Rael collapses in exhaustion from chasing the Raven and helplessly watches the tube containing his sexual organs floating away in the ravine. Hearing Gabriel panting so hard that he can barely force the notes out at the end, one senses that he really *has* been chasing the Raven, running around on the stage. Listening to the re-recorded version, there is no evidence of any physical discomfort.

Finally, from a historical point of view some other details are omitted from the *Genesis Archive 1967–75* version, such as the story Gabriel tells the audience between "Anyway" and "Here Comes The Supernatural Anaesthetist." That missing story is as follows:

Ladies and Gentlemen, Mr. Phil Collins on my immediate left.

Those of you familiar with the problems of drummers—the afflictions—will know the only way the lumps and bumps can be correctly removed, is the operation, the severing of the sexual organs. This is performed in this Colony of Slippermen—mark the word, Slippermen—by notorious Doktor Dyper, reformed sniper, who for a very small fee will guarantee to remove your very own windscreen wiper.

[cheers from audience]

And the windscreen wipers of Rael and his brother John are neatly deposited into small yellow plastic—fully sterilised, don't worry—tubes. And all of a sudden a big black bird comes out of the air, grabs Rael's little yellow plastic tube, flies all the way down the narrow tunnel, drops it into a large area of gushing water called "Ravine," where Rael sees his drowning brother John.

Given that Gabriel's stories were one of the distinctive features of the vintage era of Genesis, fondly remembered by fans, it is curious that this story was omitted altogether. Another casualty of the editing process was a group improvisation of about 1:15 in length, in E minor, that preceded "The Lamia," perhaps because of what appears to be a firecracker explosion during it. Still, it presents another rare glimpse at the kind of group improvisation the band briefly explored during the *Lamb* period, and its omission on the *Genesis Archive 1967–75* version is regrettable.

About half of the 102 shows on the *Lamb* tour were recorded, a greater proportion than that of previous tours. Of course, given that the set list on this tour was virtually unchanged from show to show, with the exception of encores, comparing bootlegs does not reveal as much musical variety. Gabriel's stories of Rael, however, do occasionally change from performance to performance, and of course recording circumstances result in a wide range of recording quality. One of the most widely bootlegged shows, the April 15, 1975 show at the Empire Pool, Wembley (UK), was originally taped for radio broadcast. Excerpts from the show were condensed into a one-hour radio format, and further excisions were made on 1970s bootleg albums to fit the time constraints of vinyl. Thus, that one show exists under a number of titles (including *Lamb Stew*, *The Light Goes Down on Empire*, and *Awed Man Out*) and with a variety of set lists, most of which do not contain the complete show. Other recordings exist which contain complete performances, such as those of the Los Angeles and Providence (US), and Manchester and Birmingham (UK) shows.

Reflecting on the importance of *The Lamb* soon before Genesis's triumphant performance at the Empire Pool, Wembley, Gabriel told *Melody Maker*: "You can say the characters are far-fetched, the music over ornate, that we're riding on my costumed success. There, I've done it for you. However, in maybe ten years a group will emerge to take what we do a lot further. I look upon us as an early, clumsy prototype" (Bell, 1975, p. 14). Certainly Gabriel's anticipations to critical objections indicate that he was sensitive to the changes in critical opinion about progressive rock that were already stirring in Britain and beyond in 1975. More interesting, however, is his prediction that "in maybe ten years a group will emerge to take what we do a lot further." As the 1970s continued, rock's penchant for theatrical spectacle blossomed. Pink Floyd's 1980 staged performances of *The Wall*—with crashing airplanes, monstrous floating marionettes designed by British artist Gerald Scarfe, and the construction of an enormous wall made up of approximately 420 fireproof cardboard bricks—was so elaborate that it could only be performed at four venues (for multiple nights at each location) around the world. Genesis's staging of *The Lamb* may certainly be seen as "an early, clumsy prototype" of such endeavors. The multi-faceted slide projections behind the band are echoed in later, much larger concert spectacles such as U2's *Zooropa* tour. Of course, the available sound and lighting technology developed at a rapid pace along with the needs of these bands; Genesis in 1975 simply did not have at their disposal, either financially or technologically, what Pink Floyd had in 1980 or U2 in 1994. But the elaborate costumes and theatrics Gabriel employed, along with the unusual move of performing an entire dramatic production as the concert's set list (setting aside other, older material for only the encores), display a concern with rock theatre as a total spectacle—seen also in contemporary tours by artists such as David Bowie, Alice Cooper, and Funkadelic—that was not a significant factor in concert performances of just two or three years before. *The Lamb* was a product of its time, but it also pointed toward things to come.

Gabriel's prediction that other bands may emerge to "take what we do a lot further" also points, musically, to the emergence of "neo-progressive" rock in the 1980s and 1990s, and to the fanatic exactitude of progressive-rock tribute bands. The sound of the Genesis era, and especially *The Lamb*, was the touchpoint for neo-progressive rock, the most commercially successful example being Marillion.[6] At the same time, over the years there have been at least 25 Genesis tribute bands ("Overnight Job: Tribute Bands," n.d.); while some "cover" the more commercial Phil Collins era, most seem to specialize in the material between *Trespass* and *The Lamb*—in short, the "vintage" Gabriel years.

For such bands, *The Lamb* remains a touchstone of musical and theatrical prowess. Partly, this is due to the album's status as Gabriel's "swan song" with the group, after which—progressive rock wisdom has it—the band took a sharp artistic nosedive by pursuing commercial success (this is not entirely true, of course, as *A Trick of the Tail* and *Wind and Wuthering* both have much to recommend them). *The Lamb* is also revered because of its mystique as a tour that was reportedly Genesis's most visually ambitious, yet suffered from the least visual documentation; since virtually every performance had technical difficulties of some sort, the band never felt satisfied enough with the shows to have them professionally filmed. Thus, compared to re-creating concerts of the *Selling England By The Pound* era, for example, re-enacting *The Lamb* amounts to a kind of musical archaeology. For such bands as England's ReGenesis and Canada's The Musical Box, "covering" Genesis involves more than mastering the music's complexities; it also requires a full re-enactment of the original concert experience and every attendant nuance therein, from lighting and costumes to vintage (often now-rare and expensive) musical instruments matching the exact models used by the original musicians (a development that has interesting parallels with the "original instruments"

---

6   For example, Marillion's *Misplaced Childhood* (1985)—the group's highest-charting (number 47) album in the US as well as a number 1 hit in the UK—contains a number of Genesis timbral/stylistic references besides the oft-cited resemblance of the group's original vocalist Fish to Peter Gabriel. In the opening section "Pseudo Silk Kimono" and elsewhere, Steve Rothery's guitar uncannily resembles the sighing sound that Steve Hackett imparted to his solos on "The Carpet Crawlers" and "Firth of Fifth." The introduction to "Bitter Suite" recalls the modal drone-based improvisations of "Silent Sorrow in Empty Boats" and the opening to "The Colony of Slippermen." The most striking resemblance to *The Lamb*, however, is found in the song "Lords of the Backstage," which in its deep pedal tones, insistent keyboard arpeggios, and asymmetrical meter particularly recalls "Back in N.Y.C."

movement in the performance of Baroque music). Why would any band go to such lengths to re-create every nuance of a musical performance that took place more than 30 years ago? The members of ReGenesis offer some reasons:

Because we like Genesis
Because we're mad
Because the music is a challenge to any musician, both technically and in terms of
    getting all the right sounds
Because Genesis don't play it anymore …
Because a lot of people keep turning up to our gigs!

(Sollow, 2001)

Both ReGenesis and The Musical Box have, in fact, made their mark as top-notch Genesis tribute bands by tackling *The Lamb*. At the 2001 "G2" Genesis fan convention in Guildford, UK, ReGenesis presented a staged performance of the full *Lamb*, recorded and released as *Lamb for Supper* (Mystic Records MYS CD 149, 2001). Unlike Giraffe's performance at the 1994 ProgFest, ReGenesis performed the entire album from beginning to end. However, they took some liberties with the staging, updating certain slides and other visuals to give the performance a contemporary flavor, and thus their "tribute" stops short of historical re-enactment. Instead, such a performance might be likened to a revival of a classic Broadway show, retaining the musical content but updating the dramatic elements.

The Musical Box ("The Musical Box: The Lamb Lies Down on Broadway", n.d.), on the other hand, aims for historically exact detail. Pictures on the group's web site, showing scenes from a Musical Box *Lamb* performance alongside shots from the Genesis tour, show how carefully the staging, costumes, and lighting parallel the original concert spectacle. In re-creating these details, the band are assisted by their artistic director, "resident Genesis historian" Serge Morissette. Profiling the group for a Canadian Broadcasting Corporation feature, Guy Leshinski commented:

A Musical Box show is no mere tribute; it is a revival. The band evokes the experience of a Genesis concert from the misty past. The lighting, the sets, even the musicians' gestures are choreographed from painstaking study of archival footage. Though its lineup has varied through the years, the Musical Box has guarded its fidelity with care. (Leshinski, 2005)

The personnel has changed over the years since the band's inception in 1993 but the current line-up as of 2007 consists of vocalist Denis Gagné (who, like Gabriel, plays flute, oboe, and bass drum), guitarist François Gagnon, bassist/ guitarist Sébastien Lamothe, keyboard player David Myers, and percussionist Martin Levac.

The Musical Box has been active re-enacting Genesis since November 1993, when the band performed *Selling England By The Pound* at the Montreal Spectrum to commemorate the twentieth anniversary of that album's release (Leshinski, 2005). The band premiered their fully staged re-creation of *The Lamb* on October 11, 2000, again at the Montreal Spectrum. It was this feat that earned the band international fame; not only did the show have to be re-created from a painstaking assemblage of still photographs, bootleg audio recordings and silent film footage, but they even hired the slide operator from Genesis's original tour to assemble the 1,120 slides (Leshinski, 2005). Gagné worked about eight hours a day for two months to recreate Gabriel's "Slipperman" costume in exact detail, and Lamothe's bass was custom built according to specifications provided by Mike Rutherford (Leshinski, 2005). The Musical Box was the only band to have been granted a license by Gabriel and Genesis to re-create the show ("The Musical Box: The Lamb Lies Down on Broadway"); the band were also allowed to listen to the master multi-track tapes of *The Lamb* in Genesis's Surrey studios, noting subtle instrumental details that were barely audible in the final mix (Leshinski, 2005). The Musical Box undertook a successful world tour of *The Lamb* that, while not as extensive as the original, lasted almost as long; it is estimated that the band have played for over 250,000 people around the world, with 110 shows in 2004 alone (Leshinski, 2005). After the band's license to perform *The Lamb* expired in 2006, they went on to mount similar recreations of the *Foxtrot* and *Selling England By The Pound* tours in 2006 and 2007, with similar painstaking historical detail and again to great success. Members of Genesis have seen Musical Box shows (and, in the case of Steve Hackett and Phil Collins, joined the band onstage for live performances) and commented that, from a technical perspective, they were often better than the originals, since—in the case of *The Lamb*, at least—performances were almost never without some technical difficulties. Meanwhile, Genesis fans who were too young or not fortunate enough to have seen Genesis in its prime have been known to travel halfway around the world to see a Musical Box show, and hopes remain high that the group will one day tour *The Lamb* again.

For the enduring appeal that *The Lamb Lies Down on Broadway* has enjoyed, it is somewhat surprising that Tony Banks has said, "I don't think [the album] advanced our career in America at all. It was OK, but I don't think we won people over particularly." He continues:

> The album wasn't a great success, we have to be honest about this, it did alright and although some of the crowds were good, I don't remember it being as nearly as well received as the previous tour, because it didn't have as many good live songs. Some of the songs like "In The Cage" worked well live, but just kind of faded away, so you got most of your applause for "It" which wasn't the best of live songs. (Russell, 2004, p. 208)

Certainly there is an element of truth to this statement, in that some shows were indeed cancelled because of a lack of ticket sales toward the end of the European leg of the tour. But Banks's general jaundice toward *The Lamb* is also certainly colored by the feelings of being betrayed by Peter, who grew up with him in Charterhouse and who was in effect living a lie as Genesis's front man for virtually the entire *Lamb* tour. Every performance, Banks knew, put them one show closer to the point when Gabriel would leave them. That must have been a terrible burden to bear, playing the same set in the same order night after night.

If Banks is right, however, that *The Lamb* simply wasn't that successful, its stature has—unlike many progressive rock albums—actually grown over the years; Mike Rutherford acknowledges, "I do think that we have been colored very much by people's reaction to *The Lamb*" (Gallo, 1980, p. 68). Gabriel's determination to steer the band away from fantasy and myth subjects and toward a contemporary, realistic protagonist has actually helped the album age reasonably well. As Mike Rutherford put it: "For once we were writing about subject matter which was neither airy-fairy, nor romantic. We finally managed to get away from writing about unearthly things which I think helped the album" (Fielder, 1984, p. 90).

At the same time, critics of progressive rock do cite *The Lamb* as evidence of the genre's obscurantism. Rutherford says, "I think it's a great album, and I stand by it very much. There are some great bits in there, but a lot of people got put off it because they just didn't get around to listening to the whole thing. That's what a lot of the criticism is down to" (Gallo, 1980, p. 68). Responding to the critique that *The Lamb* is too obscure, Gabriel says "I think probably that is right, but we were pushed from every side. There was a release date to expect, and a tour to start … . I can look objectively perhaps about some points in it that I was defensive about beforehand, but … I'm still proud of what I did, and what they did" (Gallo, 1980, p. 155).

In his otherwise excellent book *I'll Take You There: Pop Music and the Urge for Transcendence* (2005), Bill Friskics-Warren discusses the notion of spiritual transformation in the work of a number of performers, whom he classifies by spiritual archetypes—mystics (Van Morrison, Al Green, Moby, etc.), Dystopian "naysayers" (Nine Inch Nails, the Sex Pistols, etc.), and prophets (Curtis Mayfield, U2, Public Enemy, etc.)—yet in so doing he curiously makes no mention of progressive rock. Such a blanket omission may be indicative of the general indifference given the genre by modern rock historians, but it is also inexcusable; in its visionary subject matter, Romantic aesthetics and technological adventurism, progressive rock is a genre that is manifestly "about" transcendence. Macan (2006) even cites transcendence as one of the foundational principles of progressive rock ideology, along with idealism, authenticity, "the artist as prophet figure," and the modernist doctrine of progress (p. xxxviii). Regarding transcendence, Macan writes that the idea is "fairly modern (think Schiller, Schopenhauer, E. T. A. Hoffman, Nietzsche) in its specifics," but more generally it can be traced "back to neo-Platonism and the belief that an ultimate Good, Beauty, and Truth exists, and is imperfectly expressed in great art, the contemplation of which can lead one ever closer to the ultimate good, that is, God" (2006, p. xxxix). One can find many transcendent or sublime moments in *The Lamb*: The moment when the "wall" engulfs Rael in "Fly on a Windshield," the alternating delicacy and majesty of "Hairless Heart," Hackett's guitar work on "The Carpet Crawlers," Gabriel's impassioned performance in "The Chamber of 32 Doors," Tony Banks's otherworldly aquatic ripplings and

Mellotron surges that grace "The Lamia," and the group-created sense of real-time chaos and claustrophobia in "The Waiting Room." In the frustratingly finite world of the 1970s, such glimpses of the sublime offered welcome relief and escape, reminding us that it was still possible to transcend the mundane through the power of the imagination.

Paul Stump (1997) singles out the music of Genesis as representing something of an apex in progressive rock's mastery of studio resources, noting that "the methodical organization of sound which characterized Progressive can also lead to immense and indelible musical *jouissance*, due to the structural ambition that mastery of the recording studio can bestow upon recording artists." He continues:

> The intervallic developments and crashing climaxes of Genesis's "Firth of Fifth," for example, use a harmonic language not that much more advanced than most mainstream pop music. Yet for me it is as goose-pimply thrilling as any Gladys Knight or Jimi Hendrix performance, for the simple reason that the application of new structural techniques to the placing and deployment of emotional triggers in the music—diminished seventh chords, cycles of fifths, etc.—in a quasi-classical format, and the organization of the orchestral-style soundstage upon which these are subjected to timbral manipulation to enhance emotional effect, is a result of studio exactitude and perseverance as well as the adrenalizing jolt of creative ecstasy. Studio mastery did not begin and end with Progressive—but its centrality to the way Progressive used its own quirky language is unique in rock and pop history. (p. 352)

Careful listening to *The Lamb* reveals plentiful examples of such *jouissance*, or delight, in the arranging capabilities presented by the studio. For example, in no previous Genesis album does one find the variety of percussion that one finds on this album, including vibraphone (on "Fly on a Windshield" and "The Lamia" for example), xylophone (on "Anyway"— listen at [0:50–0:58], perhaps portraying the "pale horse" on which Death is supposed to ride), glockenspiel and finger cymbals ("Cuckoo Cocoon"), temple blocks (the introduction to "The Colony of Slippermen"), ratchet ("The Grand Parade of Lifeless Packaging"), and various whistles ("The Grand Parade of Lifeless Packaging"). In his inventive and colorful use of percussion on this album Collins approaches the multi-percussion variety of his progressive-rock peer Carl Palmer; however, it can also be pointed out that Collins's "extra" percussion cameos call far less attention to themselves than Palmer's do, and that whereas Palmer's use of orchestral percussion sometimes appears to be for the sake of variety alone, Collins is far more purposeful and subtle in his multi-percussion touches.[7]

---

[7]   A similar observation might be made in comparing the keyboard styles of Tony Banks with Keith Emerson or Rick Wakeman; in fact, the text for the *Lamb* tour program guide sardonically noted, "Banks wisely kept his keyboard playing melodic and lyrical instead of succumbing to the obvious desire to create a Third World War like so many of his peers and contemporaries" (McMahan, 1998, p. 398).

It is because of this combination of stylistic uniqueness, studio experimentation and sublime aesthetic experience that Stump points out progressive rock offers that Armando Gallo is able to assert: "In its concept and execution, *The Lamb Lies Down on Broadway* was a milestone not only in Genesis' career, but in the history of the recording industry" (1980, p. 68). Certainly, it was a time of rapid change and waning innocence in the music industry. As Robert Fripp (in the King Crimson *Great Deceiver* boxed-set booklet) and others have attested, bands were forced into extended periods of arduous touring to pay back studio-budget advances from the record labels; the labels also invariably controlled the royalties on those recordings, so the only real income a band could get was from touring and merchandising (such as T-shirts) associated with those tours. Furthermore, the phenomenal success of Peter Frampton's *Frampton Comes Alive!* and Fleetwood Mac's *Rumours*, both in 1976, led to massive changes in the way the industry promoted its artists; suddenly every major release was *expected* to sell in the quantities demonstrated by those two releases, and artists with a top-draw track record were given the lion's share of available promotion funds. This made it more difficult for less marketable artists to survive and for new artists to establish themselves. Progressive rock in particular was seen as a "rich man's rock," as the huge banks of keyboards used by Keith Emerson, Rick Wakeman, and so forth were beyond the reach of the average garage-band musician. All of these factors, combined with the economic stagnation in the UK, ultimately came together to spawn the rise of punk rock. Meanwhile, the music business had learned to "play it safe" under the dual pressures of economic slowdown and the desire for ever-higher profit margins.

Genesis themselves seemed to reflect on the music industry's shift toward privileging the bottom line over the artistic impulse in their song "Down and Out," which opened the 1978 *... And Then There Were Three* album. Like Pink Floyd's better known "Have a Cigar" (*Wish You Were Here*, 1975), the lyrics adopt the persona of a high-powered music executive, though musically the song is a distant cousin of "Back in N.Y.C." (albeit with a more complex asymmetrical meter). Given that both *... And Then There Were Three* and its successor, *Duke*, were decisive shifts away from the band's earlier high-progressive style and toward the brand of streamlined pop that they would adopt in the 1980s (on *Abacab*, *Genesis*, and *Invisible Touch*), the song can be read retroactively as a kind of early warning from the group to their core progressive audience. Thus, the pairing of *The Lamb* with *Invisible Touch* as polar opposites in Giraffe's introduction to the *Lamb* performance at 1994's ProgFest is telling. Gallo is correct in his assertion that *The Lamb Lies Down on Broadway* is a milestone in the music industry, but mainly because 1975 seems to have been the music industry's last year of countercultural idealism.

Appendix

"Once again the stage is set for you": *The Lamb* tour itinerary

Note: The information in this appendix has been culled from several sources—fan sites and tape trading lists and Genesis bootleg discographies on the web (most notably the Genesis Movement's "Gig Guide: The Lamb Lies Down on Broadway" (n.d.) and Paul Russell's excellent *Genesis: A Live Guide 1969 to 1975* (2004), which provides annotated reviews of every extant performance tape uncovered as of 2004. Russell's reviews, in fact, indicate that a great deal of audience-traded tapes exist beyond those indicated here; I have simply indicated those that have been 'professionally' packaged and traded with titles. Where there are discrepancies in details (regarding venue name, for example), I have followed Russell.

1974

Date	Venue	City	Country
29 Oct	City Hall	Newcastle	UK
	Note: Possibly fan club preview; cancelled due to Hackett's hand injury		
30 Oct	City Hall	Newcastle	UK
	Note: Cancelled due to Hackett's hand injury		
01 Nov	Palace Theatre	Manchester	UK
	Note: Cancelled due to Hackett's hand injury		
02 Nov	Palace Theatre	Manchester	UK
	Note: Cancelled due to Hackett's hand injury		
04 Nov	Empire Pool, Wembley	London	UK
	Note: Cancelled due to Hackett's hand injury		
06 Nov	Usher Hall	Edinburgh	Scotland
	Note: Cancelled due to Hackett's hand injury		
07 Nov	Usher Hall	Edinburgh	Scotland
	Note: Cancelled due to Hackett's hand injury		
08 Nov	Hippodrome	Bristol	UK
	Note: Cancelled due to Hackett's hand injury		
09 Nov	Hippodrome	Bristol	UK
	Note: Cancelled due to Hackett's hand injury		
11 Nov	Hippodrome	Birmingham	UK
	Note: Cancelled due to Hackett's hand injury		

Date	Venue	City	Country
12 Nov	Hippodrome	Birmingham	UK
	Note: Cancelled due to Hackett's hand injury		
20 Nov	Auditorium Theatre	Chicago, IL	US
	Note: First concert performance of *The Lamb*		
21 Nov	Auditorium Theatre	Chicago, IL	US
22 Nov	Indiana Convention Centre	Indianapolis, IN	US
	Note: Bootlegged as *Indianapolis 22/11/74; Indianapolis '74*		
23 Nov	Ambassador Theatre	St. Louis, MO	US
25 Nov	Allen Theatre	Cleveland, OH	US
	Note: Bootlegged as *Cleveland '75, Cleveland First Night*. Gabriel had made his decision to leave the band during the Cleveland stint; Russell's evaluation of the tape (2004, pp. 106–107) indicates that the band was not at their best on this particular night. Was this the night he had told them?		
26 Nov	Allen Theatre	Cleveland, OH	US
	Note: Bootlegged as *The Lamb in Cleveland*		
27 Nov	Veterans Memorial Coliseum	Columbus, OH	US
28 Nov	Masonic Temple	Detroit, MI	US
29 Nov	National Guard Armory	Fort Wayne, IN	US
30 Nov	Syria Mosque	Pittsburgh, PA	US
01 Dec	Lyric Theatre	Baltimore, MD	US
	Note: Bootlegged as *The Baltimore Show*		
02 Dec	Warner Theatre	Washington, DC	US
04 Dec	Mosque Theatre	Richmond, VA	US
05 Dec	Tower Theatre	Philadelphia, PA	US
06 Dec	Academy of Music	New York, NY	US
	Note: Bootlegged as *The Lamb Still Canned in N.Y.C.* (Eeklair GL002) and *The Lamb Lives in N.Y.C.*		
07 Dec	Academy of Music	New York, NY	US
	Note: Bootlegged as *The Lamb Lies on the Academy, Rael in N.Y.C.*		
08 Dec	Palace Theatre	Providence, RI	US
	Note: Bootlegged as *Rael Imperial Aerosol Kid, Rael Imperial* (Highland HL059/60#G7), *Providence, Rhode Island 8th Dec. 1974* (Hogweed Project HW 14), *Brother John is Number Nine* (Alternative Recording Company GNV018), *Palace Theatre R.I.*, and *Carpet Crawlers in the Palace Theatre*.		
09 Dec	Music Hall	Boston, MA	US
	Note: Bootlegged as *The Boston Lamb* (Digital Brothers Production) and *Boston Music Hall* (BURP 032).		
11 Dec	Palace Theatre	Albany, NY	US
12 Dec	Palace Theatre	Waterbury, CT	US

Date	Venue	City	Country
	Note: Bootlegged as *Palace Theatre Waterbury* (Burp II 03) and *Real Imperial*.		
13 Dec	Capitol Theatre	Passaic, NJ	US
14 Dec	Market Square Arena	Kansas City, MO	US
15 Dec	Forum	Montreal, Quebec	Canada
	Note: Bootlegged as *Move Over Casanova*.		
16 Dec	Maple Leaf Gardens	Toronto, ON	Canada
	Note: Bootlegged as *Toronto '74*.		
17 Dec	The Dome	Rochester, NY	US
18 Dec	Century Theatre	Buffalo, NY	US

1975

Date	Venue	City	Country
10 Jan	Convention Hall	W. Palm Beach, FL	US
	Note: Bootlegged as *Supper's Ready with a Little Lost Lamb* (Colosseum CD 97-C-25 A/B), *West Palm Beach, Florida 10th Jan. 1975* (Hogweed Project HW 05), *West Palm Beach '75* (BURP 009), *West Palm Beach '75* (SAB 06), *Digital West Palm Beach* (Digital Brothers Production), and *The Lamb Lives*; erroneously bootlegged as *The Lamb Descends on Waterbury*.		
11 Jan	Civic Centre	Lakeland, FL	US
	Note: Bootlegged as *From One Fan to All Others* (Stonehenge STBX 016/017/018), *The Lamb Lives Backstage* (Backstage BKCD 033/034), *Lakeland 11.1.75* (SAB 09); *The Lamb on the Rainbow, Lakeland '75*, erroneously bootlegged as *Rael Visits San Diego*.		
12 Jan	Municipal Auditorium	Atlanta, GA	US
15 Jan	Music Hall	New Orleans, LA	US
17 Jan	Houston Music Hall	Houston, TX	US
18 Jan	McFarland Auditorium	Dallas, TX	US
	Note: Cancelled		
19 Jan	Civic Centre Music Hall	Oklahoma City, OK	US
	Note: Erroneously bootlegged as *Live at the Music Hall Tulsa*.		
20 Jan	McKey Auditorium, University of Colorado at Boulder	Boulder, CO	US

Date	Venue	City	Country
	Note: In light of progressive rock's fan base rooted in the university and college circuit, noted by both Stump (1997) and Macan (1997, 2006), it is noteworthy that this performance was one of only two such venues on the *Lamb* tour, showing just how far from those roots progressive rock had gone since its late-1960s origins.		
22 Jan	Community Theatre	Berkeley, CA	US
23 Jan	Old Waldorf Astoria	San Francisco, CA	US
24 Jan	Shrine Auditorium	Los Angeles, CA	US
	Note: This show was professionally recorded and portions were filmed by a German television crew. It was, along with the April 15 Empire Pool performance, the most widely bootlegged of the *Lamb* tour. It has appeared in bootleg form as *Twilight Alehouse* (Flashback WorldProductions 10.80.0109), *As Through Emerald City* (Amazing Kornyfone TAKRL 1945, Amazing Kornyfone TAKRL 19413/183), *Shrine Auditorium Los Angeles 24 January 1975* (BURP 019/AV07), *Shrine 75, Live in Los Angeles* (TM Productions GEN750124TM), *Revelation Without a Cause* (Wizard WRMB 313), and in streaming audio form on the *Wolfgang's Shrine* web site. A version with considerable post-production (see Chapter 6) was released on the *Genesis Archive 1967–1975* box set. Video clips from the German Treffpunkt broadcast were bootlegged on *Treffpunkte* (MPEG), *Genesis Collection 1973 & 1975* (DVD, GMDVD 08), *Genesis Collection 1972–1975* (DVD, GMDVD 11), and *The Lamb Lies Down on Treffpunkt*.		
25 Jan	Fox Theatre	San Diego, CA	US
26 Jan	Community Theater	Berkeley, CA	US
	Note: Cancelled—but see January 22 entry!		
28 Jan	Civic Centre		Phoenix, AZ
29 Jan	Golden Hall Community Centre	San Diego, CA	US
01 Feb	Queen Elizabeth Theatre	Vancouver, BC	Canada
	Note: Cancelled.		
01 Feb	Kansas Memorial Hall	Kansas City, MO	US
02 Feb	Grand Valley State College	Grand Rapids, MI	US
	Note: This was the other collegiate date on the *Lamb* tour (see January 21, Boulder, CO entry). Silent home-movie audience footage from this show has been bootlegged as *Genesis Collection 1973 & 1975* (DVD GMDVD 08) and *The Lamb Lies Down on Grand Rapids* (DVD). There is also a bootleg audio recording, *Grand Rapids '75*.		
03 Feb	Memorial Coliseum	Fort Wayne, IN	US
04 Feb	Arie Crown Theatre, McCormick Place	Chicago, IL	US

Date	Venue	City	Country
	Note: To conclude the US leg of the tour, Genesis returned to Chicago, where they had debuted *The Lamb*, for a return performance—this time at the somewhat larger Arie Crown Theater. By now, apparently, word had gotten out that this was a show worth filming; parts of the performance were filmed by an audience member with a silent home-movie camera and since bootlegged as *The Lamb Lies Down on Chicago* (DVD). The band took a two-week hiatus before resuming performances in Europe.		
19 Feb	Ekeberghallen	Oslo	Norway
21 Feb	Falkoner Theatrit	Copenhagen	Denmark
22 Feb	Niedersachsenhalle	Hannover	Germany
23 Feb	Eissporthalle	Berlin	Germany
	Note: Portions of this performance were filmed with a silent home-movie camera and bootlegged as *Berlin '75* (DVD, Raelmatrix Productions). Bootlegged as *The Lamb Lies Down on Berlin* and as *Eissporthalle, Berlin, 23.2.75*.		
24 Feb	Theater Carré	Amsterdam	The Netherlands
	Note: Bootlegged as *The Digital Brothers in Amsterdam* (Digital Brothers Productions) and as *Amsterdam '75*. A second performance on 25 February is accounted by some sources.		
26 Feb	Palais des Grottes	Cambrai	France
	Note: Bootlegged as *Cambrai, France 26 February 1975* (BURP 030), *Cambrai '75* and as *Palais des Grottes 26/2/75*.		
28 Feb	Salle des Expositions	Colmar	France
01 Mar	Palais des Sports	Dijon	France
02 Mar	Palais des Sports	St. Etienne	France
	Note: Bootlegged as *The Lamb Over Saint Etienne* with the erroneous date of May 27, 1975.		
03 Mar	Palais des Sports	Paris	France
	Note: Bootlegged as *Palais des Sports 3/3/75*.		
06 Mar	Pavilhao dos Desportos	Cascais	Portugal
07 Mar	Pavilhao dos Desportos	Cascais	Portugal
	Note: Bootlegged as *Lamb Tour in Portugal*.		
09 Mar	Pabellon Nuevo	Barcelona	Spain
	Note: Bootlegged as *Lamb in Badalona*.		
10 Mar	Pabellon Nuevo	Barcelona	Spain
11 Mar	Pabellon Real Madrid	Madrid	Spain
17 Mar	Palais des Sports	Paris	Versailles
	Note: A return engagement to Paris, where they had performed two weeks previously. Bootlegged as *The Lamb over Paris*.		
22 Mar	Salle des Expositions	Annecy	France
	Note: Bootlegged as *Annecy, 22/3/75*.		
24 Mar	Palasport Parco Rufino	Turin	Italy

Date	Venue	City	Country

Note: Sadly, this was to be the only *Lamb* performance in the country that had provided Genesis with vital support while they were still struggling to find an audience in their homeland just a few years previously. Unfortunately, fans and police clashed at this show, with the use of tear gas and several injuries as a result (Russell, 2004, p. 150). The performance was fortunately bootlegged as *The Real Last Time* (Stonehenge STCD 2004/2005), *Torino Palasport*, and *Torino '75*.

Date	Venue	City	Country
26 Mar	Stadhalle	Offenburg	Germany
27 Mar	Messezentrum	Nurnburg	Germany
29 Mar	Festhalle	Bern	Switzerland
30 Mar	Saarlandhalle	Saarbrucken	Germany
01 Apr	Friedrich Ebert Halle	Ludwigshafen	Germany

Note: Bootlegged as *Ludwigshafen '75*.

02 Apr	Killesberghalle	Stuttgart	Germany

Note: Bootlegged as *Live in Stuttgart 1975*.

03 Apr	Jahrhunderthalle	Frankfurt	Germany

Note: Bootlegged as *Revelation on Broadway* (Highland HL267/268), *Master of Frankfurt '75*, *There's Always Magic in the Air* (PRRPGS001).

04 Apr	Circus Krone	Munich	Germany
05 Apr	Stadthalle	Heidelberg	Germany
06 Apr	Philipshalle	Düsseldorf	Germany

Note: Bootlegged as *The Lamb Lies Down on Düsseldorf*.

07 Apr	Westfalenhalle 3	Dortmund	Germany

Note: Bootlegged as *The Lamb Lies Down on Dortmund*, *German Melody of 1975*, *Digital Lambs in Dortmund* (Digital Brothers Production).

08 Apr	Congresshalle	Hamburg	Germany

Note: Silent film footage of this performance has been bootlegged on *Genesis Collection 1973 & 1975* (DVD GMDVD 08). Bootlegged as *Hamburg Germany 4/8/75*.

10 Apr	Martinihal Centrum	Groningen	Holland

Note: Bootlegged as *Groningen '75*, Eeklair GL 41075, MUPPET 17 (MUPPET 17), *A Blaze of White Light* (PRRPGS009).

11 Apr	Ahoy Sportpaleis	Rotterdam	Holland

Note: Bootlegged as *Masters of Rotterdam*, *Rotterdam 1975*.

12 Apr	Vorst Nationale	Brussels	Belgium

Note: Bootlegged as *The Belgian Connection '75* (RMG TBC75024), *The Other Brussels '75*, *Brussels 12.04.1975*

The group now turned to their native England, performing at the cities where concerts had been cancelled at the beginning of the tour because of Hackett's hand injury.

14 Apr	Empire Pool, Wembley	London	UK
15 Apr	Empire Pool, Wembley	London	UK

Date	Venue	City	Country

Note: The second Wembley date is the most widely bootlegged concert on the *Lamb* tour. Professionally recorded by the BBC, and syndicated for US broadcast by the Westwood One radio network, the show has over the years been broadcast in a number of different time formats (with accordingly different omissions from the set lists). These broadcasts, as well as (evidently) the original soundboard master tapes, are the source for a bewildering variety of bootleg packages. Among the bootlegs of the show are: *The Light Goes Down on Empire* (Highland HL271), *The Audience at Empire Pool, Genesis—Live in London 1975* (Super Golden Radio Shows SGRS 022), *Lamb Stew* (RS Records CD 21), *Last Supper*, *The Waiting Room* (Flashback WorldProductions 10.89.0108), *Live in London 1974* [*sic*] (Live Storm LSCD 51143), *Awed Man Out* (Amazing Kornyfone Label TAKRL 1975 and ACL 008), *A Perfect Vintage* (TM Productions and Hamilton A/V 150475-2), *Perfect Wembley, Empire Pooled* (Coaster Factory), *We Are the Lamia of the Pool* (PRRP 010), *Westwood One* (Superstar Concert Series 98-18), *The Carpet Crawlers* (Chapter One CO25134), *Wembley '75 Complete Pre-FM* (AV 01), *British Tour 1975* (Bird Brain Records RSB-002), *On Broadway, Another Gold Record*, and *Stereo Pop Special – Vintage In Concert No. 313* (BBC TS 313 – CN 4248/S).

| 16 Apr | Gaumont Theatre | Southampton | UK |

Note: Bootlegged as *Drumming Melody of 1975* (RMG DMON118), *Live in Southampton 1975*.

| 19 Apr | Empire Theatre | Liverpool | UK |

Note: Silent audience film footage of this performance has been bootlegged as *Empire Theatre '75* (MPEG) and on the DVD *Genesis Collection 1973 & 1975* (GMDVD 08).

22 Apr	Usher Hall	Edinburgh	UK
23 Apr	Usher Hall	Edinburgh	UK
24 Apr	City Hall	Newcastle	UK
25 Apr	City Hall	Newcastle	UK
27 Apr	Palace Theatre	Manchester	UK

Note: Bootlegged as *Palace Theatre, Manchester 27 Apr. 75* (Hogweed Project HW 02); also bootlegged with the erroneous name *Apollo Theatre, Manchester*.

| 28 Apr | Palace Theatre | Manchester | UK |

Note: Bootlegged as *Second Night Palace Theatre, Palace Theatre, Manchester 28 Apr. 75* (Hogweed Project HW 08).

| 29 Apr | Colston Hall | Bristol | UK |
| 30 Apr | Colston Hall | Bristol | UK |

Note: Bootlegged as *Bristol 1975*.

| 01 May | Hippodrome | Birmingham | UK |

Note: Bootlegged as *Birmingham, UK 1st May 1975* (Hogweed Project HW 11) and *Hippodrome, Birmingham May 1, 1975* (BURP 005).

| 02 May | Hippodrome | Birmingham | UK |

Date	Venue	City	Country
	Note: Bootlegged as *Birmingham England May 2, 1975* (FAde 001), *The Story of Rael* (Highland HL 254/255), *Tales of Ordinary Madness* (Dream Weaver Records DWR 396078-2), and *Swelled and Spent* (Amazing Kornyfone Label TAKRL 2980).		
08 May	Sports Palace	Antwerp	Belgium
	Note: Veracity of this date/performance is disputed; Russell (2004, p. 177) indicates that the mainland Europe leg of the tour began with the May 10 Kiel show.		
10 May	Ostseehalle	Kiel	Germany
	Note: The return to the European continent after the UK shows was added on in order to recoup financial losses the tour had up to this point incurred (Russell, 2004, p. 177). Bootlegged as *Kiel '75* and as *The Lamb Lies Down on Kiel* (DVD, silent home-movie camera footage).		
11 May	Grugahalle	Essen	Germany
12 May	Rhein am Main Halle	Wiesbaden	Germany
	Note: Bootlegged as *The Lamb in Wiesbaden*.		
13 May	Stadthalle	Bremen	Germany
15 May	Palais des Sports	Rheims	France
	Note: Bootlegged as *Echoes of the Broadway* (Highland HL 403/404), *Rheims Remastered*, and *The Lamb Lies Down ... The May 1975 Live EP* (Rus Foley RFEP 5); erroneously bootlegged as *Paris '75*.		
16 May	Palais des Sports	Rheims	France
18 May	Velodromo Anoeta	San Sebastian	Spain
	Note: Bootlegged as *Rael is Not Afraid of ETA, San Sebastian '75 Remastered*.		
20 May	Palais des Sports	Paris	France
21 May	Palais des Grottes	Cambrai	France
23 May	Salle des Expositions	Colmar	France
25 May	Palais des Sports	Dijon	France
27 May	Palais des Sports	Besancon	France

Bibliography
"Searching printed word"

Abrams, Meyer Howard, et al., eds. 1987. *The Norton Anthology of English Literature*. 5th ed. New York: W. W. Norton and Co.

Adorno, Theodor. 1989. "Popular Music." In *Introduction to the Sociology of Music*, trans. E. B. Ashton, 21–38. New York: Continuum.

Alexander, Susan. 1983. "'I'm a Drummer First'" (interview with Phil Collins). *Modern Drummer 7*, 11 (November): 8–13, 48–52.

Auslander, Philip. 2006. *Performing Glam Rock*. Ann Arbor: University of Michigan Press.

Bangs, Lester. 1973. "The Progressives: Rock Stylizations from Brahms to the Auto-Destruct Guitar." In Richard Robinson and the editors of *Creem* (eds.), *Rock Revolution: From Elvis to Alice: The Whole Story of Rock and Roll*, 87–102. New York: Curtis Books.

Baudrillard, Jean. 1989. *America*, trans. Chris Turner. New York: Verso.

Baxandall, Lee. 1969/2003. "Spectacles and Scenarios: A Dramaturgy of Radical Activity." *Performance: Critical Concepts in Literary and Cultural Studies*, ed. Philip Auslander, 3: 253–265. London: Routledge.

Bell, Max. 1975. "Gabriel's Cosmic Juice." *New Musical Express* (March 15): 14–15.

Bennett, Andy. 2004. "New Tales from Canterbury: The Making of a Virtual Scene." In Andy Bennett and Richard A. Peterson (eds.), *Music Scenes: Local, Translocal, and Virtual*, 205–220. Nashville, TN: Vanderbilt University Press.

Bowler, Dave, and Dray, Bryan. 1993. *Genesis: A Biography*. London: Sidgwick & Jackson.

Bright, Spencer. 1988. *Peter Gabriel: An Authorized Biography*. London: Sidgwick & Jackson.

Campbell, Joseph. 1968. *The Hero With a Thousand Faces*. Princeton, NJ: Princeton University Press.

Carroll, Peter. 1982. *It Seemed Like Nothing Happened: The Tragedy and Promise of America in the 1970s*. New York: Holt, Rinehart and Winston.

Chambers, Iain. 1985. *Urban Rhythms: Pop Music and Popular Culture*. Houndmills: Macmillan.

Charone, Barbara. 1974. "Zombie twits make good: A journey into worm world with Genesis." *Creem 6*, 12 (December): 34–37.

Clecak, Peter. 1983. *America's Quest for the Ideal Self: Dissent and Fulfillment in the 60s and 70s*. New York: Oxford University Press.

Conway, Flo, and Siegelman, Jim. 1978. *Snapping: America's Epidemic of Sudden Personality Change*. New York: Delta Books.

Couture, François. n.d. "The Lamb Lies Down on Broadway—Overview." <http://www.allmusic.com/cg/amg.dll?p=amg&token=ADFEAEE47816D34DA971 20CF802A47C6B275F329C742F281116E495AD1A93240841E73ED40A1C 6CCB9E577B479AAB32FAE5E0ED9CFED468DA1&sql=10:86vsa9cgb23 g>, accessed March 15, 2006.

Covach, John. 2006. *What's That Sound?: An Introduction to Rock and its History.* New York: W. W. Norton.

Covach, John, and Boone, Graeme, eds. 1997. *Understanding Rock: Essays in Musical Analysis.* New York: Oxford University Press.

Currie, The Christopher [*sic*]. 1998. "Tentative Review by The Christopher Currie: Genesis—The Lamb Lies Down on Broadway." INTERNET: <http://www. tranglos.com/marek/yes/tr_77.html>, accessed September 12, 2006.

Evans-Wentz, W. Y., trans. 1960. *The Tibetan Book of the Dead.* 3rd edition. New York: Oxford University Press.

Everett, Walter. 1999. *The Beatles as Musicians: Revolver through the Anthology.* New York: Oxford University Press.

———. 2001. *The Beatles as Musicians: The Quarry Men through Rubber Soul.* New York: Oxford University Press.

Fielder, Hugh. 1984. *The Book of Genesis.* New York: St. Martin's Press.

Finegan, Jason, McMahan, Scott, et al. 1994. "The Annotated Lamb Lies Down on Broadway." <http://www.rawbw.com/~marka/music/lamb.html>, accessed March 15, 2006.

Fripp, Robert. 1992. *King Crimson: The Great Deceiver Live 1973-1974* (liner notes). KC DIS 1 / Caroline 4 1597 2.

Friskics-Warren, Bill. 2005. *I'll Take You There: Pop Music and the Urge for Transcendence.* New York: Continuum.

Frith, Simon. 1973. "Sweet Notes." *Creem* (November): 42–44+.

———. 1983. *Sound Effects.* London: Constable.

———. 1996. *Performing Rites: On the Value of Popular Music.* Cambridge, MA: Harvard University Press.

Frum, David. 2000. *How We Got Here.* New York: Basic Books.

Gabriel, Peter. 1974. *The Lamb Lies Down on Broadway* (liner notes). Atco.

Gallo, Armando. 1980. *Genesis: I Know What I Like.* Los Angeles: D.I.Y. Publishing.

———. 1986. *Peter Gabriel.* London: Omnibus Press.

Garofalo, Reebee. 1997. *Rockin' Out: Popular Music in the USA.* Boston: Allyn and Bacon.

"Genesis on Green Pages: The Lamb Lies Down on Broadway." n.d. <http://www. venco.com.pl/~piotrus/greenpages/genesis/la~a.htm>, accessed October 2, 2007.

GenesisFan.net. n.d. "The Lamb Lies Down on Broadway Story." <http://genesisfan. net/content/view/14>, accessed October 2, 2007.

"Gig Guide: The Lamb Lies Down on Broadway." n.d. <http://www.genesis-movement. co.uk/php/listtour.php?tourid=6&username=all#>, accessed July 10, 2007.

Gillett, Charles. 1972. *The Sound of the City.* New York: Dell.

Goethe, Johann Wolfgang von. 1880. *Faust*, trans. Bayard Taylor. Cambridge: The Riverside Press.

——. 1992. *Faust: A Tragedy, Part One*, trans. Martin Greenberg. New Haven: Yale University Press.

Harrigan, Brian. 1975. "How Genesis brought their Lamb to market." *Melody Maker 50*, 16 (April 19): 31.

Hewitt, Alan. 2000. *Opening the Musical Box: A Genesis Chronicle*. London: SAF Publishing, Ltd.

Hinton, Graham, and Wood, Robin. 1995–98. "EMS Synthi Range 1969–1979." <http://users.tinyonline.co.uk/ian.simpson/ian.simpson/ems%20prods.htm>, accessed April 20, 2007.

"Historia en inglés de The Lamb Lies Down on Broadway—Genesis." n.d. <http://www.ferhiga.com/progre/notas/notas-genesis-tlldob-ingles.htm>, accessed October 2, 2007.

Holm-Hudson, Kevin, ed. 2002. *Progressive Rock Reconsidered*. New York: Routledge.

——. Forthcoming. "A study of maximally smooth voice leading in the mid-1970s music of Genesis." In John Covach and Mark Spicer (eds.), *Sounding Out Rock: Analytical Essays in Popular Music*. Ann Arbor: University of Michigan Press.

Hoppe, Uwe. 1998. "Peaceful Shades of Green: The Pastoral Element in the Works of Early Genesis (1969–1971)." INTERNET: <http://genesis-path.net/gen_pastoral.html>, accessed March 15, 2006.

Huxley, Aldous. 1998. *Brave New World*. New York: Harper Perennial Classics.

James, William. 1925. *The Varieties of Religious Experience: A Study in Human Nature*. New York: Longmans, Green and Co.

Jung, Carl Gustav. 1969. *The Archetypes and the Collective Unconscious*, trans. R. F. C. Hull. 2nd edition. Princeton, NJ: Princeton University Press.

——. 1971. *The Essential Jung*, ed. Joseph Campbell, trans. R. F. C. Hull. New York: The Viking Press.

Killen, Andreas. 2006. *1973 Nervous Breakdown: Watergate, Warhol, and the Birth of Post-Sixties America*. New York: Bloomsbury.

"The Lamb Lies Down on Broadway—Genesis—Traduções." n.d. <http://whiplash.net/materias/traducoes/052446-genesis.html>, accessed October 2, 2007.

"The Lamb Story." n.d. <http://members.aol.com/inthecage9/lambtext.html>, accessed October 2, 2007.

Leshinski, Guy. 2005. "High Fidelity." <http://www.cbc.ca/arts/music/musicalbox.html>, accessed May 12, 2007.

Lilly, John C. 1973. *The Center of the Cyclone: An Autobiography of Inner Space*. New York: Bantam Books.

Logan, Nick, and Woffinden, Bob. 1977. *The Illustrated Encyclopedia of Rock*. New York: Harmony Books.

Macan, Edward. 1997. *Rocking the Classics: English Progressive Rock and the Counterculture*. New York: Oxford University Press.

———. 2006. *Endless Enigma: A Musical Biography of Emerson, Lake and Palmer*. Chicago: Open Court Press.

McClary, Susan. 1983. "Pitches, Expression, Ideology: An Exercise in Mediation." *Enclitic* (Spring): 76–86.

McMahan, Scott. 1998. *The Genesis Discography 1967–1996: "The scattered pages of a book by the sea ..."* <http://cyberreviews.skwc.com/genesis.html>, accessed April 11, 2006.

Markowitz, Michael. 2003. "The New Newcomers." *The Gotham Gazette* (June 2). <http://www.gothamgazette.com/article/issueoftheweek/20030602/200/407>, accessed May 10, 2006.

Marsh, Dave, and Swenson, John, eds. 1979. *The Rolling Stone Record Guide*. New York: Rolling Stone Press/Random House.

Martin, Bill. 1998. *Listening to the Future: The Time of Progressive Rock, 1968–1978*. Chicago: Open Court Press.

Matthews, R.C.O., ed. 1982. *Slower Growth in the Western World*. London: Heinemann.

Moore, Allan F. 2001. *Rock: The Primary Text*. 2nd edition. Burlington, VT: Ashgate.

Morse, Tim. 1999. "Classic Tracks: Genesis' 'The Lamb Lies Down on Broadway.'" <http://mixonline.com/mag/audio_classic_tracks_genesis/index.html>, accessed April 5, 2006.

"The Musical Box: The Lamb Lies Down on Broadway." n.d. <http://themusicalbox. net/main/page_lamb.html>, accessed April 20, 2007.

The Musical Box. n.d. "The Musical Box: The Lamb Lies Down on Broadway—A Few Facts." <http://themusicalbox.net/main/lamb_facts.html>, accessed April 20, 2007.

"Overnight Job: Tribute Bands." n.d. <http://genesisresource.8m.com/bands.htm>, accessed April 20, 2007.

Partridge, Robert. 1974. "Why I Killed the King" (interview with Robert Fripp). <http://www.rocksbackpages.com/article.html?ArticleID=6470>, accessed October 2, 2007.

Platts, Robin. 2001. *Genesis: Inside & Out (1967–2000)*. Burlington, Ontario: Collector's Guide Publishing.

Robertson, David Brian, ed. 1998. *Loss of Confidence: Politics and Policy in the 1970s*. University Park, PA: Pennsylvania State University Press.

Ross, Ron. 1975. "Why Genesis Wouldn't Chop Up The Lamb." *Circus 9*, 6 (March): 66–70.

Rothstein, Edward. 1995. *Emblems of Mind: The Inner Life of Music and Mathematics*. New York: Avon Books.

Russell, Paul. 2004. *Genesis: A Live Guide 1969 to 1975*. London: SAF Publishing, Ltd.

Salem, Roger. 2000. "The Art of Illusion—or the Art of Flattery?" <http://genesis-path.net/TMB_montreal2000.html>, accessed March 31, 2006.

Scerba, Amy. 1999. "Changing Literary Representations of Lilith and the Evolution of a Mythical Heroine." <http://feminism.eserver.org/lilith>, accessed December 19, 2006.

Schoenberg, Arnold. 1975. "New Music, Outmoded Music, Style and Idea." In *Style and Idea: Selected Writings of Arnold Schoenberg*, ed. Leonard Stein, trans. Leo Black. Berkeley: University of California Press.

Seay, Davin, with Neely, Mary. 1986. *Stairway to Heaven: The Spiritual Roots of Rock 'n' Roll—From the King and Little Richard to Prince and Amy Grant*. New York: Ballantine Books.

Sinclair, David. 1992. *Rock on CD: The Essential Guide*. London: Kyle Cathie, Ltd.

Smith, Martin J., and Kiger, Patrick J. 2006. *Oops: 20 Life Lessons from the Fiascoes that Shaped America*. New York: Collins.

Sollow, Stephanie. 2001. "ReGenesis—*Lamb for Supper*—Live, 2001" (review). <http://www.progressiveworld.net/regenesis.html>, accessed April 20, 2007.

Spicer, Mark. 2001. "British Pop-Rock Music in the Post-Beatles Era: Three Analytical Studies." Ph.D. dissertation, Yale University.

———. 2005. "Genesis's *Foxtrot*." *Philomusica-Online*. <http://www.unipv.it/britishrock1966-1976/pdf/spicereng.pdf>, accessed May 10, 2007.

Stump, Paul. 1997. *The Music's All That Matters: A History of Progressive Rock*. London: Quartet Books.

Walters, Barry. 1986. "Hit Me" (review of Peter Gabriel's *So*). *Village Voice 31*, 28 (July 15): 67.

Welch, Chris. 1974. "Plodding Genesis." *Melody Maker 49*, 47 (November 23): 41.

———. 1975. "Gabriel's Ladder." *Melody Maker 50,* 11 (March 15): 13.

Wells, H. G. 1897. *The Invisible Man: A Grotesque Romance*. New York: Harper & Brothers Publishers.

Whitburn, Joel. 1995. *The Billboard Book of Top 40 Albums*. 3rd edition. New York: Billboard Books.

Wilding, Philip. 2000. "The Book of Revelations." *Classic Rock* (February): 17–25.

Willis, Paul. 1978. *Profane Culture*. London: Routledge and Kegan Paul.

Yesfans.com. n.d. "The Lamb Lies Down on Broadway—Your Interpretations!" <http://www.yesfans.com/archive/index.php/t-21988.html>, accessed October 3, 2006.

Index